Collins Primary Literacy

Teacher's Guide 6

Jonathan Rooke and Karina Law
Series editor: Kay Hiatt

William Collins' dream of knowledge for all began with the publication of his first book in 1819. A self-educated mill worker, he not only enriched millions of lives, but also founded a flourishing publishing house. Today, staying true to this spirit, Collins books are packed with inspiration, innovation and practical expertise. They place you at the centre of a world of possibility and give you exactly what you need to explore it.

Published by Collins
An imprint of HarperCollins*Publishers*
77–85 Fulham Palace Road
Hammersmith
London
W6 8JB

Text © 2007 Jonathan Rooke and Karina Law
Illustrations and design © HarperCollins*Publishers* Limited 2007

Series editor: Kay Hiatt

10 9 8 7 6 5 4 3 2

ISBN 978 0 00 722669 6

British Library Cataloguing in Publication Data
A Catalogue record for this publication is available from the British Library.

Acknowledgements
The authors and publishers wish to thank the following for permission to use copyright material:
PCM 9a: PFD for the text from "Give and Take" by Roger McGough, from *Good Enough To Eat* © Roger McGough 2002; PCM 12a: The Orion Publishing Group for the text from *Macbeth* from *Stories from Shakespeare* retold by Geraldine McCaughrean, text © Geraldine McCaughrean, 1994; PCM 14b: The Watts Publishing Group Limited for the text from *Nature's Fury: Volcano!* by Anita Ganeri, text © Anita Ganeri, 2006 (Franklin Watts 2006); PCM 15a: Macmillan for "Spin Me A Web, Spider" by Charles Causley, from *Collected Poems for Children*, reprinted with permission of David Higham Associates Ltd; PCM 15b: Faber and Faber Limited for "Spider's Song" by Judith Nicholls from *Magic Mirror and other Poems* by Judith Nicholls, © Judith Nicholls 1985, reprinted with the kind permission of the author

Illustrations: Kevin Sutherland, Humberto Blanco, Martin Ursell, Jo Taylor, Abigail Conway

Every effort has been made to trace copyright holders and to obtain their permission for the use of copyright material. The authors and publishers will gladly receive any information enabling them to rectify any error or omission in subsequent editions.

Browse the complete Collins catalogue at
www.collinseducation.com

Printed by Martins the Printers, Berwick upon Tweed

Mixed Sources
Product group from well-managed forests and other controlled sources
www.fsc.org Cert no. SW-COC-1806
© 1996 Forest Stewardship Council
FSC

Contents

Welcome to Collins Primary Literacy

Collins Primary Literacy is designed to help you deliver a creative, enjoyable and interactive approach to literacy learning.

Excellence and Enjoyment – A Strategy for Primary Schools encouraged teachers to be creative and innovative in how they teach because *"children learn better when they are excited and engaged"*.

This programme has been developed to help you do just that, while fulfilling all the requirements of excellent teaching, with teaching and learning moving at a challenging pace towards the end-of-year expectations and beyond.

Integral to *Collins Primary Literacy* are:

- engaged learning that motivate and stimulate the literacy session
- differentiated activities that suit each child's learning needs
- assessment and progression so children work at the right level of challenge – and move on.

Talking to learn

Collins Primary Literacy has incorporated all aspects of the 12 strands of the renewed Framework with a strong emphasis on the importance of integrated speaking, listening and drama activities. At the heart of the programme is the teaching and learning strategy of talking to learn, that:

> *"…Children are more confident with words, expressions, ideas and different types of language if they have experienced them in conversation first. Ideas which have been orally rehearsed are better articulated on paper."* (Primary National Strategy)

For example, in *Collins Primary Literacy* children are encouraged to clarify thinking by working in pairs and groups, or orally rehearsing writing with someone else.

Thinking to learn

Collins Primary Literacy's enjoyable and engaging activities build on children's experience and previous learning. It provides ideas and resources which embed key teaching and learning principles in flexible literacy sessions that build up to create a unit. Each unit incorporates a block of sessions that sustain progression over a number of weeks towards a final outcome. This encourages a "classroom as workshop"

approach, with an emphasis on reflecting on the processes involved as you work toward the finished product. This encourages reflective, critical thinking in children who become self-evaluating learners.

An overview of the programme

Each unit is structured around the investigation of fantastic texts from fiction, non-fiction, poetry and plays to interactive texts such as video, film and audio texts. The ideas in the Teacher's Guide are further supported by lively Pupil Books, an interactive software, photocopiable master sheets (PCMs) and Homework Books full of activities, which engage children and help them to consolidate and apply their learning.

For *Collins Primary Literacy* 3, 4, 5 and 6 the programme consists of:

Interactive software
including shared texts

Pupil Book

Homework book

Teacher's Guide

The **Interactive Software** includes:

- **Warm up**: a multimedia introduction to the unit themes
- **Explore**: a range of fantastic texts to read and explore with the whole class, with ready-made annotations that highlight key objectives plus annotation tools to make your own
- **Workpad**: ready-prepared frames that facilitate shared investigation of the texts
- **Plan**: frames that support thinking and planning
- **Write**: frames where children create and publish their own work
- **Practise**: differentiated grammar and spelling activities with built-in result tracking.

The **Pupil Book** contains a range of lively differentiated activities for children working independently, in pairs or groups, including comprehension, speaking and listening, and writing.

The **Homework Book** delivers engaging activities that consolidate and extend key skills.

The **Teacher's Guide** provides unit-by-unit teaching sequences, with clear links to objectives, a wide range of interactive ideas for learning and built-in opportunities for regular assessment; plus yearly planning charts, PCMs, Assessment Sheets for writing and series overview.

Supporting the writing process

The ideas in *Collins Primary Literacy* are based on what works in classrooms, supporting your teaching of the writing process, for example, through the choice of quality texts to investigate and model writing on, exemplars for demonstration writing, advice on working with small groups and pairs, incorporating grammar activities directly related to outcomes, and lots more activities on the software, in the PCMs and in the Homework Book.

Supporting flexible approaches in the classroom

The units have been written so that you can easily adapt them to suit the children currently in your class.

For example, you could:

- place the unit within a thematic approach to delivering literacy within the wider curriculum, e.g. Unit 3 This is Your Life in *Collins Primary Literacy* Year 6 sits well within the History curriculum
- run units alongside a thematic approach, as revision and consolidation units
- extend a session within a unit if you need more time to consolidate a particular aspect, e.g. spending more time on speaking, listening

and drama activities so that children can clarify their thinking

- merge two sessions where children's skills are well established, giving more time for an aspect that needs developing, e.g. getting the most out of small-group discussion
- build upon the children's ideas and feedback and create new routes through the unit
- use a unit on poetry as part of an Arts week in school.

Supporting teaching and learning strategies

Today's Primary classroom is likely to reflect aspects of these learning and teaching strategies:

- incorporating a range of teaching and learning styles (aural, visual and kinaesthetic)
- bringing thinking skills to the fore
- planning interesting contexts for learning with creative approaches and outcomes
- delivering a problem-solving approach with key questions to set the class learning in active and co-operative ways
- looking for more breadth and depth of literacy teaching through incorporating all of the four language modes: speaking, listening, reading and writing.

Collins Primary Literacy fully supports these strategies. It places you the teacher at the heart of the classroom as the facilitator and enabler who gets children thinking and taking responsibility for their own decision making. The resources and the teaching and learning approaches will challenge children to think and be creative, and the expectations are high.

You also have a vital role as demonstrator and support-giver. *Collins Primary Literacy* provides numerous ideas and resources for you in this area. For example:

- engaging children through discussion, using the Warm up section of the software
- demonstrating writing using ready-prepared examples provided on the software
- using the Workpad, Plan and Write software sections to model thinking, note-making and planning strategies
- working with children as researchers using the internet and other materials
- joining discussion groups to listen to views and take part in the discussion
- responding to children
- expecting them to articulate what they have learned as part of reviews.

Working together as equal partners

You and your class are very much working as equal partners where children's views and understandings are respected and used as part of the learning.

Classroom as a workshop

Collins Primary Literacy units are based on the authors' own experiences of working with children. The ideas are there because they get the best from children. They will help to support a workshop-style, active, talking classroom where children can think for themselves and develop their critical thinking by frequently working in partnership with another child or within a small group. This makes for a stimulating, challenging and creative classroom environment where every child works to their full ability.

Planning for speaking, listening and responding, group discussion and interaction and drama

The best way to incorporate these key aspects of learning is through interesting contexts within lessons. The renewed Framework for the Primary National Strategy places speaking, listening and responding, group discussion and interaction and drama at its heart, as the first four strands of learning.

They are integrated throughout *Collins Primary Literacy*.

Speaking and listening – thinking and learning

A range of teaching and learning strategies has been built into the programme. These are likely to be features of your own teaching style already, but if any are less familiar, are very easy to assimilate and will become second-nature to your work with children.

Using ICT as an integrated part of the lesson

Under your watchful eye, children are encouraged to use the Internet as part of developing their research skills. Suggestions are made on how to integrate ICT into your literacy session, for example to prepare for presentations, both oral and written. Children are

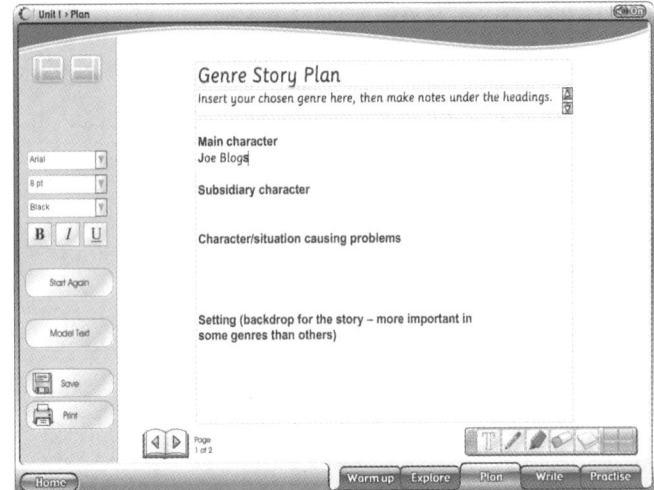

Example planning screen from Collins Primary Literacy *Interactive Software.*

encouraged to become skilled users of ICT, as part of thinking about the audience for writing, and its purpose. There are also, of course, a wide range of opportunities for reading and writing activities using ICT provided on the *Collins Primary Literacy* software.

Linking to the wider curriculum

The adoption of a thematic approach in primary schools is growing. Every unit of *Collins Primary Literacy* has clear links to other areas of the curriculum built in.

Curriculum links

Citizenship: Taking part – developing skills of communication and participation

Geography: How can we make our local area safer?

Support for National Tests

This is offered through interesting activities which have been designed for children to use independently. These give an indication of what children can do – and what coverage may still be needed. Revision units are included in *Collins Primary Literacy* 6, with exemplar reading and writing tasks that children can undertake in test conditions and reflect on their performance.

How to use this guide

Collins Primary Literacy Teacher's Guides provide teachers with practical planning and teaching support, helping you to assess and identify the needs of each child, and to teach essential literacy skills in the content of an engaging and stimulating block of lessons.

This Teacher's Guide has 7 main sections:

Welcome to *Collins Primary Literacy* – pages 4 to 5

Collins Primary Literacy series editor, Kay Hiatt, introduces *Collins Primary Literacy* and explains how it benefits teachers and children.

Planning support – pages 8 to 17

These pages are a practical planning tool designed to help you plan and adapt the materials to suit your class's needs. All the information you need is at your fingertips with an at-a-glance synopsis of each unit, including the learning focus, strategy objectives, supporting materials and where to find them, and links to the wider curriculum.

Structure and features – pages 18 to 27

This section outlines the content and structure of *Collins Primary Literacy*, including an overview of where to find what.

Teaching notes – pages 28 to 123

Unit-by-unit teaching notes provide clear, practical ideas and activities within a suggested teaching sequence, with guidance for assessment, differentiation, speaking, listening and drama, and paired/group work.

Photocopiable activity sheets – pages 124 to 158

Each unit is supported by a number of photocopiable activity sheets which can be used to consolidate, practise or extend the objectives of the related session.

Ideas for your literacy session – pages 159 to 162

This section provides practical ideas for generic techniques that really work to implement your literacy sessions, focusing on drama and discussion.

Assessment support – pages 163 to 176

This section shows how *Collins Primary Literacy* has built assessment for learning into every unit, and how this benefits you and your class. Photocopiable assessment sheets are provided on PCMs 166 to 174.

Unit by unit planning chart

Unit	Unit focus	PNS strand objectives
1 Fairytales, Fantasy and Beyond *Fantasy and fairy stories*	**Speaking and listening:** Use discussion and feedback to explore different genres; tell and evaluate oral stories. **Reading:** Understand how genres use certain types of character and formulaic plots that follow a clear plan. **Writing:** Write a short story using the features of a chosen genre. **Assessment focus:** writing a story in a chosen genre **Curriculum links** **Citizenship:** Children's rights – human rights; Living in a diverse world	**1. Speaking:** Use a range of oral techniques to present … engaging narratives; Tailor the structure, vocabulary and delivery of a talk or presentation so that it is helpfully sequenced and supported by gesture or other visual aids as appropriate; Use techniques of dialogic talk to explore ideas **2. Listening:** Analyse and evaluate how speakers present points effectively through use of language and gesture **3. Group discussion:** Understand and use a variety of ways to criticise constructively and respond to criticism **4. Drama:** Improvise using a range of drama strategies and conventions to explore themes such as hopes, fears and desires **6. Word structure and spelling:** Use a range of appropriate strategies to edit, proofread and correct spelling in their own work, on paper and on screen **7. Understanding and interpreting text:** Appraise a text quickly, deciding on its value, quality or usefulness; Understand underlying themes, causes and points of view; Understand how writers use different structures to create coherence and impact **9. Creating and shaping text:** Set their own challenges to extend achievement and experience in writing; Use different narrative techniques to engage and entertain the reader; Select words and language drawing on their knowledge of literary features and formal and informal writing **10. Text structure and organisation:** Use varied structures to shape and organise text coherently; Use paragraphs to achieve pace and emphasis **11. Word structure and spelling:** Express distinctions of meaning … by constructing sentences in varied ways
2 Heroes and Villains *Spy fiction*	**Speaking and listening:** Use feedback techniques to evaluate reading and writing, and to support the creative writing process. **Reading:** Understand how genres use character types and plot formulas. **Writing:** Write a short story using the features of a specific genre. **Assessment focus:** writing a spy thriller **Curriculum links** **Design and Technology:** Draw plans for the design of a spy gadget **Citizenship:** Discuss responsibilities and responses when people are threatened by others' actions on the world	**1. Speaking:** Use the techniques of dialogic talk to explore ideas, topics or issues **3. Group discussion:** Understand and use a variety of ways to criticise constructively and respond to criticism **4. Drama:** Consider the overall impact of a live or recorded performance, identifying dramatic ways of conveying characters' ideas and building tension **6. Word structure and spelling:** Use a range of appropriate strategies to edit, proofread and correct spelling in their own work, on paper and on screen **7. Understanding and interpreting text:** Understand how writers use different structures to create coherence and impact **9. Creating and shaping text:** Set their own challenges to extend achievement and experience in writing; Use different narrative techniques to engage and entertain the reader; Select words and language drawing on their knowledge of literary features and formal and informal writing **10. Text structure and organisation:** Use varied structures to shape and organise text coherently; Use paragraphs to achieve pace and emphasis **11. Sentence structure and punctuation:** Express subtle distinctions of meaning … by constructing sentences in varied ways
3 This is Your Life *Biography and autobiography*	**Speaking and listening:** Evaluate how speakers present points effectively. **Reading:** Evaluate, read, interpret and select information and distinguish between fact and opinion. **Writing:** Write a biography to suit a particular audience and purpose. **Assessment focus:** writing a biography **Curriculum links** **History:** What was it like for children in the Second World War?	**1. Speaking:** Use a range of oral techniques to present persuasive arguments and engaging narratives **2. Listening:** Analyse and evaluate how speakers present points effectively through language and gesture **6. Word structure and spelling:** Use a range of appropriate strategies to edit, proofread and correct spelling in their own work, on paper and on screen **7. Understanding and interpreting text:** Appraise a text quickly; Understand underlying themes, causes and points of view **9. Creating and shaping text:** Use different narrative techniques to engage and entertain the reader; Select words and language drawing on their knowledge of literary features and formal and informal writing **10. Text structure and organisation:** Use varied structures to shape and organise texts coherently **11. Sentence structure and punctuation:** Express subtle distinction of meaning, including hypothesis, speculation and supposition, by constructing sentences in varied ways

Texts	Related resources	Unit overview
The Golden Goose by Sara and Stephen Corrin from *The Faber Book of Golden Fairytales*, Faber and Faber Ltd *The Sea of Trolls* by Nancy Farmer, Simon and Schuster UK Ltd *Rescuing Dad* by Pete Johnson, Corgi Yearling Books Interview with author Philip Reeve *Mortal Engines* by Philip Reeve, Scholastic Ltd *The Adventure of the Dented Computer* by Simon Cheshire from *An Oxford Anthology of Mystery Stories* by Dennis Hamley, Oxford University Press	PCM 1a: group fairytales under headings PCM 1b: make up a story using the cues on three genre cards PCM 1c: use a planning frame to plan their story Homework 1a: continue a fantasy story Homework 1b: spot the genres of some texts Software: Workpad 1: genre chart Workpad 2: tips for oral storytelling Workpad 3: evaluating storytelling Workpad 4: answering questions on science fiction Workpad 5: character web Workpad 6: excitement graph Plan: plan a story in a chosen genre. A modelled version for a science fiction story is provided Write: a modelled opening for a science fiction story is provided Practise: powerful verbs	This unit is designed to last three weeks. During the unit, children will read examples of different fiction genres, explore them through oral storytelling and drama, and then write their own story parodying one of the genres. **Phase 1: *Engage (sessions 1–6)*** Children identify the specific features of a range of genres, tell oral stories in a particular genre and transform them into a written narrative. **Phase 2: *Explore (sessions 7–11)*** Children extend their exploration of genres to compare the science fiction and mystery genres and consider how authors use parody to create humorous texts. **Phase 3: *Create (sessions 12–15)*** Children write, present and publish a story in a genre of their choice, constructing sentences in varied ways.
Point Blanc by Anthony Horowitz, Walker Books Ltd *Goldfinger* by Ian Fleming *Agent X – Super Spy* by Jonathan Rooke	PCM 2a: find vivid details of characters PCM 2b: invent an evil villain for a new spy story PCM 2c: plan their spy thriller PCM 2d: plan an exciting spy thriller plot Homework 2a: design a gadget for a spy hero Homework 2b: describe a villain's lair Software: Workpad 1: character web Workpad 3: key features of main characters Workpad 4: create a villain Workpad 5: plot a spy thriller Workpad 6: create a spy storyline Plan: plan a spy thriller Write: a model describing the setting is provided Practise: ordering sentences into a paragraph	This unit is designed to last two weeks. During the unit, children will read passages from three spy thriller stories and write their own spy thriller. **Phase 1: *Engage (sessions 1–4)*** The class develops their knowledge of genres, focusing on the spy thriller genre with an emphasis on characterisation. **Phase 2: *Explore (sessions 5–6)*** The class invents their own characters for a spy thriller and develops their understanding of how a spy thriller plot works. **Phase 3: *Create (sessions 7–10)*** The class plans and writes a spy thriller, constructing sentences in varied ways and considering presentation and publishing.
Coming to England by Floella Benjamin, Puffin Books *Boy: Tales of Childhood* by Roald Dahl, Jonathan Cape *Roald Dahl: A Biography* by Jeremy Treglown, Faber and Faber Ltd Obituary – Alfred Andersen from *The Guardian* 23 November 2005 Assorted information on Anne Frank Interview with Bert Leatherbarrow talking about Charles Wintergarden Assorted material to create the Charles Wintergarden biography	Homework 3a: make a Trading Card biography Homework 3b: write the biography of a friend or family member Software: Workpad 1: produce a timeline Workpad 2: compare biography and autobiography Workpad 3: compare a biography and autobiography of Roald Dahl Workpad 5: create a mind map Plan: complete a timeline for a life. A modelled version is provided Write: write a biography. Modelled sentences are provided Practise: spelling	This unit is designed to last two weeks. During the unit, the class will read passages from biographies and autobiographies and write a biography. **Phase 1: *Engage (sessions 1–3)*** Children read and compare biographical and autobiographical writing and identify language features. **Phase 2: *Explore (sessions 4–7)*** Children analyse the construction of biographies and create their own biography for an oral presentation. **Phase 3: *Create (sessions 8–10)*** Children write a biography, reflecting on how biographers select, interpret and present information.

Unit	Unit focus	PNS strand objectives
4 The Power of Imagery *Personification in poetry*	**Speaking and listening:** Use the techniques of dialogic talk to explore ideas. **Reading:** Explore how poets use powerful forms of imagery including personification. **Writing:** Write poetry using personification and simile and metaphor. **Assessment focus:** writing a poem personifying rain **Curriculum links** **Geography:** Connecting ourselves to the world	**1. Speaking:** Use the techniques of dialogic talk to explore ideas, topics or issues **3. Group discussion and interaction:** Understand and use a variety of ways to criticise constructively and respond to criticism **6. Word structure and spelling:** Use a range of appropriate strategies to edit, proofread and correct spelling in their own work, on paper and on screen **7. Understand and interpret texts:** Understand underlying themes, causes and points of view; Understand how writers use different structures to create coherence and impact **9. Creating and shaping texts:** Select words and language drawing on their knowledge of literary features and formal and informal writing **10. Text structure and organisation:** Use varied structures to shape and organise texts coherently
5 A Quest for Adventure *Quest adventure stories*	**Speaking and listening:** Use dialogue to explore ideas, listen and respond constructively. **Reading:** Understand the features of the quest adventure genre, and the effect of having different reading pathways in a text. **Writing:** Write a short branching text with different reading pathways, using elements of a specific genre. **Assessment focus:** writing a quest adventure **Curriculum links** **History:** Who were the ancient Greeks?	**1. Speaking:** Use techniques of dialogic talk to explore ideas, topics or issues **3. Group discussion and interaction:** Understand and use a variety of ways to criticise constructively and respond to criticism **6. Word structure and spelling:** Use a range of appropriate strategies to edit, proofread and correct spelling in their own work, on paper and on screen **7. Understanding and interpreting texts:** Understand how writers use different structures to create coherence and impact **8. Engaging with and responding to texts:** Sustain engagement with longer texts, using different techniques to make the text come alive **9. Creating and shaping texts:** Use different narrative techniques to engage and entertain the reader; Select words and language drawing on their knowledge of literary features and formal and informal writing; Integrate words, images and sounds imaginatively for different purposes **10. Text structure and organisation:** Use varied structures to shape and organise text coherently **11. Sentence structure and punctuation:** Express subtle distinctions of meaning, including hypothesis, speculation and supposition, by constructing sentences in varied ways; Use punctuation to clarify meaning in complex sentences **12. Presentation:** Select from a wide range of ICT programs to present text effectively and communicate information and ideas
6 Getting the Facts Straight *Writing in a journalistic style*	**Speaking and listening:** Use a range of oral and drama techniques to present news reports. **Reading:** Engage with texts that can be used to inform, persuade, mislead and sway the reader. **Writing:** Use journalistic techniques to write news reports. **Assessment focus:** writing a radio news report **Curriculum links** **Geography:** Passport to the world (television news reporting), What's in the news?	**1. Speaking:** Use a range of oral techniques to present persuasive arguments and engaging narratives **2. Listening:** Make notes when listening for a sustained period and discuss how note taking varies depending on context and purpose **6. Word structure and spelling:** Use a range of appropriate strategies to edit, proofread and correct spelling in their own work, on paper and on screen **7. Understanding and interpreting text:** Appraise a text quickly; Recognise rhetorical devices used to argue, persuade, mislead and sway the reader **9. Creating and shaping text:** Use different narrative techniques to engage and entertain the reader; Select words and language drawing on their knowledge of literary features and formal and informal writing **10. Text structure and organisation:** Use varied structures to shape and organise texts coherently **11. Sentence structure and punctuation:** Express subtle distinction of meaning, including hypothesis, speculation and supposition, by constructing sentences in varied ways

Texts	Related resources	Unit overview
"Xmas" by Wes Magee from *A Fifth Poetry Book* edited by John Foster, Oxford University Press "Silver" by Walter de la Mare from *The Complete Poems of Walter de la Mare* "Snow and Snow" by Ted Hughes from *Collected Poems for Children*, Faber and Faber Ltd *Wake up* by Christine Chen "The Warm and the Cold" by Ted Hughes from *Collected Poems for Children*, Faber and Faber Ltd "Reader: But What is Poetry? Adrian:" by Adrian Mitchell from *The Orchard Book of Poems*	PCM 4a: personify an everyday object PCM 4b: write similes describing different sorts of rain PCM 4c: record ideas to personify rain Homework 4a: create surprising metaphors Homework 4b: extend simple sentences to make them richer Software: Workpad 4: active verbs used to personify an alarm clock Workpad 5: describe the images and sound of rain Plan: personify different characteristics of rain using a grid. A modelled version using light, temporary rain is provided Write: a modelled verse of a personification poem on rain is provided Practise: active and passive sentences	This unit is designed to last two weeks. During the unit, the class will read, compare and write poetry that uses different types of imagery, focusing on personification. **Phase 1: *Engage* (sessions 1–5)** The class reads and responds to a range of personification poetry and begins to explore personification. **Phase 2: *Explore* (sessions 6–7)** Children read poetry that uses other forms of imagery, such as similes and surprising metaphors. **Phase 3: *Create* (sessions 8–10)** Children gather personification and imagery ideas and write personification poems.
Bellerophon and the Flying Horse retold by Pamela Oldfield, from *Stories from Ancient Greece*, Kingfisher Books *Beowulf* by Kevin Crossley-Holland, Oxford University Press *Valdemar's Quest* by Jonathan Rooke	PCM 5a: identify the features of a quest adventure PCM 5b: write notes on two trial choices Homework 5a: use non-finite clauses to make writing come alive Homework 5b: include adverbials of time in sentences Software: Workpad 1: list the elements of a quest story Workpad 2: identify the story elements in a quest adventure Workpad 4: follow the pathways through a branching text Workpad 5: write the next section of a branching text Plan: plan a quest adventure using a frame with alternative pathways. A modelled version is provided Write: modelled sections of the story are provided Practise: adverbs	This unit is designed to last two weeks. During the unit, the class will read and explore stories with different reading pathways in the form of quest adventures, learn to create stories with different reading pathways, then write a branching quest adventure. **Phase 1: *Engage* (sessions 1–3)** Children read and identify the features of quest adventures and understand their narrative structure, setting and function of characters. **Phase 2: *Explore* (sessions 4–5)** Children explore how authors can shape a branching text by constructing different reading pathways for the same story. **Phase 3: *Create* (sessions 6–10)** Children create their own branching text with alternative reading pathways in the form of a quest adventure.
Television news report Audio news report *Inflatable Goal Posts* and *Speed Restriction Near School* from Delta Radio Game of the Week review: *Sensible Soccer* from www.firstnews.co.uk 9–15 June 2006 "Maradona puts England out of the World Cup" from *The Times* 23 June 1986 "Woman, 27, found after two decades lost in jungle" from *The Guardian* 19 January 2007 Interview with Rescue helicopter pilot coastguard Marsh by Jonathan Rooke "Who stole our goal posts?" from *Alton Herald* 16 June 2006 *Orphaned albino hedgehog arrives at Bordon Sanctuary* from Delta Radio	PCM 6a: compare different types of reports PCM 6b: note the features of newspaper and radio reports PCM 6c: make notes for their news report Homework 6a: write a review of a programme or film Homework 6b: write a review of an electronic game Software: Workpad 1: note the features of types of journalistic writing Workpad 6: write a report Workpad 8: write a radio news report Plan: plan a newspaper report on an alien landing Write: a modelled version of part of the report is provided Practise: punctuation	This unit is designed to last three weeks. During the unit, the class will read, compare and write newspaper and radio reports. **Phase 1: *Engage* (sessions 1–3)** The class reads and compares a range of newspaper reports and magazine articles, radio, television and online news reports. **Phase 2: *Explore* (sessions 4–9)** The class analyses newspaper, magazine and radio features and reports identifying style, structure and audience with some focus on fact, opinion and ethics. **Phase 3: *Create* (sessions 10–15)** Children make notes, plan, write and perform newspaper and radio news reports.

Unit	Unit focus	PNS strand objectives
7 How to Write Like an Author *Different authorial voices and styles*	**Speaking and listening:** Use a range of oral and aural techniques to investigate the writing styles of different authors, including drama and reading with expression. **Reading:** Identify and describe the writing styles of different authors. **Writing:** Write an imaginative story experimenting with some of the author techniques identified. **Assessment focus:** writing a chapter in the style of an author **Curriculum links** **Citizenship:** Children's rights – human rights	**1. Speaking:** Use a range of oral techniques to present … engaging narratives **2. Listening and responding:** Listen for language variation in informal contexts; Analyse and evaluate how speakers present points effectively through use of language and gesture **7. Understanding and interpreting texts:** Understand underlying themes, causes and points of view **8. Engaging with and responding to texts:** Read extensively and discuss personal reading with others, including in reading groups; Sustain engagement with longer texts, using different techniques to make the text come alive **9. Creating and shaping texts:** Use different narrative techniques to engage and entertain the reader; Select words and language drawing on their knowledge of literary features **10. Text structure and organisation:** Express subtle distinctions of meaning by constructing sentences in varied ways
8 The Great Debate *Non-fiction: Presenting a balanced argument*	**Speaking and listening:** Participate in a whole-class debate using the language of debate. **Reading:** Study how effective arguments are constructed in journalistic writing. **Writing:** Write a balanced report on a controversial issue. **Assessment focus:** writing a guide for parents on the use of computer games by children **Curriculum links** **Citizenship:** Choices; In the media	**1. Speaking:** Use a range of oral techniques to present persuasive arguments; Participate in whole-class debate using the conventions and language of debate, including standard English **2. Listening:** Analyse and evaluate how speakers present points effectively through use of language and gesture **7. Understanding and interpreting texts:** Understand underlying themes, causes and points of view **9. Creating and shaping texts:** In non-narrative texts, establish, balance and maintain viewpoints **11. Sentence structure, punctuation:** Express subtle distinctions of meaning, including hypothesis, speculation and supposition, by constructing sentences in varied ways
9 Finding a Voice *Poetry*	**Speaking and listening:** Use the techniques of dialogue to explore issues and respond to suggestions made when reading and writing poems. **Reading:** Understand how poets use different structures to create impact. **Writing:** Use varied structures to shape and organise poems. **Assessment focus:** writing a poem on an issue of concern **Curriculum links** **Citizenship:** Choices; Children's rights – human rights	**1. Speaking:** Use the techniques of dialogic talk to explore ideas, topics or issues **2. Listening and responding:** Analyse and evaluate how speakers present points effectively through use of language **3. Group discussion and interaction:** Understand and use a variety of ways to criticise constructively and respond to criticism **4. Drama:** Improvise using a range of drama strategies and conventions to explore themes such as hopes, fears and desires; Consider the overall impact of a live or recorded performance, identifying dramatic ways of building tension **7. Understanding and interpreting texts:** Understand underlying themes, causes and points of view; Understand how writers use different structures to create coherence and impact **8. Engaging with and responding to texts:** Read extensively and discuss personal reading with others, including in reading groups **9. Creating and shaping texts:** Select words and language drawing on their knowledge of literary features and formal and informal writing **10. Text structure and organisation:** Use varied structures to shape and organise texts coherently **12. Presentation:** Use different styles of handwriting for different purposes with a range of media, developing a consistent and personal legible style; Select from a wide range of ICT programs to present text effectively and communicate information and ideas

Texts	Related resources	Unit overview
The Suitcase Kid by Jacqueline Wilson, Random House Children's Books *The Reptile Room* by Lemony Snicket, HarperCollins New York *The Bad Beginning* by Lemony Snicket, HarperCollins New York	PCM 7a: write notes on the techniques used by the two authors PCM 7b: plan their story using some questions Homework 7: match some passages to the author Software: Workpad 1: make notes on author techniques Workpad 3: fill in a grid on author techniques Workpad 4: list techniques of two authors Workpad 5: list author techniques to use in own writing Plan: plan a chapter in the style of an author. Modelled plans for two authors are provided Write: a modelled start of a chapter in the style of an author is provided Practise: ordering clauses in a sentence	This unit is designed to last two weeks. During the unit, children will compare the writing of two authors and write a chapter for a story based on the techniques used by one of them. **Phase 1: *Engage (sessions 1–3)*** Children begin to identify a range of author techniques including point of view, narrative voice, language choice and use of dialogue. **Phase 2: *Explore (sessions 4–5)*** Children compare two authors, exploring their distinctive styles and continuing to identify author techniques. **Phase 3: *Create (sessions 6–10)*** Children write a narrative experimenting with some of the identified author techniques.
Mobile phones – good or bad? by Sarah Vittachi "Expert spells it out" from *The Guardian* 12 January 2005 "Posturing on lifestyle" from *Herts and Essex Online* "A good sport" from *The Guardian* 28 April 2005	PCM 8a: highlight arguments for and against mobile phones PCM 8b: prepare an argument PCM 8c: grade a discussion text PCM 8d: plan a balanced argument for a parent guide Homework 8a: identify persuasive words and phrases Homework 8b: identify the benefits and drawbacks of on-screen entertainment Software: Workpad 1: note arguments for and against mobile phones Workpad 3: formal to informal language Workpad 4: arguments for and against computer games Workpad 5: list more arguments for and against computer games Plan: plan a guide for parents by writing notes under headings. A modelled version is provided Write: children look at a modelled guide on a different subject giving arguments for and against Practise: using connectives to show opposing points of view	This unit is designed to last three weeks. During the unit, the class will read persuasive texts and balanced arguments, participate in an oral debate and write an argument. **Phase 1: *Engage (sessions 1–4)*** The class reads and responds to a persuasive text and a balanced report. **Phase 2: *Explore (sessions 5–7)*** Children explore arguments on paper and through debate, and analyse discursive reports, identifying formal and persuasive word, sentence and text level features. **Phase 3: *Explore (sessions 8–9)*** Children prepare for and participate in whole-class debate. **Phase 3: *Create (sessions 10–15)*** The class extracts information from opposing texts and organises ideas into a plan for a written balanced argument.
"Beyond de Bell" by Benjamin Zephaniah from *Talking Turkeys*, Viking Books "What's in a Name?", "Descriptions" and "Putting the Boot In" by Malorie Blackman from *Cloudbusting*, Random House Group "Billy Doesn't Like School Really" by Paul Cookson from *Elephant Dreams*, Macmillan "Bully" by John Coldwell from *The Works 6 Assembly Poems* "Give and Take" by Roger McGough from *Good Enough to Eat*	PCM 9: write a poem in the style of a poet Homework 9a: collect words on an issue for a poem Homework 9b: write down their feelings on two pictures Software: Workpad 6: make up new verses in the style of a poem Workpad 7: list things we take from the earth and what we give back Plan: write new verses of a poem in a given format. Some modelled verses are provided Write: a modelled version of a poem is provided Practise: similes	This unit is designed to last one week. During the unit, the class will read poems around issues, compare poets' styles and write a poem based on a structure of a poem. **Phase 1: *Engage (sessions 1–2)*** Children read and respond to linked poems by the same poet on bullying. **Phase 2: *Explore (sessions 3–4)*** Children explore poems by different poets about bullying and the environment. **Phase 3: *Create (session 5)*** Children choose an issue, then write a poem that communicates their feelings about it.

Unit	Unit focus	PNS strand objectives
10 Time Travelling *Short story with flashback*	**Speaking and listening:** Use dialogue and role play to explore the events and characters' feelings in a story with flashback. **Reading:** Understand how writers use flashback in stories to create impact. **Writing:** Write a short story on an historical event and include flashback. **Assessment focus:** writing a short story using flashback **Curriculum links** **Citizenship:** Children's rights – human rights; How do rules and laws affect me; Local democracy for young citizens	**1. Speaking:** Use a range of oral techniques to present persuasive arguments and engaging narratives **2. Listening and responding:** Make notes when listening for a sustained period and discuss how note-taking varies depending on context and purpose **7. Understanding and interpreting texts:** Understand underlying themes, causes and points of view; Understand how writers use different structures to create coherence and impact **9. Creating and shaping texts:** Use different narrative techniques to engage and entertain the reader; Integrate words, images and sounds imaginatively for different purposes **10. Text structure and organisation:** Use varied structures to shape and organise texts coherently
11 Walk to School *Non-fiction, formal writing*	**Speaking and listening:** Listen and write notes on the key points of a non-fiction text; make oral presentations on an issue and discuss their effectiveness. **Reading:** Read and respond to non-fiction texts on an issue. **Writing:** Write a brochure or a web page using a combination of different non-fiction texts. **Assessment focus:** writing a brochure or website page on a local issue **Curriculum links** **Citizenship:** Taking part – developing skills of communication and participation **Geography:** How can we make our local area safer?	**1. Speaking:** Use the techniques of dialogic talk to explore ideas or issues **2. Listening and responding:** Identify ways in which spoken language varies according to differences in the context and purpose of its use **3. Group discussion and interaction:** Understand and use a variety of ways to criticise constructively and respond to criticism **7. Understanding and interpreting texts:** Understand how writers use different structures to create coherence and impact **9. Creating and shaping texts:** Select words and language drawing on their knowledge of literary features and formal and informal writing; Integrate words, images and sounds imaginatively for different purposes **10. Text structure and organisation:** Use varied structures to shape and organise texts coherently **11. Sentence structure and punctuation:** Express subtle distinctions of meaning, including hypothesis, speculation and supposition, by constructing sentences in varied ways **12. Presentation:** Select from a wide range of ICT programs to present text effectively and communicate information and ideas
12 Plays and Performance *Playscripts*	**Speaking and listening:** Engage in discussion to explore themes and issues in plays and reflect on and respond to criticism given by others. **Reading:** Read and study plays to increase understanding of their structure and purpose. **Writing:** Write a play scene taking into account features of plays studied. **Assessment focus:** writing a scene for a play in which something unexpected happens **Curriculum links** **Citizenship:** Choices; Living in a diverse world	**1. Speaking:** Explore ideas, topics or issues **2. Listening and responding:** Analyse and evaluate how speakers present points effectively through the use of language and gesture **3. Group discussion and interaction:** Understand and use a variety of ways to criticise constructively and respond to criticism; Adopt a range of roles in discussion and contribute in different ways such as promoting, opposing, exploring and questioning **4. Drama:** Improvise using a range of drama strategies and conventions to explore themes such as hopes, fears and desires; Devise a performance considering how to adapt the performance for a particular audience **7. Understanding and interpreting texts:** Understand underlying themes, causes and points of view; Understand how writers use different structures to create coherence and impact **9. Creating and shaping texts:** Use different narrative techniques to engage and entertain the reader; Select words and language drawing on their knowledge of literary features and formal and informal writing **10. Text structure and organisation:** Use varied structures to shape and organise texts coherently

Texts	Related resources	Unit overview
Maggie's Window by Marjorie Darke from *The Oxford Anthology of Mystery Stories*, Oxford University Press News report from *The Morning Post*, June 1914	PCM 10a: write a day in Maggie's diary PCM 10b: plan a story using flashback Homework 10a: write a newspaper report Homework 10b: find the meaning of words from the past Software: Workpad 2: a diary writing frame Workpad 3: a timeline that plots the sequence of events in a story Workpad 4: make notes in a spidergram Plan: plan the progression of a story from the opening paragraph. A model plan is provided Write: a model of the next paragraph is provided Practise: changing word definitions	This unit is designed to last two weeks. During the unit, the class will read a complete short story which includes flashback and write their own story using the same technique. **Phase 1: *Engage (sessions 1–3)*** Children read a mystery story and consider how the author has used the narrative technique of flashback. **Phase 2: *Explore (sessions 4–5)*** Children explore the issues that underpin the story, reflect on the story's historical setting and explore it through discussion, drama and research. **Phase 3: *Create (sessions 6–10)*** Children write their own short story on a similar theme, experimenting with narrative techniques such as flashback or time travel.
"Letter to the Editor" by Karina Law "First Walking Bus launched in Sittingbourne" from *Kent Messenger* 2006 *Hop on board the Walking Bus* from www.kentwalkingbus.org *What do you think of the walking bus?*; *Courthouse School walking bus rules for children*, *Letter to parents* from www.foe.co.uk	PCM 11a: identify informal language PCM 11b: plan a presentation on an idea for helping the local community Homework 11a: find and use connectives Homework 11b: answer questions for a newspaper report Homework 11c: write a formal letter of complaint Software: Workpad 3: key points in a report Workpad 6: change informal to formal language Plan: plan a presentation. A model using the Walking Bus scheme is provided Write: write a brochure or website. A model is provided Practise: connectives	This unit is designed to last three weeks. During the unit, the class will read letters, newspaper and website articles and write non-fiction texts on an issue. **Phase 1: *Engage (sessions 1–5)*** Children read and respond to different types of non-fiction texts, including a letter, a newspaper report and a list of instructions. **Phase 2: *Explore (sessions 6–9)*** Children identify and prepare spoken presentations on how to improve their local environment. **Phase 3: *Create (sessions 10–15)*** Children write non-fiction texts using multi-media and employing a hybrid of text types for a website or brochure.
Macbeth adapted by Geraldine McCaughrean from *Stories from Shakespeare*, Orion Children's Books *Macbeth, Act IV, Scene 1* by William Shakespeare *The Railway Children* by E Nesbit adapted by Dave Simpson, Samuel French	PCM 12a: prepare a performance of a scene from *Macbeth* PCM 12b: plot characters' feelings PCM 12c: plan a play scene PCM 12d: prepare to produce a playscript Homework 12a: give the modern meanings of Shakespearean words Homework 12b: give the modern meanings of more Shakespearean words Software: Workpad 1: key events of a scene Workpad 2: key events of another scene Workpad 4: excitement graph Plan: plan a play scene. A modelled version is provided Write: a modelled play scene is provided Practise: conditional sentences	This unit is designed to last two weeks. During the unit, the class will explore part of a story retelling *Macbeth* and scenes from Shakespeare's *Macbeth* and a play version of *The Railway Children*, and write their own play scene. **Phase 1: *Engage (sessions 1–4)*** Children examine a narrative scene from *Macbeth*, exploring the themes and dilemmas of the main characters. **Phase 2: *Explore (sessions 5–7)*** Children explore through drama how a scene develops by examining *Macbeth* and another playscript (*The Railway Children*). **Phase 3: *Create (sessions 8–10)*** Children invent and write a playscript based on the drama techniques learned.

Unit	Unit focus	PNS strand objectives
13 Revision: Fiction *Planning and writing fiction*	**Speaking and listening:** Use discussion to evaluate and respond to each other's writing. **Reading:** Read texts to explore features, such as paragraphs and sentence types, to use as models for own writing. **Writing:** Attempt short and longer writing tasks in a test situation. **Assessment focus:** writing a timed story using a newspaper article	**3. Group discussion and interaction:** Understand and use a variety of ways to criticise constructively and respond to criticism **6. Word structure and spelling:** Use a range of appropriate strategies to edit, proofread and correct spelling in their own work, on paper and on screen **7. Understanding and interpreting text:** Appraise a text quickly, deciding on its value, quality or usefulness **9. Creating and shaping texts:** Set their own challenges to extend achievement and experience in writing; Use different narrative techniques to engage and entertain the reader; Select words and language drawing on their knowledge of literary features and formal and informal writing **10. Text structure and organisation:** Use varied structures to shape and organise text coherently; Use paragraphs to achieve pace and emphasis **11. Sentence structure and punctuation:** Express subtle distinctions of meaning, including hypothesis, speculation and supposition, by constructing sentences in varied ways; Use punctuation to clarify meaning in complex sentences
14 Revision: Non-fiction *Planning and writing non-fiction*	**Speaking and listening:** Use discussion and role play to explore non-fiction texts. **Reading:** Read and revise the features of different non-fiction text types. **Writing:** Write a discussion text and practise techniques for answering test questions. **Assessment focus:** writing a timed discussion text; answering questions on non-fiction texts **Curriculum links** **Geography:** The mountain environment	**1. Speaking:** Use the techniques of dialogic talk to explore ideas, topics or issues **2. Listening and responding:** Make notes when listening for a sustained period and discuss how note-taking varies depending on context and purpose **3. Group discussion and interaction:** Understand and use a variety of ways to criticise constructively and respond to criticism **7. Understanding and interpreting texts:** Understand how writers use different structures to create coherence and impact; Recognise rhetorical devices used to argue, persuade, mislead and sway the reader **9. Creating and shaping texts:** In non-narrative, establish, balance and maintain viewpoints; Select words and language drawing on their knowledge of literary features and formal and informal writing **10. Text structure and organisation:** Use varied structures to shape and organise texts coherently; Use paragraphs to achieve pace and emphasis **11. Sentence structure and punctuation:** Express subtle distinctions of meaning, including hypothesis, speculation and supposition, by constructing sentences in varied ways; Use punctuation to clarify meaning in complex sentences
15 Revision: Poetry *Reading comprehension (poetry)*	**Speaking and listening:** Discuss responses to a range of poems. **Reading:** Identify the different features of poems, including structure, organisation of ideas and the way language is used to create various effects. **Writing:** Record key features and personal responses to poems using a note-making frame. **Assessment focus:** answering questions on a poem **Curriculum links** **Science:** Interdependence and adaptation Section 6: Food chains	**1. Speaking:** Use the techniques of dialogic talk to explore ideas, topics or issues **3. Group discussion and interaction:** Understand and use a variety of ways to criticise constructively **7. Understanding and interpreting texts:** Understand underlying themes, causes and points of view; Understand how writers use different structures to create coherence and impact

Texts	Related resources	Unit overview
The Demon Headmaster by Gillian Cross, Oxford University Press *Dear Diary*, by Anna (Year 6 student)	PCM 13a: evaluate longer fiction writing Homework 13: use a range of sentences and vocabulary in a story Software: Workpad 2: put text into paragraphs Workpad 3: fill in a table on features of genres Workpad 4: use a planning frame to plan a story Plan: plan a story entitled *The Stranger*. A modelled version is provided Write: children write a story relating to a newspaper article about an escaped wolf Practise: ordering complex sentences into paragraphs	This unit is designed to last one week. During this unit, the class will practise writing short and longer fiction pieces in preparation for the National Tests. **Phase 1: *Explore and Create* (sessions 1–2)** The class explores the use of paragraphs and variety of sentences to remind them to use these in their own writing. **Phase 2: *Explore and Create* (session 3)** Children plan a longer story taking into account the features of the genre chosen. **Phase 1: *Explore and Create* (sessions 4–5)** Children write and assess a piece of longer fiction writing.
Eiger Challenge from www.mariecurie.org.uk *Sir Ranulph Fiennes' Account* from www.myspace.com "Helvellyn" from *Pathfinder Guide: Lake District Walks* compiled by Brian Conduit, Jarrold Publishing "What are volcanoes?" and "Living with volcanoes" by Anita Ganeri from *Nature's Fury: Volcano!*, The Watts Publishing Group *The Shadow of Vesuvius* by Maureen Haselhurst, Collins Education	PCM 14a: find the meaning of place names PCM 14b: write questions on a text for a test situation Homework 14a: organise a text into paragraphs Homework 14b: use connectives in different non-fiction text types Software: Plan: plan a discussion text about the risks and benefits of living near a volcano. A model plan is provided Write: a modelled version is provided Practise: formal and informal sentences	This unit is designed to last three weeks. During this unit, the class will explore non-fiction texts on a similar theme linked to the Geography topic: the mountain environment. They will practise formulating and answering questions in preparation for the National Tests and will revise the writing skills required to write different types of non-fiction. **Phase 1: *Engage* (sessions 1–5)** Children read and respond to a variety of non-fiction texts and revise the different features of each text type. **Phase 2: *Explore* (sessions 6–11)** Children read and respond to different types of non-fiction texts and gather information to develop a plan for writing a discussion text. **Phase 3: *Create* (sessions 12–15)** Children write a discussion text based on information drawn from non-fiction texts they have read.
"The Fly" and "Five Eyes" by Walter de la Mare from *The Complete Poems of Walter de la Mare* "A Fly and a Flea in a Flue" by P. L. Mannock from *The Kingfisher Book of Children's Poetry*, Kingfisher Books "Leopard" (Yoruba poem) "The Mole" by Stanley Cook from *A Third Poetry Book* edited by John Foster, Oxford University Press "Animal Riddle" by Pie Corbett from *Wacky Wild Animals*, Macmillan Children's Books "Spin Me a Web, Spider" by Charles Causley from *Collected Poems for Children*, Macmillan "Spider's Song" by Judith Nicholls from *Magic Mirror and Other Poems*, Faber and Faber Ltd	PCM 15a: analyse a poem PCM 15b: analyse a different poem Homework 15a: highlight a poem's features and make up questions on it Homework 15b: examine a poem closely Software: Workpad 5: use prompts to find the features of a poem Plan: design a planning frame to analyse a poem Write: write poems or limericks of your own Practise: prefixes and suffixes	This unit is designed to last two weeks. During this unit, the class will explore and compare poems on a similar theme and practise formulating and answering questions in preparation for the National Tests. **Phase 1: *Engage* (sessions 1–3)** Children read and respond to linked poems. **Phase 2: *Explore* (sessions 4–5)** Children explore poems by different poets about creatures great and small. **Phase 3: *Create* (sessions 6–10)** Children analyse poems on a similar theme using a note-making frame and practise responding to poems in a test situation.

Collins Primary Literacy
structure and features

Supporting you through the Teacher's Guide

The unit teaching sequence in *Collins Primary Literacy* follows three clear phases:

Phase 1 *Engage*

Phase 2 *Explore*

Phase 3 *Create*

Each phase incorporates speaking, listening, paired and small group discussion through reading, writing and comprehension activities. A clear unit focus is provided from the outset, in both the teaching notes and the Pupil Book, so children know the purpose for the activities they are doing. Children build up their understanding through progressive tasks towards a final piece which draws on the knowledge they've developed. The final outcome ranges from an extended writing piece to an oral presentation as part of an advertising campaign. Children are encouraged to work in a variety of contexts:

- as part of the whole class
- in small groups
- in pairs
- independently.

Icons in the Teacher's Guide indicate where opportunities for working in groups and pairs arise in the teaching sequence, for quick reference and easy classroom management.

 shows opportunities for paired activities

 shows opportunities for group activities

Integrated differentiation

Children working both below and above age-related expectations are catered for through interesting activities. Ideas for differentiating activities are shown by the following symbols in the resources:

 more able or extension activities

 average ability activities

 less able activities

Sentence (grammar) and word (spelling and vocabulary) activities are embedded within the programme in a coherent and progressive way, and suggestions are made for appropriate use of ICT.

Integrated assessment for learning

Assessment opportunities are threaded through units, with prompts for you to pause and assess learning of key objectives at the end of each phase, and support for assessing final outcomes at the end of each unit.

Children are encouraged to reflect on their own progress as learners, building up their confidence and raising self-esteem.

Guidance on success criteria is provided to enable you and the children themselves to monitor the success of activities – what went well, and what could be done better.

Unit plans

Each unit plan in the Teacher's Guide has a very clear structure.

Unit number and the suggested number of weeks that it can be taught over

Prior learning: a checklist for what children should already have experienced

Headline objectives for each unit written in child-friendly language for sharing with the class

PNS Framework objectives focused on in this unit

Cross-curricular links to other curriculum areas where this unit would sit well

Resources: what is provided in the materials and what to use alongside

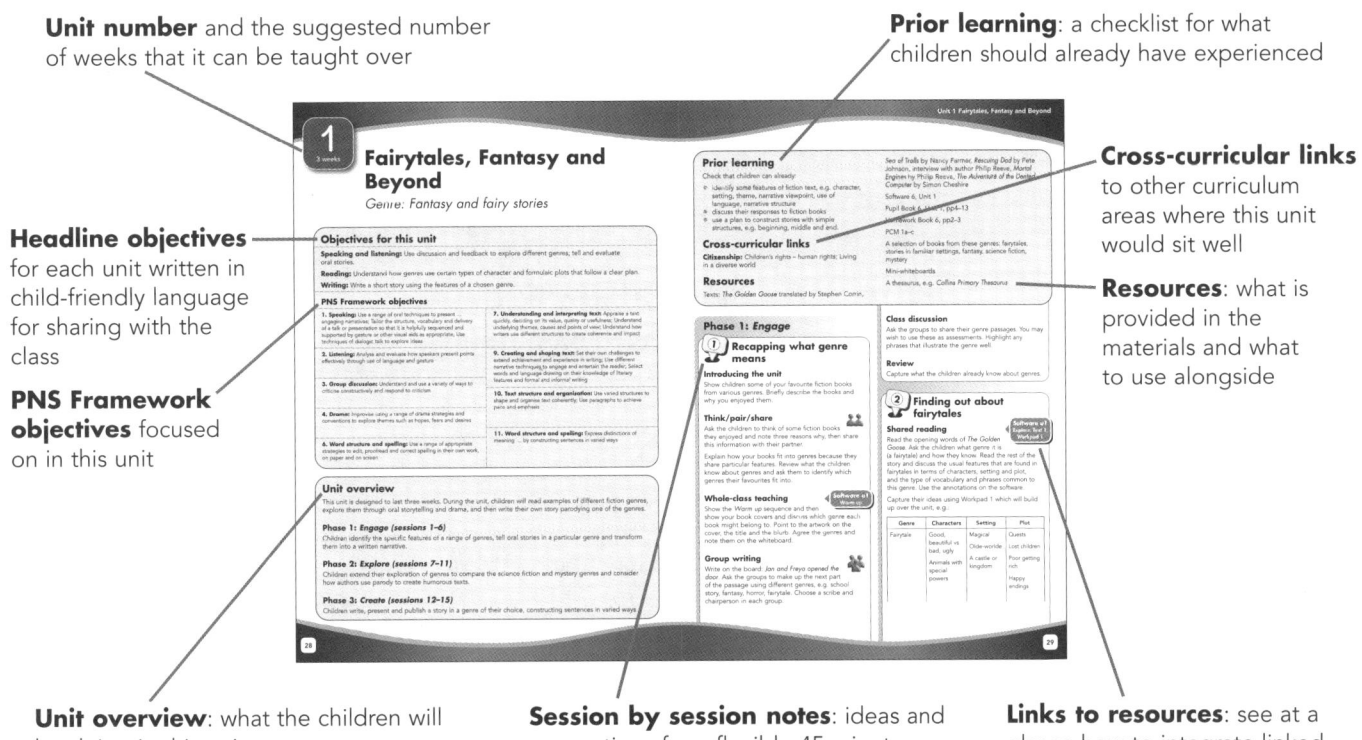

Unit overview: what the children will be doing in this unit

Phase 1: *Engage* (number of sessions)

Phase 2: *Explore* (number of sessions)

Phase 2: *Create* (number of sessions)

Session by session notes: ideas and suggestions for a flexible 45 minute literacy lesson, which can be combined to make longer sessions or followed day by day

Links to resources: see at a glance how to integrate linked resources into your session

Review: ideas for assessing what children have learned and how to progress

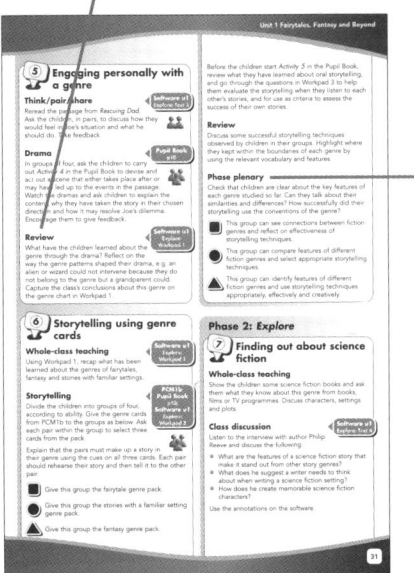

Phase plenary: a differentiated summary of where children should be at the end of each phase, linked to unit objectives

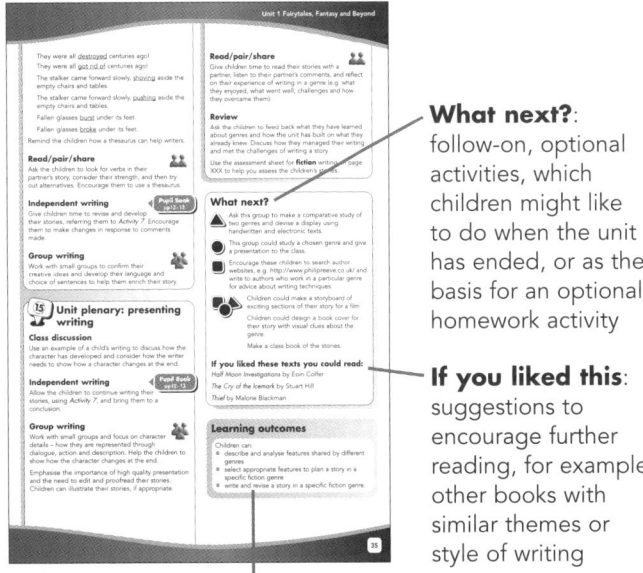

What next?: follow-on, optional activities, which children might like to do when the unit has ended, or as the basis for an optional homework activity

If you liked this: suggestions to encourage further reading, for example other books with similar themes or style of writing

Success criteria: assess children's progress at the end of the unit against these differentiated objectives

The three unit phases

A good plan supports and enhances your teaching and the children's learning. Each of the programme's unit plans have aspects of the new Primary National Strategy (PNS) objectives threaded through, including speaking and listening advice and suggestions for drama.

Every unit has three phases, broken down into easy-to-follow, numbered sessions. Each session within the phases flows seamlessly into the next, ensuring smooth progression across an extended learning sequence which may cover several weeks.

Built into each phase are your familiar teaching and learning strategies which engage and support young learners along their learning pathway.

All units have been planned like this to support your delivery in the classroom.

Phase 1: *Engage*

The importance of capturing children's interest from the beginning is a key teaching and learning strategy, and a variety of help is offered in the Teacher's Guide. The Warm up section of the software provides a stimulating "hook" into the units, with a multimedia looped sequence that gives a sidelong route into the themes children will encounter during the unit. Play it as children get ready for the session, and see their imagination and ideas fire up. The teaching notes provide ideas for questioning and focused whole-class activities to draw children into the focus for the unit.

Phase 2: *Explore*

In your teaching, you'll already use a variety of strategies to explore texts. *Collins Primary Literacy* supports these and more, with a wide range of ideas and resources for you to use with confidence in the classroom, from using a range and variety of questions that will help the children tease out meaning and reflect upon the purpose of writing, to exploring the text through using role-play, to using review sessions to share views and attitudes to the text.

Phase 3: *Create*
Written outcomes

Children find writing harder than other aspects of English. It is a complex task. Children will need to consider the likely audience for their writing, and how this affects the tone and style; the purpose of the writing, and how this affects layout; as well as sentence construction, vocabulary choices and punctuation. *Collins Primary Literacy* provides extra support to guide you though the important processes for teaching, modelling and supporting writing.

More guidance on assessing writing can be found on page 165.

Oral outcomes

Creating doesn't only mean writing. It's important to give children time to think through and talk about their writing, and *Collins Primary Literacy* recommends that some unit outcomes are based on oral work.

The value of preparing for an oral presentation as a final piece will stretch all children and, if done as group or pair work, improve their capacity to work well as a team. These are vital key skills, transferable to all other areas of learning. An oral piece might incorporate drama, presentations on the IWB (interactive whiteboard) and the ability to use a more formal speaking style. All these ideas are catered for in this programme.

Useful tools for teachers

You'll find these headings throughout the teaching sequence in *Collins Primary Literacy*, indicating where this type of teaching tool, or activity, can be applied. Use these tools for a talking, thinking, active classroom.

Think/pair/share	**Shared reading**
Group discussion	**Class discussion**
Drama activities	**Responding to the text**
Read/pair/share	**Write/pair/share**
Whole class teaching	**Paired note-making**
Reviewing work	**Demonstration writing**

Think/pair/share

This is partner work which allows children time to think about and share their views and experiences on a particular aspect of the unit.

You might take feedback from selected pairs of children using a "no-hands up" approach as part of an ensuing whole-class discussion.

Think/pair/share and the "no-hands up" approach

Many schools use this strategy. The benefits are that:

- children are given time to think about and discuss the question as part of *Think/pair/share* –so will have something relevant to say.
- children can work with different talk-partners, of the same or different gender, ability, and even age if in a mixed year class.
- quieter children, who may not contribute adequately to whole-class discussion as individuals, can feel more confident about talking in front of the class when sharing views with a partner.
- it prevents dominance by a particular child or group in whole class feedback.
- you can choose which pair to listen to, and can plan this so that different pairs get the chance to talk, avoiding the same children always answering.

Planning for group discussion

This has the same aims as *Think/pair/share*. Here you could circulate the room and join selected groups to support and genuinely participate in the discussion. This raises the status of talk in the children's eyes.

Encouraging independent group discussion

Here the group works completely independently of you. This is a key skill to develop, not only through Primary school but in later stages of education and work.

Children need guidelines for effective group discussion, and feedback from you on how to work in a group. Some suggested guidelines for these are on page 161; you can adapt these to suit your classroom or agree your own guidelines as a class.

Allowing time for quality class discussion

This enables children to hear the viewpoints of others, to make a response, to reflect upon and to learn from others' thoughts and feelings.

It could follow *Think/pair/share*, comprehension activities, shared, partner or group work. You might choose to use a "no hands-up" system to get the most out of the class. You might like to play "devil's advocate" and sometimes challenge the children's views – this also raises the quality of their thinking.

Whole-class teaching

Collins Primary Literacy offers real support for whole-class teaching, for example through ideas for explaining a particular piece of work, revisiting an aspect of the unit for further discussion and providing different types of questions, such as literal, deductive and speculative questions.

- **Literal questions**: ask that children select the **correct factual evidence** for an oral response based on the current activities e.g. paired discussion, review sessions, responding to a written text, or as a written response.
- **Deductive questions**: ask that children **work out or deduce** evidence based on hints in the text (reading between the lines) for an oral or written response, as above. These are higher-level questions, which demand more of children's reading and thinking.
- **Speculative questions**: ask that children use what they **know and deduce** to form a **reasonable hypothesis for speculative thinking**. These are higher-level questions and children find these interesting and creative experiences.

Building in drama activities

A number of different techniques are employed consistently across *Collins Primary Literacy*, including hot seating, role play, freeze-frame and decision alley. Children find these interesting and engaging and the more frequently they are employed, the better impact they have as a vital teaching and learning tool.

Using drama frequently helps children to stand outside a situation (in a book or activity), and look analytically at the causes of behaviour and reasons for both negative and positive attitudes. This approach is hugely enjoyed by children and boosts their thinking to the highest levels. More information on drama techniques can be found on pages 159 to 160.

Shared reading from excellent texts

This is really enjoyable for both teachers and children: first sharing and enjoying the text together and then exploring at the particular features which support learning objectives. Opinions from the class should be invited, and here again *Think/pair/share* is an indispensable strategy to get a comprehensive sharing of views.

First-class examples of texts have been provided in *Collins Primary Literacy*, from the best children's authors (classic and contemporary) to meaningful non-fiction to film, radio and television. All have been chosen to show how good authors work on the page or screen to create an impact on their audience. The children are also encouraged to go further outside the session with links to other related texts, and prompts to read the whole book from which the text was taken. At least one whole short story or short film is included at every level so children can investigate a complete text. Authors range from Roald Dahl, Jacqueline Wilson and Anthony Horowitz to the BBC and *The Times* to Shakespeare.

Responding to the text

Activities provide various ways for children to respond to the text, from comprehension activities in the Pupil Book, through drama activities, to drawing settings and characters, and so on. The comprehension activities have been designed to ensure that there are higher-level questions to develop children's thinking skills and make them justify their views. The questions have been differentiated so that all children are working at their ability level – but even the easier set of questions will have one or more open questions to challenge children who may be poorer readers, but high-level thinkers.

Children as readers and editors: Read/pair/share

Reading their own writing in pairs is an important evaluative tool for meaning; reading a published author together offers the chance for a shared view of the text.

Teacher at the heart of the writing process: Demonstration writing

Children really benefit from this approach where you demonstrate what writing involves, and think aloud for the children, showing them the decision-making processes involved in creating meaningful texts on paper or screen.

Overt demonstration like this helps children to see at first hand that writing is much more than just getting spelling and punctuation correct. Your running dialogue helps children to:

- **understand** that writing has a purpose – to inform, amuse, create empathy, express views, etc.
- **learn** that different forms of writing are needed for different genres and that the layout and word choices match the underlying purpose of the writing, e.g. clear instructions, a story opening to catch the interest of the reader, a persuasive poster.
- **note** that different audiences require different styles of writing, from the formal to the informal, e.g. a formal letter of complaint to a shop or an informal text message written to a very good friend.
- **wonder** at how word choices affect meaning – the impact of using *sinister* rather than *bad*, or *stench* rather than *smell*.
- **experiment** with different sentence structures within a variety of texts, such as hooking readers into stories through using different types of opening sentences, knowing that the present tense is used in explanations, and that sentences in reports can contain more than one fact if linked with appropriate connectives.
- **see** how punctuation helps the reader to understand the meaning better – from basic sentence punctuation to how to write down the actual words that someone is speaking.
- **know** that spelling does matter – and that a published piece of writing for someone else to read needs to make sense – so accurate spelling is important.
- **recognise** a well-presented piece of work – whether it is written by hand or on screen – and attempt to create similar texts themselves.

Write/pair/share

Collins Primary Literacy encourages children to write with a partner, discussing the task and experimenting with ways of setting it down. Writing can be hard and intimidating for children, so the notion of creating a text with someone else – experimenting and playing around with ideas, rereading and discussing the meaning of the text first – is a helpful and positive experience for children. Collaborative work like this eases anxieties over writing and raises overall performance, even in independent writing.

Independent or collaborative note making

This is a key research skill and children receive guidance on how best to manage this through the programme, for example they are encouraged to follow their own line of research from a basic plan.

Review: Time to hear views and extend thinking

The children are encouraged to take an active rather than a passive role to reflect upon what they've learned and think about the effectiveness of the different strategies they've used in their learning. You can challenge them further by asking them to assess their work for particular aspects, for example to read out particular sentences or to share their personal views on current work.

Summarising what children have learned: Phase plenary

This is found at the end of every phase and is an opportunity to take a snapshot of what the class should be capable of doing at that point. It's differentiated into three separate levels of ability: more able, average and less able, represented by:

 Square: Less able

 Circle: Average

 Triangle: More able

Independent writing

Children of course need to write independently, not only as an opportunity to consolidate their learning and show you what they can do but also to clarify their thinking, to express what they want to say and to experiment with ways of saying it! Assessment guidance is provided for you to assess where children are at in writing and what the next steps are at the end of each unit and also on pages 168 to 174.

Supporting you through Interactive Software

Collins Primary Literacy Interactive Software is integral to the teaching of each unit and is structured to exemplify specific learning objectives in the renewed Primary Framework. The software is creatively constructed and can be adapted to fit into a number of learning and teaching patterns. Built into the software is the familiar teaching pattern of engage, explore and create.

The Interactive Software includes:

Warm up: a multimedia introduction to the unit themes

Explore: a range of fantastic texts, including film and audio, to explore with the whole class, with ready-made annotations that highlight key objectives plus annotation tools to make your own

Workpad: frames that facilitate shared investigation of the texts

Plan: frames that support thinking and planning

Write: frames where children create and publish their own work

Practise: differentiated grammar and spelling activities with built-in result tracking.

Warm up

For each of the units there is a Warm up activity which you can use to capture the attention of the class. It's an engaging, multimodal presentation of the main ideas and themes that will be developed within the unit. It should be launched in an exciting manner to set the scene and capture the imagination. The presentation lends itself to being shown on an interactive whiteboard so that the whole class can become focused on the context of the unit. Many of the Warm up activities have sound and animation to further enhance the experience. These materials are specifically designed to promote discussion and enquiry, to set the scene for the unit and to annex the excitement of the texts to be presented in the Explore section.

The multi-purpose nature of the presentation can be very useful for groups engaged on speaking and listening tasks associated with the unit as it can be reviewed on individual machines. There is also an opportunity for further inclusion as it allows children to return to the stimulus to refresh their ideas either on their own or with the support of a Teaching Assistant.

Warm up provides a multimodal introduction to unit themes, allowing you to set the scene while engaging and inspiring the children

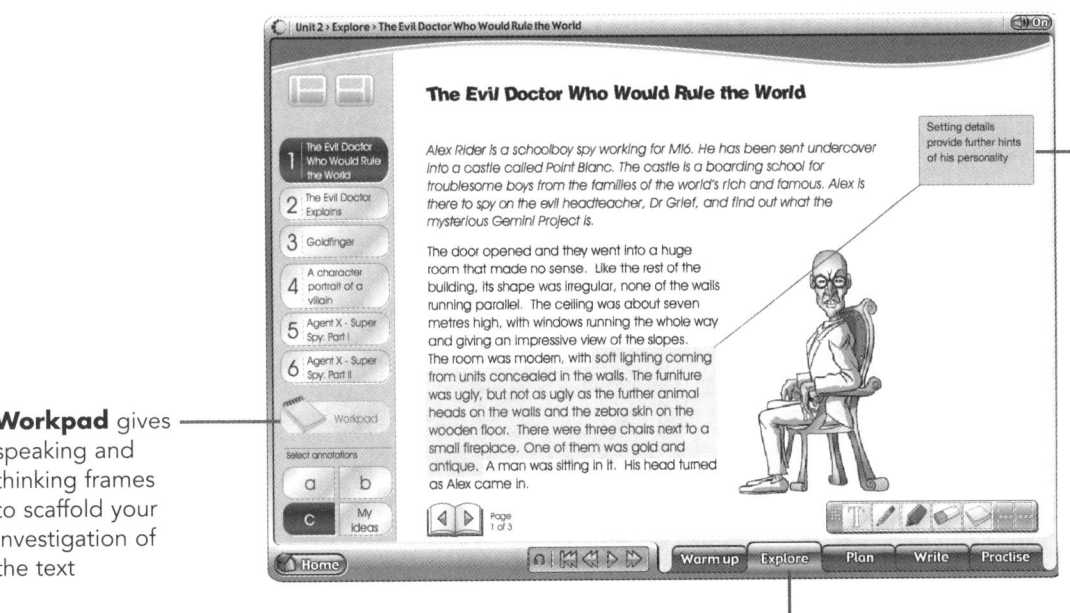

Annotations are provided ready-made to support your work with the class, highlighting key learning objectives at the click of a button

Workpad gives speaking and thinking frames to scaffold your investigation of the text

Explore provides an extensive range of exciting texts covering a variety of genres, styles and themes, including audio, multimedia and ICT texts

After the Warm up ...Explore

The *Explore* section contains the core of the teaching materials in the software and is entirely multi-purposed containing a whole range of text genres to be "read" from the screen, including ICT texts, film and audio. Here you can explore exciting texts with the children, with tools to annotate and make notes, or click to reveal ready-made annotations that support key objectives for that text, such as words and phrases that suggest a familiar setting.

Many of the texts have voiceovers so can be listened to as well as read, with playback controls.

Workpads are provided for many texts – ready-made templates to help you get started quickly on developing the key points from the text.

On to the Plan ...

Plan is a working screen, for you modelling with the class, and/or for the children working independently. Here you will find scaffolded frames especially constructed to help you or the children quickly focus on the ideas for the unit's extended writing or presentation. Text tools are available, so you can change font, size and colour to emphasise points and you can save your notes and print them if desired. These notes will support the important next stage of writing.

Write

This is the section where it all comes together; where children construct their own texts from the ideas learned during the unit and finally publish their own work. It is where they show that they have understood the objectives and it is where they powerfully and with pride show what they can do.

You can begin by modelling on the whiteboard with the whole class, with children progressing to write in small groups, pairs or independently.

Each page in *Write* has an appropriate template for the final work, with areas where text, images and sounds can be added to enhance the presentation. The final work can be saved and printed as well as published.

Practise

The activities here provide differentiated free-standing practice of grammar, spelling and vocabulary objectives linked to learning objectives from the unit. Responses to the questions are stored and an in-built tracking system records the results which you can access through the Teacher Controls for record keeping and assessment purposes.

Supporting you through the Pupil Book

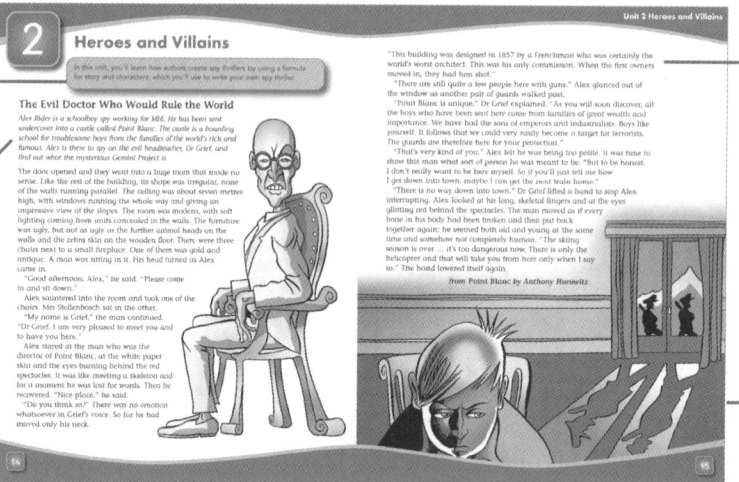

Unit overview — helps children focus on their learning goals for the unit from the outset

Text introductions put the passage into context

Exciting texts by top children's authors provide a wide range of writing styles and genres

Engaging illustrations bring the text to life

Responding to the text: clearly differentiated comprehension questions promote close reading and critical thinking

Grammar activities help children develop their essential literacy skills and apply them to writing

Writing activities provide an opportunity to consolidate and apply the skills developed during the unit

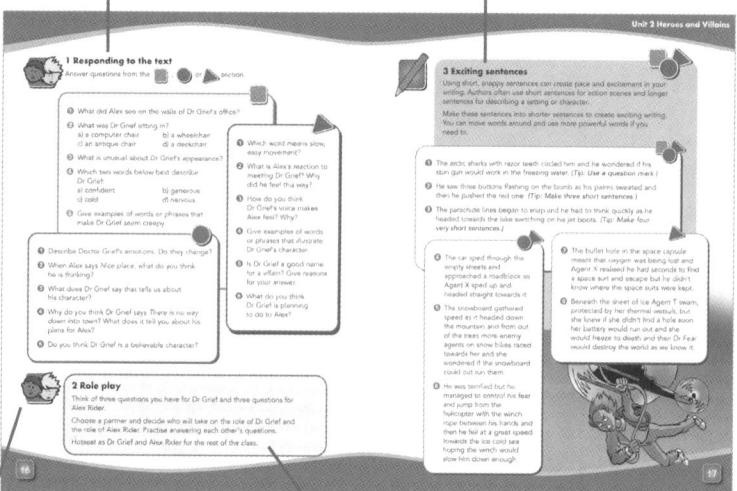

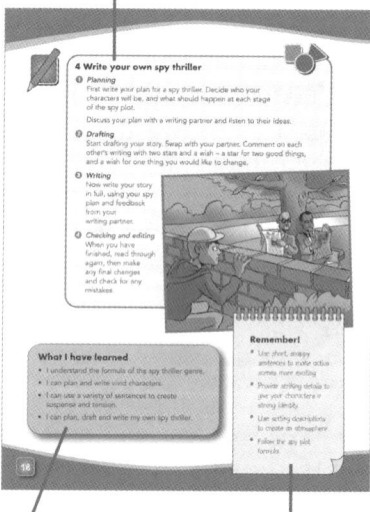

Activity icons show which activities have a writing focus and which have a speaking and listening focus

Role play engages children through drama activities, promoting higher thinking skills

What I have learned provides an overview of what the children have achieved during the unit, which they can use as success criteria for self-assessment

Remember! gives helpful suggestions to support children while they work

Encouraging interaction and giving you time to work with groups

The Pupil Book is designed for you to encourage children to work together on purposeful activities, which they'll discuss and think about as part of the unit experience. This allows you time to work with groups and pairs.

Helping children to be independent

Children are challenged to work as independently as possible.

For assessment purposes, children produce finished, independent pieces of writing as well as presentations based on research and group discussion.

Differentiated activities: *Responding to texts*

The art of creating differentiated activities takes time, as all teachers are only too aware. *Collins Primary Literacy* helps by providing activities differentiated for differently performing groups in your class. These are signalled by the three differentiation symbols, ■, ●, and ◀. Steer children towards the level that best suits them.

The comprehension questions in the section *Responding to the text* are interesting and challenging, with an emphasis on higher-level questions, for example justifying viewpoints, searching for evidence, and thinking about the writers crafting their work for particular purposes.

The less able section will also have at least one deductive/inferential question to stretch their thinking.

Assessment

Assessment is continuous throughout the units. You're encouraged to respond to what the children know and can do, supporting a personalised learning approach, rather than expecting them to fit a year group correlation. This allows children to reach their full potential. There are many and varied opportunities for assessment and self-assessment woven into the programme.

Prior learning

Collins Primary Literacy adopts using a "bottom-up" approach to learning, delivering what children actually need in literacy teaching. At the beginning of each unit is a section called *Prior learning*, which outlines what children should already know if the most is to be gained from the unit, and reminds you to revisit previous objectives for those children who need revision.

Review

Regular opportunities for you to review progress through the learning phases are built in so that you can check that progress is being made. Children are also encouraged to reflect on their own learning and what they need to do to improve.

End of phase review

These provide a series of statements which have been differentiated against the objectives for each phase, offering another opportunity to pause, reflect and check progress, to identify any areas of weakness that need consolidation, or opportunities to build in additional challenge.

General advice

Guidance for using formative and summative assessment can be found in Assessment and Progression on page 163, with support for assessing all key areas of learning, including speaking and listening, reading and comprehension, and writing.

Assessing writing

Levelled assessment sheets are provided within *Collins Primary Literacy* to help you monitor progress in children's writing against National Curriculum levels. These have been carefully developed to enable a quick check of where children are, what that means in terms of their level, and what they should be doing in order to progress. This helps you to focus your teaching for that child's needs. Levelled writing assessment sheets are provided for:

- Non-chronological reports
- Discussion
- Explanation
- Persuasion
- Recount
- Instruction
- Fiction.

Further guidance on assessing writing is provided in Assessment and Progression on page 165.

Fairytales, Fantasy and Beyond

Genre: Fantasy and fairy stories

Objectives for this unit

Speaking and listening: Use discussion and feedback to explore different genres; tell and evaluate oral stories.

Reading: Understand how genres use certain types of character and formulaic plots that follow a clear plan.

Writing: Write a short story using the features of a chosen genre.

PNS Framework objectives

1. Speaking: Use a range of oral techniques to present ... engaging narratives; Tailor the structure, vocabulary and delivery of a talk or presentation so that it is helpfully sequenced and supported by gesture or other visual aids as appropriate; Use techniques of dialogic talk to explore ideas

2. Listening: Analyse and evaluate how speakers present points effectively through use of language and gesture

3. Group discussion: Understand and use a variety of ways to criticise constructively and respond to criticism

4. Drama: Improvise using a range of drama strategies and conventions to explore themes such as hopes, fears and desires

6. Word structure and spelling: Use a range of appropriate strategies to edit, proofread and correct spelling in their own work, on paper and on screen

7. Understanding and interpreting text: Appraise a text quickly, deciding on its value, quality or usefulness; Understand underlying themes, causes and points of view; Understand how writers use different structures to create coherence and impact

9. Creating and shaping text: Set their own challenges to extend achievement and experience in writing; Use different narrative techniques to engage and entertain the reader; Select words and language drawing on their knowledge of literary features and formal and informal writing

10. Text structure and organisation: Use varied structures to shape and organise text coherently; Use paragraphs to achieve pace and emphasis

11. Word structure and spelling: Express distinctions of meaning ... by constructing sentences in varied ways

Unit overview

This unit is designed to last three weeks. During the unit, children will read examples of different fiction genres, explore them through oral storytelling and drama, and then write their own story parodying one of the genres.

Phase 1: *Engage (sessions 1–6)*

Children identify the specific features of a range of genres, tell oral stories in a particular genre and transform them into a written narrative.

Phase 2: *Explore (sessions 7–11)*

Children extend their exploration of genres to compare the science fiction and mystery genres and consider how authors use parody to create humorous texts.

Phase 3: *Create (sessions 12–15)*

Children write, present and publish a story in a genre of their choice, constructing sentences in varied ways.

Prior learning

Check that children can already:

- identify *some* features of fiction text, e.g. character, setting, theme, narrative viewpoint, use of language, narrative structure
- discuss their responses to fiction books
- use a plan to construct stories with simple structures, e.g. beginning, middle and end.

Cross-curricular links

Citizenship: Children's rights – human rights; Living in a diverse world

Resources

Texts: *The Golden Goose* by Sara and Stephen Corrin,

Sea of Trolls by Nancy Farmer, *Rescuing Dad* by Pete Johnson, interview with author Philip Reeve, *Mortal Engines* by Philip Reeve, *The Adventure of the Dented Computer* by Simon Cheshire

Software 6, Unit 1

Pupil Book 6, Unit 1, pp4–13

Homework Book 6, pp2–3

PCM 1a–c

A selection of books from these genres: fairytales, stories in familiar settings, fantasy, science fiction, mystery

Mini-whiteboards

A thesaurus, e.g. *Collins Primary Thesaurus*

Phase 1: *Engage*

1 Recapping what genre means

Introducing the unit

Show children some of your favourite fiction books from various genres. Briefly describe the books and why you enjoyed them.

Think/pair/share

Ask the children to think of some fiction books they enjoyed and note three reasons why, then share this information with their partner.

Explain how your books fit into genres because they share particular features. Review what the children know about genres and ask them to identify which genres their favourites fit into.

Whole-class teaching

Show the *Warm up* sequence and then show your book covers and discuss which genre each book might belong to. Point to the artwork on the cover, the title and the blurb. Agree the genres and note them on the whiteboard.

> **Software u1**
> **Warm up**

Group writing

Write on the board: *Jan and Freya opened the door.* Ask the groups to make up the next part of the passage using different genres, e.g. school story, fantasy, horror, fairytale. Choose a scribe and chairperson in each group.

Class discussion

Ask the groups to share their genre passages. You may wish to use these as assessments. Highlight any phrases that illustrate the genre well.

Review

Capture what the children already know about genres.

2 Finding out about fairytales

Shared reading

> **Software u1**
> **Explore: Text 1,**
> **Workpad 1**

Read the opening words of *The Golden Goose*. Ask the children what genre it is (a fairytale) and how they know. Read the rest of the story and discuss the usual features that are found in fairytales in terms of characters, setting and plot, and the type of vocabulary and phrases common to this genre. Use the annotations on the software.

Capture their ideas using Workpad 1 which will build up over the unit, e.g.

Genre	Characters	Setting	Plot
Fairytale	Good, beautiful vs bad, ugly Animals with special powers	Magical Olde-worlde A castle or kingdom	Quests Lost children Poor getting rich Happy endings

Responding to the text

Ask the children to fill in PCM 1a with the titles of all the fairytales they know with the listed features.

■ This group need think of only one fairytale for each category.

Review

Share some of the groups' titles. In discussion, reinforce how the children identify features shared by fiction within a well-known genre.

3 Finding out about fantasy

Class discussion

Briefly review the features of fairytales and explain that those of fantasy are similar. Establish what the class know about the fantasy genre from books, films or games.

Group discussion

Ask the groups to discuss their favourite fantasy books. Each group should list some features of the genre under the headings *Characters*, *Setting* and *Plot*.

Class discussion

Software u1
Explore:
Workpad 1

Share the groups' features of fantasy books and agree a class list under each heading.

Shared reading

Software u1
Explore: Text 2

Read the passage "In the Dragon's Claws" from *Sea of Trolls*. Discuss the children's response to the text, focusing on genre. What vocabulary and features show this is written in the fantasy genre? Can they see any similarities with fairytales?

Some key features of the fantasy genre are shown in the annotations.

Looking at simple and complex sentences

Pupil Book
pp4–6

Ask children to do *Activity 1* in the Pupil Book where they find examples of simple and complex sentences in *Sea of Trolls*, examine punctuation and comment on the effect created.

Storytelling

Pupil Book
pp4–6;
Software u1
Explore:
Workpad 2

Ask pairs to work orally on *Activity 2* in the Pupil Book where they make up the next scene of *Sea of Trolls*, using the vocabulary and features of the fantasy genre. Refer to the tips for storytelling in Workpad 2.

■ This group could tell it from Jack's point of view.

● This group could tell it from Thorgill's point of view.

▲ This group could tell it from the dragon's point of view.

Review

Share some of the oral stories, take feedback and highlight good use of genre. What have the groups learned from their fantasy storytelling? (e.g. the fantasy genre allows a storyteller to take the story in many directions and lets the imagination run free.)

Homework

Homework Book
p2

Activity 1a asks children to develop a storyboard to tell the next part of the story of *Sea of Trolls*.

4 Responding to stories with a familiar setting

Shared reading

Software u1
Explore: Text 3

Recap what the children have learned about genres and introduce the genre of stories with a familiar setting. Talk about books they may have read in this genre, such as those by Jacqueline Wilson and Helen Dunmore.

Read the passage "Dad's New House" from *Rescuing Dad* and discuss some of the genre features (e.g. children working out feelings and dealing with difficult circumstances, realistic and believable storyline, lots of dialogue to drive the story, settings we recognise, and sometimes the use of slang). Use the annotations on the software.

Responding to the text

Pupil Book
pp7–9

Ask the children individually to answer the questions in *Activity 3* in the Pupil Book.

Each group can complete the appropriate set of questions.

Review

Ensure the children have understood the text by discussing their answers. Can they identify any genre features in this story?

 **Engaging personally with a genre**

Think/pair/share

Software u1 Explore: Text 3

Reread the passage from *Rescuing Dad*. Ask the children, in pairs, to discuss how they would feel in Joe's situation and what he should do. Take feedback.

Drama

Pupil Book p10

In groups of four, ask the children to carry out *Activity 4* in the Pupil Book to devise and act out a scene that either takes place after or may have led up to the events in the passage. Watch the dramas and ask children to explain the content, why they have taken the story in their chosen direction and how it may resolve Joe's dilemma. Encourage them to give feedback.

Review

Software u1 Explore: Workpad 1

What have the children learned about the genre through the drama? Reflect on the way the genre patterns shaped their drama, e.g. an alien or wizard could not intervene because they do not belong to the genre but a grandparent could. Capture the class's conclusions about this genre on the genre chart in Workpad 1.

Before the children start *Activity 5* in the Pupil Book, review what they have learned about oral storytelling, and go through the questions in Workpad 3 to help them evaluate the storytelling when they listen to each other's stories, and for use as criteria to assess the success of their own stories.

Review

Discuss some successful storytelling techniques observed by children in their groups. Highlight where they kept within the boundaries of each genre by using the relevant vocabulary and features.

Phase plenary

Check that children are clear about the key features of each genre studied so far. Can they talk about their similarities and differences? How successfully did their storytelling use the conventions of the genre?

 This group can see connections between fiction genres and reflect on effectiveness of storytelling techniques.

 This group can compare features of different fiction genres and select appropriate storytelling techniques.

 This group can identify features of different fiction genres and use storytelling techniques appropriately, effectively and creatively.

 **Storytelling using genre cards**

Whole-class teaching

Software u1 Explore: Workpad 1

Using Workpad 1, recap what has been learned about the genres of fairytales, fantasy and stories with familiar settings.

Storytelling

PCM 1b; Pupil Book p10; Software u1 Explore: Workpad 3

Divide the children into groups of four, according to ability. Give the genre cards from PCM 1b to the groups as below. Ask each pair within the group to select three cards from the pack.

Explain that the pairs must make up a story in their genre using the cues on all three cards. Each pair should rehearse their story and then tell it to the other pair.

 Give this group the fairytale genre pack.

 Give this group the stories with a familiar setting genre pack.

 Give this group the fantasy genre pack.

Phase 2: *Explore*

Finding out about science fiction

Whole-class teaching

Show the children some science fiction books and ask them what they know about this genre from books, films or TV programmes. Discuss characters, settings and plots.

Class discussion

Software u1 Explore: Text 4

Listen to the interview with author Philip Reeve and discuss the following:

● What are the features of a science fiction story that make it stand out from other story genres?
● What does he suggest a writer needs to think about when writing a science fiction setting?
● How does he create memorable science fiction characters?

Use the annotations on the software.

Think/pair/share

Software u1
Explore:
Workpad 4

Ask the children, in pairs, to think about a particular science fiction book, film or TV programme and answer the questions on Workpad 4.

Review

Software u1
Explore:
Workpad 1

Briefly review their answers. Invite the children to name the key features of science fiction, and capture these on the genre chart in Workpad 1. Check that all children recognise the genre. Can they see the similarities and differences between it and other genres, particularly fairytales and fantasy?

8 Exploring science fiction settings

Shared reading

Software u1
Explore: Text 5

Read the passage from *Mortal Engines* and discuss how this genre has action, uses technology and often takes place in the future. How does this offer scope for the writer's imagination when inventing a different world? Talk about the importance of descriptive words, e.g. verbs, adjectives and noun phrases, in science fiction to paint pictures and highlight examples in the passage. Use the annotations on the software.

Interpreting text

Software u1
Explore:
Workpad 5;
Practise

Highlight the sentences in the *Mortal Engines* passage which describe Shrike the stalker. Once they can picture Shrike, encourage the children to draw the character and add labels with appropriate nouns, verbs and adjectives to the character web on Workpad 5.

Work through the exercise in *Practise* on powerful verbs, making the sentences as dramatic as possible.

Review

Reinforce the main features of science fiction and the challenges authors have when writing in that genre.

9 Finding out about mystery

Class discussion

Review what they have learned about the different genres.

Ask the class to suggest the key features of the mystery genre, drawing on examples from books, films, cartoons or TV programmes (e.g. Sherlock Holmes, James Bond, Scooby Doo).

Group discussion

In groups, ask children to make a list of features that belong to this genre on mini-whiteboards. Elect a spokesperson to give feedback. Take feedback and make a list on the whiteboard (e.g. clever detective, vital clues, detective's assistant, villain – someone you knew all along).

Shared reading

Software u1
Explore: Text 6

Share the story *The Adventure of the Dented Computer*. Discuss the children's responses to the story, e.g. what they liked, any questions, what worked well.

Whole-class teaching

Software u1
Explore:
Workpad 6,
Workpad 1

Identify key parts of the narrative structure. Point out how:

- a mystery is set up
- the key characters are introduced early
- vital clues can be found in the text
- the villain is caught
- the detective explains how he solved the mystery at the end.

Determine the level of excitement for some of these key parts and plot them on the 'hot' and 'cold' graph on Workpad 6.

Complete the genre chart on Workpad 1 for the mystery genre.

Writing a blurb

Pupil Book
pp11–12

Ask the children, in pairs, to write a blurb for *The Adventure of the Dented Computer* using the prompts in *Activity 6* in the Pupil Book.

Review

Share some of the children's blurbs.

10 Exploring parody in mystery and other genres

Class discussion

Software u1
Explore: Text 6

Look again at *The Adventure of the Dented Computer* and how the author has generated humour from the genre. Make a list of the key features of the crime/mystery genre and ask the children to identify these in the story, e.g. detective's assistant = Weasel Watson.

Explain how parody has been used to make the mystery story humorous. Discuss how these features have been subverted or played with by the author, e.g. the dopey sidekick Weasel Watson is a parody of Dr Watson in *Sherlock Holmes*.

Parody is when you take the features of a genre and exaggerate them beyond reasonable belief, introducing humour, e.g. the cleaner leaves her job to join the circus. Identify examples of humour in the text, e.g. *You didn't want to be in Thug's bad books unless you liked going to the dentist*. Use the annotations to show features of the genre and examples of parody. Ask for examples of where parody has been used in other genres.

Talk about how only the essential descriptions of setting and character are given. Examine the narrator, Kevin, and how the story is told from his point of view.

Write/pair/share

Draw attention to the way the author uses names to indicate the qualities of the characters. Ask the children to create character webs for some of the characters with words and phrases that describe them, share these with partners and explain their choices.

Drama

Divide the children into five groups. Assign four groups a character (Weasel Watson, Kevin, Thug Robinson, Mega Maurice) and one group the role of devising questions. Give each group time to discuss their characters or to devise questions for each character. Make new groups, each composed of one of each of the characters and one questioner. In their new groups hotseat each character. Explain that they are hearing the story from different characters' viewpoints.

Independent writing

Ask the children to retell the story from the viewpoint of either Weasel Watson or Thug Robinson. Share the writing with other children.

 This group writes from Weasel Watson's point of view.

 These groups write from Thug Robinson's point of view.

Homework

 *Activity 1b* asks children to identify and write notes on the genre which links to each story passage.

Homework Book p3

11 Creating and presenting a drama of a parody

Class discussion

Remind the children that features of a genre can be played with to make a humorous story. When writers do this they can create humorous situations, e.g. a nervous superhero, or a magician who can't remember any spells. Ask for examples.

Drama

Software u1 Explore: Workpad 1

Ask groups to prepare a five-minute drama of part of a story using a genre of their choosing (it can be a known story or one they make up) with some of the elements parodied. Some ideas could be to put characters together from different stories, give characters unconventional roles, or turn a character's qualities inside out, e.g.

- A fairytale with a brave princess and a cowardly prince
- A mystery with young detectives helping their not-so-bright dad
- A sci-fi with a family of aliens that act just like a human family.

Review how to plan and work together as a group.

Make the completed genre chart in Workpad 1 available for reference.

Give the children time to show their drama and take feedback from the audience.

Phase plenary

What have children learned about how genres can be used to create something new and interesting? Discuss the idea of stories having a leading genre rather than a single genre. Do they know any stories that are like this? (e.g. Harry Potter books combine fantasy and mystery.)

 This group can understand some techniques of writing in science fiction and mystery genres and describe what parody is.

 This group can discuss some techniques of writing in science fiction and mystery genres and understand what parody is.

 This group can compare techniques of writing in science fiction and mystery genres to their own writing and explain how parody works.

Phase 3: *Create*

12 Planning to write in a genre

Introduction

Tell the children they will be writing a story in their chosen genre.

Think/pair/share

After allowing time to think about what genre of story they want to write and key points, e.g. plot, setting, main characters and possible ending, ask children to share their ideas with a partner. (This will help to refine their ideas before they begin to plan. They can use their story as a basis for their plan, or reject it and start again.)

Demonstration writing

> **Software u1**
> Plan

Demonstrate planning a story. You can use the modelled planning frame for a science fiction story in *Plan*. Focus on establishing a main character and the problem they must overcome. Encourage the children to work out the ending before they begin writing by talking through your story using the prompts in the planning boxes.

Independent writing

> **PCM 1c;**
> **Pupil Book**
> pp12–13

Ask the children to use a chosen planning method and plan their own story in a particular genre. The boxes in *Activity 7* in the Pupil Book give the main features for each genre. Encourage them to use minimal notes in their planning.

 This group could use the planning grid on PCM 1c or the blank planning frame on the software.

Review

Share some story plans and ask the children whether the plans have fulfilled the criteria.

13 Writing a story in a genre

Think/pair/share

> **Software u1**
> Write

Give the children time to rehearse their plan orally with a partner so they can hear themselves working through the story to an ending. Discuss the questions in *Reviewing your story plan* on page 1 of the model text and ask them to comment on each other's endings.

Demonstration writing

> **Software u1**
> Write

Write some story sentences from a chosen genre, talking about your choices and how you might set out the rest of the story. Focus on the opening – establishing the character and the problem fairly quickly to engage the reader. (You can use the example on page 2 of the model text in *Write*.) Remind children about using paragraphs when structuring a story.

Group writing

Work with small groups to develop their openings and help them to move the story forward to an ending using paragraphs.

Independent writing

> **Pupil Book**
> pp12–13

Allow children time to complete their independent writing. They may use the blank writing frame on the software. Work with individuals and groups where appropriate.

14 Developing use of language

Class discussion

Read out some of the children's work and take feedback. If possible, display the writing.

Model ways of offering encouragement and constructive comments to help the writer – it is often helpful to give a writer time to talk about their writing.

Highlight the inclusion of effective vocabulary and using a variety of sentences, e.g. description of setting, well-chosen verbs to drive the story along, and use of simple and complex sentences for effect.

Read/pair/share

Ask children to comment on each other's writing, based on your modelling, focusing on the language used.

Ask some children to share the words, phrases and sentences they like in their partner's writing and explain why they think they work.

Exploring vocabulary

> **Software u1**
> Explore: Text 5

Tell the children that verbs are the driving force in a sentence and give writing pace and energy. Authors take time to choose the best verbs they can. Show them the examples of sentences from *Mortal Engines* and discuss how the choices Philip Reeve made are more effective than the alternatives below. Annotation set a shows these sentences.

They were all <u>destroyed</u> centuries ago!

They were all <u>got rid of</u> centuries ago!

The stalker came forward slowly, <u>shoving</u> aside the empty chairs and tables.

The stalker came forward slowly, <u>pushing</u> aside the empty chairs and tables.

Fallen glasses <u>burst</u> under its feet.

Fallen glasses <u>broke</u> under its feet.

Remind the children how a thesaurus can help writers.

Read/pair/share

Ask the children to look for verbs in their partner's story, consider their strength, and then try out alternatives. Encourage them to use a thesaurus.

Independent writing

> **Pupil Book**
> **pp12–13**

Give children time to revise and develop their stories, referring them to *Activity 7*. Encourage them to make changes in response to comments made.

Group writing

Work with small groups to confirm their creative ideas and develop their language and choice of sentences to help them enrich their story.

 Unit plenary: presenting writing

(15)

Class discussion

Use an example of a child's writing to discuss how the character has developed and consider how the writer needs to show how a character changes at the end.

Independent writing

> **Pupil Book**
> **pp12–13**

Allow the children to continue writing their stories, using *Activity 7*, and bring them to a conclusion.

Group writing

Work with small groups and focus on character details – how they are represented through dialogue, action and description. Help the children to show how the character changes at the end.

Emphasise the importance of high quality presentation and the need to edit and proofread their stories. Children can illustrate their stories, if appropriate.

Read/pair/share

Give children time to read their stories with a partner, listen to their partner's comments, and reflect on their experience of writing in a genre (e.g. what they enjoyed, what went well, challenges and how they overcame them).

Review

Ask the children to feed back what they have learned about genres and how the unit has built on what they already knew. Discuss how they managed their writing and met the challenges of writing a story.

Use the assessment sheet for **fiction** writing on page 170 to help you assess the children's stories.

What next?

 Ask this group to make a comparative study of two genres and devise a display using handwritten and electronic texts.

 This group could study a chosen genre and give a presentation to the class.

 Encourage these children to search author websites, e.g. http://www.philipreeve.co.uk/ and write to authors who work in a particular genre for advice about writing techniques.

 Children could make a storyboard of exciting sections of their story for a film.

Children could design a book cover for their story with visual clues about the genre.

Make a class book of the stories.

If you liked these texts you could read:

Half Moon Investigations by Eoin Colfer

The Cry of the Icemark by Stuart Hill

Thief by Malorie Blackman

Learning outcomes

Children can:
- describe and analyse features shared by different genres
- select appropriate features to plan a story in a specific fiction genre
- write and revise a story in a specific fiction genre.

Heroes and Villains
Genre: Spy thrillers

Objectives for this unit

Speaking and listening: Use feedback techniques to evaluate reading and writing, and to support the creative writing process.

Reading: Understand how genres use character types and plot formulas.

Writing: Write a short story using the features of a specific genre.

PNS Framework objectives

1. Speaking: Use the techniques of dialogic talk to explore ideas, topics or issues	**7. Understanding and interpreting text:** Understand how writers use different structures to create coherence and impact
3. Group discussion: Understand and use a variety of ways to criticise constructively and respond to criticism	**9. Creating and shaping text:** Set their own challenges to extend achievement and experience in writing; Use different narrative techniques to engage and entertain the reader; Select words and language drawing on their knowledge of literary features and formal and informal writing
4. Drama: Consider the overall impact of a live or recorded performance, identifying dramatic ways of conveying characters' ideas and building tension	**10. Text structure and organisation:** Use varied structures to shape and organise text coherently; Use paragraphs to achieve pace and emphasis
6. Word structure and spelling: Use a range of appropriate strategies to edit, proofread and correct spelling in their own work, on paper and on screen	**11. Sentence structure and punctuation:** Express subtle distinctions of meaning ... by constructing sentences in varied ways

Unit overview

This unit is designed to last two weeks. During the unit, children will read passages from three spy thriller stories and write their own spy thriller.

Phase 1: *Engage (sessions 1–4)*
The class develops their knowledge of genres, focusing on the spy thriller genre with an emphasis on characterisation.

Phase 2: *Explore (sessions 5–6)*
The class invents their own characters for a spy thriller and develops their understanding of how a spy thriller plot works.

Phase 3: *Create (sessions 7–10)*
The class plans and writes a spy thriller, constructing sentences in varied ways and considering presentation and publishing.

Prior learning

Check that children can already:

- identify *some* features of fiction, e.g. character, setting, theme, narrative viewpoint, use of language, narrative structure
- discuss their responses to fiction
- use a plan to construct stories with simple structures, e.g. beginning, middle and end
- have some knowledge of character and setting.

Cross-curricular links

Design and Technology: Draw plans for the design of a spy gadget

Citizenship: Discuss responsibilities and responses when people are threatened by others' actions on the world

Resources

Texts: *Point Blanc* by Anthony Horowitz, *Goldfinger* by Ian Fleming, *Agent X – Super Spy* by Jonathan Rooke

Software 6, Unit 2

Pupil Book 6, Unit 2, pp14–18

Homework Book 6, pp4–5

PCM 2a–d

Mini-whiteboards

Digital video/camera (optional)

Phase 1: *Engage*

1 Introducing the spy thriller genre

Introducing the text

> **Software u2**
> Warm up

Play the *Warm up* sequence, and ask the children what sort of story it reminds them of (spy story or thriller). Explain that they will be writing their own spy story and creating heroes and villains.

Ask if anyone has seen a spy film, e.g. James Bond or Alex Rider films. Ask them, in pairs, to discuss spy films they know. Who are the main characters? Who are their favourites? Take feedback.

Discuss how the characters in spy films are very important and the most interesting character besides the hero is the villain.

Shared reading

> **Software u2**
> Explore: Text 1

Introduce the first passage from *Point Blanc*. (The Alex Rider books by Anthony Horowitz follow the pattern of James Bond films.) Look at the way the author presents a character by focusing on a few very vivid details (e.g. his skeleton-like appearance and burning red eyes).

Think/pair/share

Ask the children, in pairs, to note the most striking details about Dr Grief, then share their ideas with another pair. Ask them quickly to sketch a picture of Dr Grief from information in the text, and to add their own words and phrases around the drawing to describe him.

Review

> **Software u2**
> Explore:
> Workpad 1,
> Text 1

Ask some children to share their work with the class, talking about the choices they made. Discuss how well they show Dr Grief's character. You could add the best suggestions to the character web in Workpad 1. Check that children understand the characteristics which make Dr Grief an evil villain. Use the annotations on the software.

2 Introducing characters in spy thrillers

Class discussion

> **Software u2**
> Explore: Text 2

Recap the passage read in Session 1 and read the second passage *The Evil Doctor Explains*. Discuss what the children thought of the two texts. What do they think about Dr Grief? Does he remind them of other characters they have read about or seen in films?

Responding to the text

> **Pupil Book**
> pp14–16

Ask each child to answer the appropriate set of questions in *Activity 1* in the Pupil Book.

Role play

> **Pupil Book**
> p16

Activity 2 in the Pupil Book asks the children, in pairs, to hotseat as Doctor Grief and Alex. Children answering questions could be filmed to capture their techniques in presenting their characters.

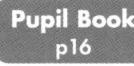

Group work

Software u2
Explore: Text 2

Ask the children to review their answers and decide what devices the author uses to present the character (e.g. action, dialogue, description, other characters' reactions, settings and possessions). In groups of three (chairperson, scribe and spokesperson), identify an example of each from the text and write it on a mini-whiteboard. You can show the annotations on the software.

Review

Share the children's findings with the class and capture them.

③ Finding out about characters

Shared reading

Software u2
Explore: Text 3

Read the passages from *Goldfinger*, which feature Ian Fleming's famous spy character James Bond.

Class discussion

Software u2
Explore:
Workpad 3;
PCM 2a

Discuss what the children already know about James Bond, and brainstorm the main types of character in this sort of spy story. Reveal the prepared spidergram in Workpad 3. Explain that they will look at four main character types: hero (e.g. Bond), controller (e.g. M, Bond's boss), villain (e.g. Goldfinger) and henchman (e.g. Oddjob).

Ask children to suggest a feature of each character and, using PCM 2a, add these to the spidergram, e.g. hero – *brave*; villain – *cunning*; henchman – *strong*; controller – *mysterious*.

Group work

Software u2
Explore:
Workpad 3;
Text 3
PCM 2a

Divide the class into four groups, assign one character type to each, and ask them to list the key features of the character on the spidergram using Workpad 3 or PCM 2a. Share each group's findings and build up a completed spidergram to use later. You can show the annotations on the software.

Review

Discuss in what ways characters in spy stories are different from those in most books. Could they be described as stereotypes? Why? The writer doesn't tell us aspects of the characters that we are often told in other genres, e.g. how they are feeling, how they get on with friends. Why is this?

④ Designing a character

Class discussion

Recap what the children have learned about the different character types in a James Bond-style spy story.

Discuss how, once a writer has a cast of characters that works well together, all they need to make a series of stories is to change the situation they find themselves in and rearrange the plot.

Write/pair/share

Software u2
Explore:
Workpad 4;
PCM 2b

Ask pairs to create a villain for a new spy thriller, using PCM 2b or Workpad 4. Display the completed spidergram from Session 3 for support. Encourage them to make up their own words for the villain's name and gadgets.

Next ask pairs to design a henchman to accompany their villain, in the same way.

Choose pairs to hotseat in the roles of their villains and henchmen.

Class discussion

Ask children to identify similarities between their villains, e.g. cruel, powerful, want to take over the world. Do the same for the henchmen. What does this tell them about this genre? (The villains and their henchmen tend to be stereotypical and easily recognisable in each story.)

Demonstration writing

Software u2
Explore: Text 4

Either model writing a character portrait of a villain, describing the character choices you are making, or use the modelled character portrait of Leo Von D'Eath on the software. The annotations illustrate the description used by the author.

Independent writing

Ask the children to write a character portrait of their villain, drawing on their Write/pair/share work.

Review

Draw out the reasons why the children think the characters in spy thrillers stay the same (e.g. as with fairytales, readers enjoy experiencing the same basic storyline – good winning over evil and overcoming impossible odds).

Homework

Homework Book
p4

Activity 2a asks children to design a gadget for a spy hero.

Phase plenary

Check that the children understand the key features of the main characters in spy thriller stories.

 This group can name some of the techniques used by authors to design a character.

 This group can understand how authors use different devices to show, rather than tell, the reader about a character.

 This group can reflect on and discuss the effectiveness of the author's choice of techniques to design a character.

Phase 2: *Explore*

(5) Plotting a spy thriller

Introducing the text

Explain that the class is now going to think about structure and plot. What have they noticed from their knowledge of the spy thriller genre about plot? (Stories in the spy thriller genre have similar structures; they work according to a similar formula.)

Think/pair/share

Ask pairs to note on their mini-whiteboards the plot devices they think make up the spy story formula.

Class discussion

> **Software u2**
> Explore:
> Workpad 5

Use the ideas from the pairs to compile a class list of plot devices, using Workpad 5. You may wish to draw from the modelled list.

Shared reading

> **Software u2**
> Explore: Text 5

Read the first part of *Agent X – Super Spy* – a short story that illustrates the spy story formula. Remind children to look for the elements of the formula in the story.

(6) Continuing plotting a spy thriller

Shared reading

> **Software u2**
> Explore: Text 6

Continue reading *Agent X – Super Spy* to the end. Ask for the children's response to the story.

Class discussion

> **Software u2**
> Explore: Text 6,
> Workpad 6

Identify the elements of the spy plot formula in the story. Show the annotations on the software. Discuss how a storyline can be created by choosing an option from each of the categories in Workpad 6. Ask for ideas that could link the story elements together.

Think/pair/share

> **Software u2**
> Explore:
> Workpad 6

Ask pairs to think up an alternative plot, using different choices from Workpad 6 and noting details on the mini-whiteboards.

Review

Share some pairs' ideas for a spy story, referring to the spy plot formula. Ask the class to evaluate the ideas using constructive feedback. Have they included all the elements for a spy story?

Phase plenary

Confirm that the children have understood the main elements of the spy plot formula.

 This group know there is a formula for the structure and plot of a spy thriller.

 This group can identify the elements of the spy plot formula and can develop their own plots and offer constructive feedback on other people's spy formula plots.

 This group can experiment with/develop their own spy formula plots for their own characters, develop a range of ideas for different parts of the structure and evaluate their effectiveness in response to constructive feedback.

Phase 3: *Create*

(7) Planning a spy thriller

Think/pair/share

The children are going to plan a spy story using what they have learned about the spy thriller genre (characters, setting and plot).

Remind them of the spy plot formula in Workpad 5. After giving time to think about their story, allow the children to share their ideas with a partner. Remind them to give constructive feedback.

> **Software u2**
> Explore:
> Workpad 5

Planning the story

Ask the children to plan their stories using the software or the planning frames on PCM 2c and PCM 2d, and their character portraits of the villains and henchmen. Also refer them to *Activity 4* in the Pupil Book for tips on planning and writing a spy thriller. They can choose to create their own hero or a James Bond/Alex Rider-style character. Remind them to think of ways to establish the main characters and to work out the ending when they plan.

Software u2
Plan;
PCM 2c, 2d;
Pupil Book
p18

Demonstration writing

Software u2
Write

Remind children that the setting for a villain's lair is very important. It sets the mood, tells the reader about the villain's character and provides the backdrop for the final action.

Demonstrate writing a setting, talking about your decisions (what you see, smell, hear, time and weather). Alternatively, you could use the sample writing in *Write*.

Homework

Homework
Book
p5

Activity 2b asks children to draw and write a setting based around a villain character.

8 Writing a spy story

Grammar work

Pupil Book
p17;
Software u2
Practise

Remind children of the effect simple and complex sentences have on writing from Unit 1. *Activity 3* in the Pupil Book explores ways to create pace and excitement in action scenes with short, snappy sentences and powerful language.

Each group can complete the appropriate set of questions.

If necessary, support this group. Alternatively, they could give their answers orally to discuss before writing them down.

Children can work through the exercise in Practise organising sentences coherently into paragraphs.

Independent writing

Software u2
Plan; Write

The children are now going to write their own spy thriller, using their plan from the previous session. Encourage them to use simple and complex sentences effectively.

Give the children time to write their spy thriller. Children may use the blank writing frame on the software.

Think/pair/share

Pupil Book
p18

Review the ideas for working with a writing partner during the writing process in *Activity 4*.

 Children could make a freeze frame of important scenes from their stories and ask each character to say what they are thinking and doing, how they got there and what they will do next.

Group writing

Work with small groups, focusing on how sentence variety and vocabulary choices support the characterisation and plot.

9 Continuing writing a spy story

Class discussion

Read out some of the children's writing and discuss how well it has worked. If possible, display the writing. Model ways of offering encouragement and constructive comments to help the writer – it can often help to give a writer time to talk about their own writing. Highlight the use of effective vocabulary and varied sentences.

Read/pair/share

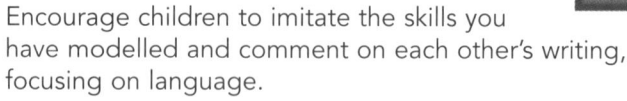

Encourage children to imitate the skills you have modelled and comment on each other's writing, focusing on language.

Ask some children to share the words, phrases and sentences they like in their partner's writing and explain why they think they work.

Independent writing

Give children time to revise and develop their writing, making changes in response to comments made.

Group writing

Work with small groups to develop their language and choice of sentences to help them to enrich their stories.

 **10 Unit plenary: presenting writing**

Demonstration writing

Software u2
Explore: Text 6

Discuss how to end their spy stories. Review the climax from the *Last-second saviour* section of *Agent X – Super Spy*. Do they think it's effective? Ask them to justify their opinions and apply conclusions to their own writing.

Independent writing

Allow the children to continue their stories and bring them to an end. Work with small groups, getting the children to focus on effective endings.

Emphasise the importance of high quality presentation. Ask the children to check and edit their stories for correct spelling and punctuation. Offer the opportunity to make illustrations if appropriate.

Review

When they have finished, give the children time to read their stories in their groups and listen to their comments. You could show some writing on the whiteboard for evaluation with the whole class.

Ask the children to discuss what they have learned, what they enjoyed and what was challenging. Ask each group to choose a spokesperson to share their thoughts with the class.

Use the assessment sheet for **fiction** writing on page 170 to help you assess the children's spy stories.

What next?

Collect chains of simple and complex sentences written by the children on a display board with captions saying why they are effective.

 Encourage the children to publish their story in a class book called *Spy Thrillers*.

 Ask the children to *swap villains* with a friend and devise another tense moment for their hero to escape from.

 Visit the website of Alex Rider author, Anthony Horowitz: http://www.anthonyhorowitz.com/ and the Alex Rider website: http://www.alexrider.com/home.

 Investigate what measures were taken during World War Two to prevent enemy spies gathering information.

If you liked these texts you could read:

Dawn Undercover by Anna Dale

Alex Rider: The Gadgets by Anthony Horowitz

Ark Angel by Anthony Horowitz

Special Agents: Final Shot by Sam Hutton

Learning outcomes

Children can:
- structure and plot a spy thriller
- use a range of devices to draw vivid characters
- use a range of simple and complex sentences to develop particular effects, e.g. suspense and tension
- write a short spy story using elements of the genre, e.g. clear plot progression, vivid characters, rich settings, vigorous action and thoughtful choice of language and sentence construction for effect
- discuss the reasons for their structural and linguistic choices.

3

2 weeks

This is Your Life

Genre: Biography and autobiography

Objectives for this unit

Speaking and listening: Evaluate how speakers present points effectively.

Reading: Evaluate, read, interpret and select information and distinguish between fact and opinion.

Writing: Write a biography to suit a particular audience and purpose.

PNS Framework objectives

1. Speaking: Use a range of oral techniques to present persuasive arguments and engaging narratives

2. Listening: Analyse and evaluate how speakers present points effectively through language and gesture

6. Word structure and spelling: Use a range of appropriate strategies to edit, proofread and correct spelling in their own work, on paper and on screen

7. Understanding and interpreting text: Appraise a text quickly; Understand underlying themes, causes and points of view

9. Creating and shaping text: Use different narrative techniques to engage and entertain the reader; Select words and language drawing on their knowledge of literary features and formal and informal writing

10. Text structure and organisation: Use varied structures to shape and organise texts coherently

11. Sentence structure and punctuation: Express subtle distinction of meaning, including hypothesis, speculation and supposition, by constructing sentences in varied ways

Unit overview

This unit is designed to last two weeks. During the unit, the class will read passages from biographies and autobiographies and write a biography.

Phase 1: *Engage (sessions 1–3)*

Children read and compare biographical and autobiographical writing and identify language features.

Phase 2: *Explore (sessions 4–7)*

Children analyse the construction of biographies and create their own biography for an oral presentation.

Phase 3: *Create (sessions 8–10)*

Children write a biography, reflecting on how biographers select, interpret and present information.

Prior learning

Check that children can already:

- recognise the language and structural features of diaries, other recounts and historical reports which use the past tense and chronological ordering of events using time connectives
- understand how texts are adapted to suit different purposes and audiences
- locate information in books and electronic texts such as websites.

Cross-curricular links

History: What was it like for children in the Second World War?

Resources

Texts: *Coming to England* by Floella Benjamin, *Boy: Tales of Childhood* by Roald Dahl, *Roald Dahl: A Biography* by Jeremy Treglown, Alfred Anderson obituary from *The Guardian*; *The Diary of a Young Girl* by Anne Frank and Susan Massotty

Software 6, Unit 3

Pupil Book 6, Unit 3 pp19–25

Homework Book 6, pp6–7

Memory box (box with six objects that have a particular significance to you)

Printouts of the historical documents about Charles Wintergarden (can be found in Software Resource Library)

Phase 1: *Engage*

1 Introduction to autobiography

Introducing the unit

> Software u3
> Warm up

Set the scene by showing the *Warm up* sequence that reveals the key points in a person's life. Discuss the root meaning of the word autobiography. It comes from the Greek: autos (self); bios (life); graphe (writing).

Class discussion

Tell the children a story from your own life. Ask them to tell a partner a similar anecdote from their own life. Have they told the whole truth, left bits out, or exaggerated? What does their partner think? What is the difference between an autobiography and a biography?

Shared reading

> Software u3
> Explore: Text 1

Read the passages from Floella Benjamin's autobiography, *Coming to England*. What do the children notice about how events are described? Use the annotations on the software and compile a list of the key features of an autobiography, e.g. focuses on key moments in chronological order, uses past tense, the first person, reveals thoughts and feelings to the audience in a confidential way. Are there any similarities to a fiction text?

Class discussion

> Software u3
> Explore: Workpad 1

Provide a short autobiography of your own life using a timeline labelled with some main events. There is an example in Workpad 1.

Demonstrate how to construct a timeline.

Born	Brother Fred born	Went to school	Lived in Paris	Became a teacher

Think/pair/share

> Software u3
> Explore: Workpad 1

Ask children to make a timeline of their life and tell their autobiography to their partner. Ask them to note down the key points of their partner's life on another timeline and compare them. Help children to understand how this timeline of their partner's life is a biography.

Review

Discuss what might happen to the timeline if another member of the family added other stories and events to it. Ask the children to bring to the next session a *memory box* of six objects that mean something to them, which they can use to tell a story about their life.

2 Autobiography as a point of view

Whole-class teaching

Show children the objects in your own memory box and tell the story they refer to. Demonstrate plotting the events on an autobiographical timeline. You could use the timeline in Workpad 1.

Think/pair/share

Children share the stories behind the objects in their memory box with a partner and plot them on an autobiographical timeline.

Independent writing

Ask children to choose one of the events on their timeline and write a short description of it, using the language features of autobiography they identified.

Review

Share some of the children's life stories, pointing out and praising use of autobiographical language features. Would the stories be different if someone else told them? Why might autobiographies be biased in how they tell events?

3 Comparing autobiography and biography

Shared reading

> **Software u3**
> Explore: Text 2

Review what the children have learned about autobiography. Ask them what they already know about Roald Dahl. Read the passage from *Boy*. What do the children think about life at Dahl's school? Find and discuss the key points in the passage. Show the annotations on the software.

Responding to the text

> **Pupil Book**
> pp19–20

Ask the children to reread the passage from *Boy* and then answer the questions in *Activity 1*.

   Each group can complete the appropriate set of questions.

Shared reading

> **Software u3**
> Explore: Text 3,
> Workpad 2

Review the children's understanding of the difference between autobiography and biography. (You could use the model comparison grid in Workpad 2.)

Read the passage from *Roald Dahl – A Biography* by Jeremy Treglown. Explain that this is a biographical account of Roald Dahl whereas the passage from *Boy* is an autobiographical account. The annotations on the software show the key features of the text.

Group discussion

> **Software u3**
> Explore: Text 3;
> **Pupil Book**
> p19

Ask each group to compare the two texts using the following questions. They should agree reasons for their answers, appointing a scribe and spokesperson. Take feedback from each group.

1 How do the two accounts of Roald Dahl's life at Repton differ?

2 Which is more likely to offer facts rather than opinions?

3 Where has the biography used other people's opinions?

4 Which account is more likely to be accurate?

5 How will Treglown's version affect readers' opinion of Dahl?

Phase plenary

> **Software u3**
> Explore:
> Workpad 3

Use the table in Workpad 3 to discuss how events are interpreted differently between biography and autobiography.

Check what children have learned about the difference between biography and autobiography and the key features of each type of writing.

   Children can describe what an autobiography and a biography are.

   Children can understand differences between autobiography and biography, identify language features and some effects these have on readers.

   Children can compare and contrast biography and autobiography and discuss how different sources of information and language features can affect readers.

Phase 2: *Explore*

4 Exploring an obituary

Shared reading

> **Software u3**
> Explore: Text 4

Introduce another type of biography – the obituary. Do the children know what an obituary is? (A short biography of a person published on their death, usually in a newspaper)

Read the obituary of Alfred Anderson (the last survivor who witnessed the alleged 1914 Christmas Truce in the trenches in France during the First World War). Use the annotations to discuss how it is composed, e.g. uses past tense and third person, comments from friends and relatives, interview material, selects most interesting events of his life, includes a photo.

Write/pair/share

Ask the children to write a 150-word obituary for a superhero for the publication *Superhero Monthly*. Each pair should agree the life history of the superhero prior to starting the obituary. Remind the children of the key features of a biography and obituary.

Review

Discuss the importance of using other people's recollections in biographical accounts and how reliable they might be. Check that children understand the steps they need to take to change a piece of text from the first to the third person.

5 Researching a biography

Whole-class teaching

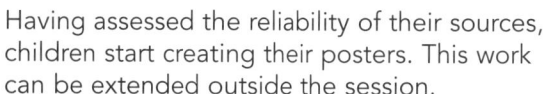
Software u3
Explore: Text 5

Read the biography of Anne Frank. Look at the ways of displaying information: discuss the layout and the way timelines and images are used to present a biography to readers. What effect does this have? (e.g. Readers can scan the page to glean information about the person quickly.) Show the annotations on the software.

Group work

Each group will make a biography poster. They should decide who the poster will be about, where to find information and how to design the poster. They should share information-finding tasks and decide what source material they will need. Review techniques for finding information in non-fiction texts, e.g. using contents and indexes, skimming and scanning. Provide access to a range of information resources, including the Internet if possible.

Review

Each group should feed back to the class on what they have decided. Discuss techniques for gathering information, and ask them to begin collecting source material.

6 Evaluating sources of information

Whole-class teaching

Software u3
Explore:
Workpad 5

Review note-making techniques such as capturing key words, using timelines and creating mind maps. You can note down your ideas on the spider diagram in Workpad 5.

Group work

Ask the groups to collect information and make notes for their poster biography from their sources.

Class discussion

Ask the groups to evaluate the evidence they have collected for their biography considering the following questions, and feed back to the class.

- How reliable is the information?
- Where did it come from?
- Is there a chance it is biased?
- Do different sources offer conflicting viewpoints?
- Could the group have interpreted the information in a different way to another reader?

Children should refer back to the source material and give examples that support their answers. Is the information fact or opinion? How do they know? (Remind children of the reading objective for this unit.)

Group work

Having assessed the reliability of their sources, children start creating their posters. This work can be extended outside the session.

Review

Discuss the responsibilities of a biographer. Draw up a class list of *dos and don'ts* for writing a reliable biography.

7 Presenting a biography

Group work

Discuss how the groups could present the information in their poster to an audience. Ask them to prepare a presentation, assigning roles. It could include a dramatised *interview* with the subject or a friend of the subject.

Group presentations

Ask the groups to present their poster biography and their *interviews* to the class. The class should provide feedback on the balance of facts and opinions, the point of view, unanswered questions and the clarity of the presentation.

Phase plenary

Discuss how the presentation, content and emphasis might differ if presented to another audience, or if there was less time to present it, e.g. a ten-second biography. Capture their top tips in preparation for writing a biography in the next phase.

Children can take notes from different sources and work in a group to compose a biographical account for presentation.

 Children can select relevant information considering the purpose of resources to compose a biographical account for a presentation.

 Children can discuss how biographers use and interpret different sources and compose a biographical account for a presentation.

Phase 3: *Create*

 **8 Planning to write a biography**

Class discussion

> **Pupil Book pp21–24; Software u3** Explore: Text 6

Using the Pupil Book and the software, look at the collection of historical documents relating to Charles Wintergarden, discovered by a relative. Listen to the interview of Charles Wintergarden's friend Bert Leatherbarrow, talking about their friendship.

The children are going to be historians and, in groups, will use their skills of inference, deduction and making connections to plan and write a short biography of Charles Wintergarden from the various sources.

Discuss deduction and inference. Explain that deduction is using clues within a text to draw a conclusion. Inference is bringing your own experience and understanding to a text to draw a conclusion, e.g. if you read a letter that had ink-smudged water stains, you could infer that these were tear stains. Knowing how you would feel if someone you loved was far away you can work out how the person was feeling when they wrote the letter. With this in mind, show the annotations on the software.

Group work

> **Pupil Book pp21–24; Software u3** Plan

Form groups. Prompt each group to agree their strategies, discuss what they have found out about Charles Wintergarden and begin to make a timeline of his life, referring to *Activity 2* and the model timeline in *Plan*.

Review

Ask the spokespersons from some groups to share their information, collecting strategies and findings.

 **9 Designing and writing a biography**

Think/pair/share

The children are going to design a biography of Charles Wintergarden based on their notes. Agree what audience they are writing for, e.g. readers who are looking for reliable, accessible information. Prompt them to discuss with a partner what they might write.

Demonstration writing

> **Software u3** Write

Write some sentences for a biography of Charles Wintergarden talking about your choices of vocabulary and sentence construction. In your modelled writing, emphasise:

- using time connectives and adverbial phrases
- giving key dates
- showing how you have interpreted source material
- giving other people's points of view about the character.

You can use the modelled text in *Write* to get started.

Guided writing

> **Pupil Book p25; Software u3** Write

Work with small groups to develop their biographies and help them to use the notes they have made. Make sure they refer to the *Remember!* tips in *Activity 3* of the Pupil Book, which focus on the features of biography. They can use the blank writing frame on the software to complete their writing.

Discuss how they should make a selection of the most interesting information and how this should faithfully reflect the evidence available. They should include quotes of some sources and understand why some information can be left out. Think about how alternative interpretations of Charles's life could be made and the reasons why they, as authors, have chosen their final interpretation.

Review

Share the challenges of using evidence to write a biography, e.g. using inference and deduction, selecting information that interests the reader, deciding which information to leave out, choosing effective quotes to make a point and keeping their personal opinions invisible.

 **10 Unit plenary: presenting a biography**

Independent writing

Allow the children to complete their biographies.

Guided writing

Work with small groups to focus on building up a whole picture from the details in the documents. Help them to respond to each other's work, checking for language features of a biography.

Editing

Emphasise the importance of high quality presentation and the need to edit, proofread and use illustrations and timelines to make information accessible.

Think/pair/share

> **Pupil Book**
> **p25**

Pairs should swap their work and listen to their partner's comments, referring to *Activity 4*. Ask them to write a few reflective lines about their experience of writing a biography, e.g. what they enjoyed, what went well, where it was a struggle, how they overcame challenges.

Compile the biographies into a class book or display.

Review

Check that the children can distinguish between a biography and an autobiography. Discuss how they met the challenges of writing a biography and if it has changed the way they read autobiographies and biographies.

Use the assessment sheet for **recount** writing on page 174 to help you assess the children's biographies.

What next?

 Children can work through the exercise in *Practise* on spelling.

> **Software u3**
> **Practise**

 *Activity 3a* asks children to make a Trading Card biography for a favourite sports or pop star personality.

> **Homework Book**
> **p6**

 Children collect obituaries from newspapers and discuss them.

 Children search for information on a modern historical figure from different sources and compare them. Why do the sources provide different information?

 *Activity 3b* asks children to write a biography of one of the members of their family.

> **Homework Book**
> **p7**

 Children design and write an autobiography using photos and objects, e.g. certificates, tickets.

 Children visit a local home for the elderly and conduct interviews that lead to writing a biography. They then present a book to the home with the children's biographies of all the residents.

If you liked these texts you could read:

Autobiographies of authors on their websites

A biography or autobiography of a hero

Learning outcomes

Children can:

- describe the differences between a biography and an autobiography
- reflect on the range of ways writers can select, interpret and present information in biographies and autobiographies and discuss the impact this can have in a range of contexts, e.g. obituaries
- use information sources to compile a biography.

The Power of Imagery
Genre: Personification in poetry

Objectives for this unit

Speaking and listening: Use the techniques of dialogic talk to explore ideas.

Reading: Explore how poets use powerful forms of imagery including personification.

Writing: Write poetry using personification and simile and metaphor.

PNS Framework objectives

1. Speaking: Use the techniques of dialogic talk to explore ideas, topics or issues	**7. Understanding and interpreting texts:** Understand underlying themes, causes and points of view; Understand how writers use different structures to create coherence and impact
3. Group discussion and interaction: Understand and use a variety of ways to criticise constructively and respond to criticism	**9. Creating and shaping texts:** Select words and language drawing on their knowledge of literary features and formal and informal writing
6. Word structure and spelling: Use a range of appropriate strategies to edit, proofread and correct spelling in their own work, on paper and on screen	**10. Text structure and organisation:** Use varied structures to shape and organise texts coherently

Unit overview

This unit is designed to last two weeks. During the unit, the class will read, compare and write poetry that uses different types of imagery, focusing on personification.

Phase 1: *Engage and Explore (sessions 1–5)*

The class reads and responds to a range of personification poetry and begins to explore personification.

Phase 2: *Engage and Explore (sessions 6–7)*

Children read poetry that uses other forms of imagery, such as similes and surprising metaphors.

Phase 3: *Create (sessions 8–10)*

Children gather personification and imagery ideas and write personification poems.

Prior learning

Check that children can already:

- identify and discuss similes and metaphors
- use verb tenses consistently
- understand the differences between narrative and poetic forms
- draw upon their imagination to create images.

Cross-curricular links

Geography: Connecting ourselves to the world

Resources

Texts: *Xmas* by Wes Magee, *Silver* by Walter de la Mare, *Snow and Snow* by Ted Hughes, *Wake up* by Christine Chen, *The Warm and the Cold* by Ted Hughes, *Reader: But what **is** Poetry? Adrian:* by Adrian Mitchell

Software 6, Unit 4

Pupil Book 6, Unit 4, pp26–30

Homework Book 6, pp8–9

PCM 4a–c

Mini-whiteboards

Phase 1: *Engage and Explore*

1 Explaining personification poetry

Introducing the texts

Discuss how the class will explore personification poems. Explain the differences between metaphors, similes and personification. (Personification is a form of metaphor: non-human subjects and abstract ideas are described as if they own human characteristics.)

Class discussion

Software u4
Warm up

Show the *Warm up* sequence which reveals an atmospheric scene and use it as a stimulus for discussion.

Shared reading

Software u4
Explore: Text 1, Text 2

Read the poem *Xmas*. Ask the children to describe the two scenes portrayed in the poem.

Reread it, this time drawing children's attention to the active verb *huddles* in:

> *The frost-bitten garden*
> *Huddles under a duvet of snow.*

Why does the poet choose to describe the garden as if it were a person? Why is *duvet* an appropriate metaphor for snow?

Look at other examples of personification in the poem (*Not a twig stirs*, *Holly awaits the advent of balloons*, *the TV set glows tipsy with joy*). Explain that by giving non-human subjects human actions, the reader is able to identify more closely with the subject described. Use Annotation sets a and b on the software to show active verbs and examples of personification in the poem.

Introduce *Silver*. Ask the children what they think is being personified in this poem. Reread the first four lines, asking a volunteer to mime the movements of the moon. Which active verbs are being used to describe the moon's graceful movements (walks, peers, sees)? Point out that the adverbs (slowly, silently) help to convey the moon's gentle, soothing qualities. Show these features using the annotations on the software.

Clarify the meaning of *shoon* – shoes.

Responding to the texts

Pupil Book
pp26–27

Ask the children to reread *Xmas* and *Silver* and to answer the appropriate set of questions individually, in pairs or as a guided group.

Each group can complete the appropriate set of questions.

Review

Select two questions from each set and discuss responses as a class. Ask the children to consider which poem they think uses personification most effectively and why.

2 Exploring an extended personification poem

Shared reading

Software u4
Explore: Text 3

Ask the children to describe different characteristics of snow they have encountered.

Read aloud *Snow and Snow*, gathering initial impressions. What strikes them about the character of each of the verses? (Snow is personified as a *he* in some verses and a *she* in others.) Do they think the characters are the same in alternating verses or is each character different? (Different characteristics of snow are explored in each of the five verses.)

Draw attention to the use of metaphor. Why is *wedding lace* an appropriate metaphor for the snow's transformation of the landscape? Annotation set a shows the characteristics of snow and Annotation set b shows examples of metaphor.

Explain some of the less familiar vocabulary used in the poem (waifish, falters, foxwrap, frail, muffled, gloaming).

Role play

Pupil Book p29

Divide the class into five groups, each focusing on one verse of the poem. (The second verse is particularly challenging so may require a teacher-led guided group.)

Ask each group, working in pairs, to describe the images created in their minds when they read about the characters and the scene in their verse. Can they identify the active verbs?

Ask them to create a short mime to represent the actions of the *character* created in their verse, rehearsing it with the poem read aloud.

Alternatively, children could interpret a verse of their choosing by drawing the images conjured up in their minds.

Review

Ask pairs/groups to perform their mimes to a reading of their verse. Allow the class to comment on how effective each mime is in relaying the images and characters represented in the verse. Encourage children to explain what they were trying to capture through their mimes, looking back at the language used in the poem. (Active verbs can be displayed using Annotation set c.)

③ Playing with personification

Class discussion

Software u4 Explore: Text 4

Experiment with personification using the context of familiar non-human objects. Ask children to brainstorm the non-human objects they encounter as they wake up and get ready for school. (You could bring in some props, e.g. toothbrush, comb, mirror, towel, breakfast bowl, TV, school uniform, school bag, lunch box, shoes, car, bike.)

To introduce the poem *Wake up*, ask what they think their alarm clock would say to them if it were a person. How would it behave? How would they respond to it if it were a person?

Read aloud *Wake up*, drawing attention to the active verbs used. Note the rhythm and use of rhyme/near rhymes. Show Annotation sets a and b on the software.

Exploring vocabulary

Software u4 Explore: Workpad 4

Show the example in the table in Workpad 4 that categorises the verbs

associated with how an alarm clock might sound, look, move and behave if it were personified.

Sentence work

Pupil Book pp29–30; PCM 4a

Refer back to the non-human objects discussed earlier.

Ask the children, in pairs, to generate active verbs for two of the objects in the chart on PCM 4a or using the blank table on the software, considering how each would sound, look, move and behave. Refer them to *Activity 3* in the Pupil Book.

Referring to the appropriate section, ask the pairs to compose orally and write full sentences using the subjects and verbs from the completed table and a range of conjunctions.

Review

Look at a few sentences and ask the children to evaluate them. How effective are the active verbs chosen in personifying the inanimate objects?

④ Capturing ideas for writing weather poems

Shared reading

Software u4 Explore: Text 1, Text 2

Refer children back to the personification of the moon in *Silver* and the snow in *Xmas* (read selected sections). In *Silver*, the moon "walks" and "peers". What other active verbs can the children think of to describe how the moon might move and behave if it were a person? Pie Corbett describes the moon in *Poetman*:

> The moon grins
> A thin-lipped smile

Grammar work

Software u4 Practise

Children can recognise and group active and passive sentences in the activity in *Practise*.

Class discussion

Software u4 Warm up

Share the images and sound effects of winter weather conditions in *Warm up*. Brainstorm types of weather (e.g. hurricane, thunder, lightning, fog, blizzard, sunshine, etc.). Discuss how, if each of the weather conditions were human, they might move, look, sound and behave, e.g.

- sun (greets, glances, smiles, glares, stares, creeps)
- wind (sprints, darts, runs, plays).

Group discussion

Select a weather condition for each group to focus on. Using a large sheet of paper, with the title of the weather written in the centre, ask each group to write down as many active verbs as possible to personify that weather condition. Change over or *boomerang* the sheet to the next group, so that they can consider a different weather condition. Continue to *boomerang* the sheet until each group has considered each weather condition. Remind children to consider sounds, looks, movements and behaviour.

Review

Compare the active verbs generated for different weather conditions.

5 Forming complex sentences to develop personification

Class discussion

Talk about using active verbs as a starting point to creating sentences that develop the personification. (Show the sheets of *boomerang verbs*.) Recap on how conjunctions can be used to join clauses when adding detail, e.g.

The wind moaned in the trees <u>while</u> the sky wept.

or

While the sky wept, the wind moaned in the trees.

Model further ways of creating complex sentences by joining two clauses. Show how complex sentences can begin with an -ing verb (non-finite verb):

<u>Smiling</u> from cheek to cheek, the sun <u>waved</u> at the waking world below.

Write/pair/share

Children, in pairs, create sentences on the theme of weather on their mini-whiteboards, using the class list of active verbs and others. They can start with a simple sentence, using an active verb, then improve it by joining ideas using a comma and *ing*-ending verb at the beginning, as in the example.

Prepare children to create, from one of their sentences, a mime of the weather's action for the class to interpret.

Review

Select pairs to mime and read aloud their sentences to the class, leaving blank the subject name so that the class can try to interpret the subject being personified. Children can evaluate how imaginative each

personification is and the effectiveness of the active verbs used.

Phase plenary

Check that children understand how to personify inanimate objects using active verbs and that they can describe why personification may be used by poets instead of straightforward description.

 Children can begin to understand the concept of personification in poetry and, with support, create sentences using active verbs.

 Children understand the purpose of personification in poetry and can begin to create complex sentences using active verbs.

 Children can describe the purpose of personification in poetry and readily create complex sentences using active verbs.

Phase 2: *Engage and Explore*

6 Exploring similes in imagery

> **Software u4**
> **Explore: Text 1,**
> **Text 5**

Shared reading

Talk about the effects of other types of imagery, i.e. similes and metaphors. Refer the children back to examples of metaphors used in *Xmas* in *Explore* Text 1. Click on the Annotation set c button to reveal them.

Introduce *The Warm and the Cold*. This poem includes personification but is structured around similes to describe a winter dusk scene.

Pick out examples of similes to analyse, by highlighting them, reminding children that similes (and metaphors) describe by making comparisons. The similes are shown in Annotation set a.

Think/pair/share

Select similes from the poem for children to examine in pairs. Ask them to explain why particular images have been used, e.g. *Freezing dusk is closing like a slow trap of steel* denotes the feeling of entrapment caused by the harsh temperatures.

Which similes strike the children most? Why would poets choose to use similes? How are they similar to personification? What makes an effective simile?

> **Software u4**
> **Explore:**
> **Workpad 5**

Class discussion

Discuss the images and sound of rain in its different forms. Ask the children to describe the different characteristics of rain, e.g. light, temporary rain, drizzle, steady rain, shower, rainstorm, monsoon. Display Workpad 5.

Write/pair/share

Ask the children, in pairs, to compose orally, then write similes to describe different types of rain. Use the example given on PCM 4b.

Review

Children share their best similes. Encourage them to evaluate whether the similes are appropriate for the type of rain described.

7 Exploring surprising metaphors

Shared reading

Remind children of the difference between metaphors and similes, giving examples, e.g. the simile *Freezing dusk is closing like a slow trap of steel* would become *Freezing dusk is a slow trap of steel* in a metaphor. Ask why poets use metaphors instead of similes.

Introduce the poem *Reader: But what **is** Poetry? Adrian:* This poem describes poetry by offering a series of surprising, surreal metaphors.

Group discussion

Ask the children to read the poem in groups and to discuss what the metaphors tell them about what Adrian Mitchell thinks and feels about poetry.

Ask them which metaphors they like the most and why. Discuss possible meanings of more challenging metaphors. You can display the metaphors in the poem using Annotation set a.

Write/pair/share

Show children visual images of a season. Ask them, in pairs, to think of and record metaphors to describe the season, e.g. *Summer is that special birthday present you've been waiting for all year round. Summer drenches the world in golden syrup.*

Review

Share some of their metaphors and talk about using similes and metaphors when writing their own personification poems.

Phase plenary

Check that the children can recognise examples of imagery.

 Children can identify similes and metaphors in personification poems and begin to create them, with support.

 Children can identify and create similes and metaphors and understand their purpose in personification poems.

 Children can analyse and create similes and metaphors and explain their purpose in personification poems.

Phase 3: *Create*

8 Planning to write a personification poem

Class discussion

Software u4 Explore: Text 3

Reread the poem *Snow and Snow*. The children will base a personification poem on it but using the theme of rain.

Remind them of their previous work on rain and brainstorm what *personalities* they would attribute to different types of rain, e.g. light rain as playful, temporary rain as moody.

Remind them that in *Snow and Snow*, each verse develops a different *character* of snow by describing carefully how the snow behaves in a particular situation. In each case, the setting as well as the character is described vividly. They will attempt to describe rain in a similar way.

Demonstration writing

Software u4 Plan

Using the *Personifying rain* skeleton frame on page 1 of the modelled writing in *Plan*, model how to begin personifying one characteristic of rain using active verbs. Record the situations where people encounter this kind of rain and note how people respond to it on page 2. (The examples use light, temporary rain.)

Write/pair/share

PCM 4c

Ask children, in pairs, to choose a different type of rain and to use a blank skeleton frame to build up their own ideas. (Ensure that each type of rain is covered as a class.)

Review

Software u4 Plan

Share a variety of skeleton frames and record notes for each type of rain so that children can refer to these ideas when writing their poems. Collate ideas on the grid in *Plan* page 3.

 **9** ## Modelling writing of a personification poem

Demonstration writing

 Software u4 Write

Model the verse shown on page 1 of the modelled writing, demonstrating explicitly how these ideas have been developed from the skeleton frames/planning grid. Point out the active verbs used to *humanise* the subject and the description of details that help to give the reader a clear picture of the setting. Note how complex sentences have been used to extend ideas.

Paired writing

Pupil Book p30

Children work in pairs to draft a verse at a time about rain, drawing on ideas recorded on skeleton frames/class planning grid. They may use the blank writing frame on the software.

Review

Ask the children to share their first drafts with another pair without telling them the kind of rain they have chosen. Can they work out which kind of rain is being personified? What tips can they give to improve the verse?

 **10** ## Unit plenary: improving and publishing the poem

Demonstration writing

Software u4 Write

Remind children of their similes about rain. Demonstrate how they could improve their personification rain verses by including a simile. Model inserting a simile in the verse on page 2 of the modelled writing.

Paired writing

Pupil Book p30

Ask children to include similes and/or metaphors in their draft personification poems to make them more vivid.

Think/pair/share

With a response partner, ask the children to consider how their poems could be improved.

Write/pair/share

Children can publish their poems as part of a class book, *Rain and Rain*. They can illustrate each verse interpreting details from the poem.

Review

Children evaluate their poetry and discuss what they have enjoyed and what they have learned.

Poetry writing is very subjective, so there is no assessment sheet for poetry writing. Instead, discuss the children's poems with them, either in small groups or individually.

What next?

 Ask children to look out for the occurrence of imagery in narrative writing and to note down particularly good sentences, similes or metaphors to add to a class list.

 In art lessons, personify still-life objects or themes, e.g. fruit, the forest, perhaps observing first, then creating personified versions which emphasise striking characteristics of the object or responses to the theme.

 Using the skeleton frame, children practise further poetry writing on the theme of weather, using ideas brought out in the unit.

 Using the skeleton frame, children practise further poetry writing on a different theme, such as the traffic or the sea.

 *Activity 4a* asks children to write a poem using amusing and surprising metaphors on a theme of their choice.

Homework Book p8

 *Activity 4b* asks children to add non-finite clauses to lines of personification to make them richer.

Homework Book p9

If you liked these texts you could read:

Other poems by Adrian Mitchell, Ted Hughes, Wes Magee and Walter de la Mare

Learning outcomes

Children can

- respond to, analyse and compare poetry that uses imagery
- respond to poetry through dialogue and mime
- plan, write and improve an extended poem that uses powerful imagery.

5
2 weeks

A Quest for Adventure
Genre: Quest adventure stories

Objectives for this unit

Speaking and listening: Use dialogue to explore ideas, listen and respond constructively.

Reading: Understand the features of the quest adventure genre, and the effect of having different reading pathways in a text.

Writing: Write a short branching text with different reading pathways, using elements of a specific genre.

PNS Framework objectives

1. Speaking: Use techniques of dialogic talk to explore ideas, topics or issues

3. Group discussion and interaction: Understand and use a variety of ways to criticise constructively and respond to criticism

6. Word structure and spelling: Use a range of appropriate strategies to edit, proofread and correct spelling in their own work, on paper and on screen

7. Understanding and interpreting texts: Understand how writers use different structures to create coherence and impact

8. Engaging with and responding to texts: Sustain engagement with longer texts, using different techniques to make the text come alive

9. Creating and shaping texts: Use different narrative techniques to engage and entertain the reader; Select words and language drawing on their knowledge of literary features and formal and informal writing; Integrate words, images and sounds imaginatively for different purposes

10. Text structure and organisation: Use varied structures to shape and organise text coherently

11. Sentence structure and punctuation: Express subtle distinctions of meaning, including hypothesis, speculation and supposition, by constructing sentences in varied ways; Use punctuation to clarify meaning in complex sentences

12. Presentation: Select from a wide range of ICT programs to present text effectively and communicate information and ideas

Unit overview

This unit is designed to last two weeks. During the unit, the class will read and explore stories with different reading pathways in the form of quest adventures, learn to create stories with different reading pathways, then write a branching quest adventure.

Phase 1: *Engage (sessions 1–3)*
Children read and identify the features of quest adventures and understand their narrative structure, setting and function of characters.

Phase 2: *Explore (sessions 4–5)*
Children explore how authors can shape a branching text by constructing different reading pathways for the same story.

Phase 3: *Create (sessions 6–10)*
Children create their own branching text with alternative reading pathways in the form of a quest adventure.

Prior learning

Check that children can already:

- discuss various features of a fiction text, e.g. narrative structure, author intention
- discuss responses to fictional and imaginative texts
- use a variety of sentences and appropriate vocabulary to develop character, setting and narrative drive
- navigate interactive non-linear (ICT) texts

Cross-curricular links

History: Who were the ancient Greeks?

Resources

Texts: *Bellerophon and the Flying Horse* by Pamela Oldfield, *Beowulf* by Kevin Crossley-Holland, *Valdemar's Quest* by Jonathan Rooke

Software 6, Unit 5

Pupil Book 6, Unit 5, pp31–36

Homework Book 6, pp10–11

PCM 5a–b

Phase 1: *Engage*

1 Introducing quest adventure narratives

Introducing the text

> **Software u5**
> **Warm up**

Watch the *Warm up* sequence and ask what it evokes. Discuss stories that have a quest, e.g. *Lord of the Rings*, *The Hobbit*, *Jason and the Golden Fleece*. Ask if they know any electronic games that have a quest where the player makes choices, e.g. Jak and Daxter. Tell them that later they will compose a quest adventure story.

Shared reading

> **Software u5**
> **Explore: Text 1**

Read *Bellerophon and the Flying Horse*. Discuss how the story has particular elements: a hero, a journey, and a quest.

Think/pair/share

> **PCM 5a**

Ask children, in pairs, to cut out the cards on PCM 5a and match up the elements of a quest story to their purpose in the story, then match them to the section in the story of *Bellerophon and the Flying Horse* where the elements can be found. (These elements are based on the ideas of the author Christopher Vogler.)

Review

> **Software u5**
> **Explore:**
> **Workpad 1,**
> **Text 1**

Discuss children's answers and fill in the grid on Workpad 1. Check children understand the function of each story element of this quest adventure. You could use the annotations on the software.

2 Consolidating understanding of quest adventure elements

Class discussion

> **Software u5**
> **Explore:**
> **Text 2;**
> **Workpad 2**

Remind children of *Bellerophon and the Flying Horse* and recap on the elements of a quest adventure.

Briefly look at the shortened story version of *Beowulf*. Ask children to identify the story elements of this quest adventure.

Check their answers against the annotations on the software. Discuss any differences. Use Workpad 2 to record the agreed answers. Do the children see that heroes leave a safe space to enter an unsafe space where they pursue their quest?

Responding to the text

> **Software u5**
> **Explore: Text 3;**
> **Pupil Book**
> **pp31–32**

Read through the passage in which Beowulf comes face to face with the monster, Grendel. Use the annotations to discuss the elements of quest adventure found in the passage.

Ask children to reread the passage from *Beowulf* and complete *Activity 1* in the Pupil Book.

Each group can answer the appropriate set of questions.

Review

Discuss some answers to the questions to develop children's understanding of a quest story.

 **3** ## Developing ideas for a quest adventure

Independent note-making

Ask children to invent and, on separate pieces of paper, draw, label and/or note a few words or phrases to describe their own hero, a menace, and a setting where an ordeal could take place.

Think/pair/share

Children talk about their drawings to a partner. Encourage listeners to nod, use eye contact, ask for elaboration and clarification and offer ideas.

When these are complete, pin them to the wall for children to refer to when they write their own quest adventures.

Grammar work

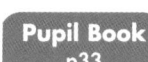 **Pupil Book p33**

Explain that quest stories use non-finite clauses to make the adventure come alive. *Activity 2* in the Pupil Book asks them to find the non-finite verbs in a passage.

Review

Discuss answers to the questions and ask for examples of sentences with non-finite clauses to confirm understanding.

Homework

Homework Book p10

Activity 5a asks children to construct sentences using non-finite clauses.

Phase plenary

Confirm that children are beginning to develop ideas for a quest adventure and understand the main elements.

 This group understands the main features of a quest adventure and can describe the functions of the main characters.

 This group can describe the main features of a quest adventure and develop different characters and settings for a quest adventure.

 This group can discuss choices available to them in characters, setting and genre for a quest adventure and take risks developing characters and settings.

Phase 2: *Explore*

 **4** ## Creating different reading pathways through a branching text

Shared reading

Software u5 Explore: Text 4, Workpad 4

Read part 1 of the passage from *Beowulf*. Workpad 4 illustrates a narrative structure showing a branching text. Analyse the first passage using Annotation set a. Point out that the ordinary world where the hero and quest are introduced is the first part of any quest adventure.

The next part (Part 2) describes the passage when the hero has left the ordinary world and entered the extraordinary world. Show how the hero has to make a choice at the end of this section, using Annotation set b.

Shared writing

Software u5 Explore: Text 4, Workpad 4

Choose one of the paths. Write with the children the beginning of the next section and end with a choice for the reader to make. You may wish to use the model in Part 3 of Text 4 – Beowulf is left with the choice of running away or jumping in the river. Show Annotation set c and introduce an adverbial time phrase, such as *a little way down the river*, and explain what its purpose is in a quest story: to show the passage of time.

Independent writing

Children write their own version of one of the choices offered by the old man on the misty moor ending their version with a choice. They could try to include non-finite clauses to create excitement.

Grammar work

Software u5 Practise

Children can work through the exercise in *Practise* on adverbs.

Review

Read out some of the versions. Discuss use of language, e.g. non-finite clauses, atmosphere and excitement.

Homework

Homework Book p11

Activity 5b asks children to practise using adverbial phrases by inventing sentences.

5 Consolidating understanding of reading pathways

Shared reading

Select one of the children's pieces of writing from Session 4 and share how you might write the next step/section for the two choices offered. Give suggestions for two new choices at the end of this section. Emphasise use of language, development of character and handling of quest adventure elements.

Independent writing

Software u5
Explore:
Text 5,
Workpad 5

Divide the children into two groups. Look at *Valdemar's Quest*, a quest story opening, and use the annotations to discuss the features of the story and the quest that has been set. Display Workpad 5 to show the two choices the hero has, and assign a road to ask each group to follow. Each child then writes what happens next. Remind them that in this section the hero will meet a menace, and face another choice about how to overcome this: the hero's trial.

Review

Each child should swap with a partner from the other group and evaluate each other's section for use of language, atmosphere, excitement, characterisation and quest adventure elements. The children then take their writing partner's section and write the next section against one of the choices. When they have finished, children exchange these so they can see what their writing partner has done with their story.

Phase plenary

Ask some children to read aloud some of their partners' stories and share what they thought worked well. Check that children understand the key features of a quest adventure, and how alternative reading pathways can be constructed. What effects do these create?

 This group knows what an alternative reading pathway is and can compose a section of a reading pathway.

 This group understands what an alternative reading pathway is and can use appropriate language to compose a section of an alternative reading path.

 This group can evaluate the effects of alternative reading paths on the audience and use exciting language to compose a section of an alternative reading path.

Phase 3: *Create*

6 Using a planning frame for a quest adventure with alternative pathways

Demonstration writing

Software u5
Plan

Show children the planning frame for a quest story with alternative writing pathways. Choose a hero, a quest, a menace and a trial and make notes in the appropriate planning boxes. The example on the software is based on the Greek myth of Andromeda and the Sea Monster. In the actual myth, Perseus falls in love with Andromeda who is tied to a cliff face and goes on a quest to release her. A sea monster threatens to kill her but Perseus slays the monster and rescues Andromeda.

Tell the children that it is important to decide how their version of the story begins and ends. Discuss possible ways that the hero might succeed in overcoming the menace and write an ending in the Trial box, e.g. Perseus arrives on a dolphin's back and drives away the sea monster or charms it to sleep. In the end he unchains Andromeda and returns to the ordinary world.

Independent writing

PCM 5b

Ask children to write alternative journey pathways in which Perseus has a confrontation and is somehow prevented from reaching Andromeda.

Read/pair/share

Give the children time to read their journey pathways to a writing partner.

Review

Discuss how using different reading pathways affects the reader's experience, e.g. they can interact with the story. What challenges does this present for the writer? What benefits? Brainstorm tips for writing a quest adventure:

- Know the end of the quest adventure before writing.
- Start in the ordinary world where the hero is given the quest.
- Continue when the hero enters the extraordinary world and makes a choice between paths.
- Use exciting language, including non-finite clauses and adverbial phrases.

7 Planning different story pathways and using literary language

Demonstration writing

 Software u5 Write

Use the modelled writing of a story on page 1 of the software and discuss how the language could be made to sound more exciting and literary. Then review the updated paragraph on page 2.

Sentence work

Pupil Book p34

Ask children, in pairs, to rewrite the passage in *Activity 3*, selecting some words and phrases and using some of their own.

■ This group need only use five words and phrases.

Class discussion

Listen to some of the children's work and identify how using literary language has improved the reading experience for the readers.

Shared planning

Software u5 Plan

Recap on the planning frame for a quest adventure made in Session 6 and the tips for writing a quest adventure.

Independent writing

Pupil Book p35

Give children time to construct their plans using the planning frame in *Activity 4*. They might like to choose a hero, a menace and a trial from the ideas on the classroom wall display from Session 3.

Review

Share some plans and discuss any new tips to add to the list for writing a quest adventure.

8 Writing a quest adventure with a different reading path

Demonstration writing

Software u5 Write

Demonstrate how to write some text for one of the boxes from the frame. You may wish to use the model of some text for the choice box on page 3 of the software.

Independent writing

Pupil Book p36

Children write their quest adventure using their planning frames and the hints in *Activity 5*.

Give the children opportunities to share their work with writing partners.

Guided writing

Focus on these with guided writing groups:

- use of literary language
- a clear sense of the end of the story, and how the reading pathways move towards this
- characterisation, especially of the hero
- use of a variety of sentences, adverbials of time and non-finite clauses
- choices that lead to the ending.

Encourage children to evaluate each other's writing and pose questions that will help the writer.

Review

Ask some children to read aloud some passages and emphasise aspects that strengthen their story.

9 Writing and enhancing quest adventures with different reading paths

Shared writing

Explain how pages of a quest adventure can be designed to heighten the reader's experience. What advantages would creating the text electronically give the reader/writer?

Discuss how children could:

- use illustration and animation
- direct readers to an alternative reading path, e.g. using hyperlinks
- use sound effects
- change the font size and design.

Independent writing

Pupil Book p36

Give the children time to write their quest adventures based on their plan and *Activity 5*. Then ask them to design their pages justifying their choices and discussing the intended effects on the audience. They can work on paper or on screen using either the blank writing frame on the software or a word processing package as appropriate.

Review

Discuss successes and challenges and any innovations the children might have made to their quest adventure or design, e.g. adding a choice button, for the audience to read an alternative reading path.

 **10** # Unit plenary: evaluating quest adventures

Independent writing

Children finish writing and designing their quest adventure on paper or on screen.

Read/pair/share

Children read their quest adventure to a partner who comments on the coherence of the story leading to an ending; the choice of reading pathways; the quality of language and the design of the pages.

Review

Ask the children to identify successes in their writing partner's quest adventure, saying why it worked. Discuss what the children have learned about planning a narrative with different reading pathways.

Use the assessment sheet for **fiction** writing on page 170 to help you assess the children's quest adventures.

What next?

 Children use suitable internet sites to find out about the story of Beowulf.

 These children could write another quest adventure with more reading pathways.

 XFactor Quest Adventure. In turn, groups of children write an episode of a quest adventure story each day that ends with a choice. Each day the class vote for their choice. Another group writes the next episode the following day in response to the vote and so on. This could run on the school intranet.

 Watch a suitable quest adventure film such as *Star Wars* or *Eragon* over several days and identify the different elements of a quest adventure.

If you liked these texts you could read:

A version of Beowulf, e.g. *Beowulf* by Kevin Crossley-Holland, *Beowulf: A New Telling* by Robert Nye or *Beowulf* by Michael Morpurgo and Michael Foreman

The Firework-maker's Daughter by Philip Pullman

The Hobbit by J R R Tolkien

Eragon by Christopher Paolini

Learning outcomes

Children can:
- identify the features of a quest adventure
- understand how a quest adventure can include a choice of two or more pathways
- plan, write and publish a quest adventure with different reading pathways.

6
3 weeks

Getting the Facts Straight
Genre: Writing in a journalistic style

Objectives for this unit

Speaking and listening: Use a range of oral and drama techniques to present news reports.

Reading: Engage with texts that can be used to inform, persuade, mislead and sway the reader.

Writing: Use journalistic techniques to write news reports.

PNS Framework objectives

1. Speaking: Use a range of oral techniques to present persuasive arguments and engaging narratives

2. Listening: Make notes when listening for a sustained period and discuss how note taking varies depending on context and purpose

6. Word structure and spelling: Use a range of appropriate strategies to edit, proofread and correct spelling in their own work, on paper and on screen

7. Understanding and interpreting text: Appraise a text quickly; Recognise rhetorical devices used to argue, persuade, mislead and sway the reader

9. Creating and shaping text: Use different narrative techniques to engage and entertain the reader; Select words and language drawing on their knowledge of literary features and formal and informal writing

10. Text structure and organisation: Use varied structures to shape and organise texts coherently

11. Sentence structure and punctuation: Express subtle distinction of meaning, including hypothesis, speculation and supposition, by constructing sentences in varied ways

Unit overview

This unit is designed to last three weeks. During the unit, the class will read, compare and write newspaper and radio reports.

Phase 1: *Engage (sessions 1–3)*
The class reads and compares a range of newspaper reports and magazine articles, radio, television and online news reports.

Phase 2: *Explore (sessions 4–9)*
The class analyses newspaper, magazine and radio features and reports identifying style, structure and audience with some focus on fact, opinion and ethics.

Phase 3: *Create (sessions 10–15)*
Children make notes, plan, write and perform newspaper and radio news reports.

Prior learning

Check that children can already:

- understand the language and structural features of a range of non-fiction genres
- use a range of questions.

Cross-curricular links

Geography: Passport to the world (television news reporting), What's in the news?

Resources

Texts: Television news report *CBBC Newsround*, Audio news reports *Inflatable Goal Posts* and *Speed Restriction Near School* from Delta Radio, Game of the Week review: *Sensible Soccer* from www.firstnews.co.uk, "Maradona puts England out of World Cup" from *The Times*, "Woman, 27, found after two decades lost in jungle" from *The Guardian*, "Who stole our goal posts?" from *Alton Herald*, Interview with Rescue helicopter pilot Coastguard Marsh by Jonathan Rooke, *Orphaned albino hedgehog arrives at Bordon sanctuary* from Delta Radio website

Software 6, Unit 6

Pupil Book 6, Unit 6, pp37–45

Homework Book 6, pp12–13

PCM 6a–c

A range of magazines and newspapers, online news channels and aural formats, e.g. local radio reports. Children can bring in their own magazines and newspapers

Recording equipment

Mini-whiteboards

Phase 1: *Engage*

① Comparing and contrasting journalistic writing

Introducing the unit

Software u6
Warm up

Discuss the magazines and newspapers that the children have in their house and what they read. Show and compare and contrast some articles from magazines and newspapers in the *Warm up* sequence.

Group work

Provide some magazine and newspaper articles. In groups, children sort and compare some of the reports, writing notes based on the headings:

- Type of article: review, feature, news
- Audience
- Language (e.g. chatty, formal)
- How it begins.

Review

Share some of the children's findings. Develop some shared understandings about paper-based journalistic writing.

② Comparing electronic journalistic writing

Watching a television news report

Software u6
Explore: Text 1, Workpad 1; PCM 6a

Show the children the television news report from *CBBC Newsround*. How effective is this form in communicating the news? How is it different from print-based journalism? (Use of pictures, sound, reported at the time news events are unfolding, audience includes everyone.) Ask children to write notes on PCM 6a, or use Workpad 1.

Group discussion

Software u6
Explore: Text 7, Workpad 1; PCM 6a

Play the radio report in *Explore* Text 7 on page 1 of the software. In groups, children identify how effective this form of news is, using the grid on PCM 6a or Workpad 1. Groups elect a spokesperson to share their ideas.

Write/pair/share

Software u6
Explore: Text 4, Workpad 1; PCM 6a

Show children the web-based news report in *Explore* Text 4 from *The Guardian* about a girl who was lost in the jungle, or allow them to explore suitable websites in the ICT suite. Ask children again to fill in PCM 6a or Workpad 1.

Class discussion

Software u6
Explore:
Workpad 1;
PCM 6a

Consider these questions with the class:

- What have you learned about electronic journalism?
- In what ways do different news sources offer different services? e.g.
  - Electronic: reports news as it happens
  - Print-based journalism: can be more reflective and explores news in depth – explaining as well as reporting.

Complete Workpad 1 or PCM 6a.

Independent writing

Software u6
Explore:
Workpad 1;
PCM 6a

Referring to Workpad 1 or PCM 6a, children write a paragraph or two summarising the differences between print- and electronic-based journalism. In pairs, they rehearse their summary before writing, and then share paragraphs after writing.

3 Reading and understanding features and reviews

Shared reading

Software u6
Explore: Text 2

Read the *Sensible Soccer* computer game review.

Think/pair/share

Software u6
Explore: Text 2

Ask children to reread the *Sensible Soccer* computer game review. Ask them, in pairs, to discuss the article's audience, purpose and form (how it is made). They can share their ideas with another pair and select a spokesperson.

Class discussion

Software u6
Explore: Text 2

Look at the annotations on the software which list the features of *Sensible Soccer*. Use this as a starting point to make a shared list about the features of review writing.

Responding to the text

Pupil Book
pp37–38

Ask the children to answer the questions in *Activity 1* on the *Sensible Soccer* game review.

 Each group can complete the appropriate set of questions.

Phase plenary

Check children understand the difference between different print-based and electronic-based media, talking about them in terms of audience, form and purpose.

 Children can describe different forms of journalistic writing.

 Children can compare different forms of journalistic writing and are aware how audience and purpose affect them.

 Children can reflect on and discuss how audience and purpose affect the forms of different journalistic writing.

Phase 2: *Explore*

4 Identifying fact and opinion

Class discussion

Arrange for a teacher to come into the classroom and remove a piece of equipment or behave in an uncharacteristically comic way. Ask the children, in groups, to discuss what has just happened, what they think they have seen and why it might have happened. Receive comments from the groups and make a list on the board.

Discuss the difference between fact (based on evidence and the same information whoever offers it) and opinion (based on the way a person perceives an event which may vary in detail and emphasis from person to person).

Write/pair/share

Draw a simple two-columned grid with the two headings "Fact" and "Opinion" for the children to copy. Ask them, in pairs, to sort their ideas into either fact or opinion.

Children share their grids with another pair to justify what is in each column.

Role play

Allow the children to hotseat yourself and the teacher, giving them time to categorise the responses.

Review

What have they learned about fact and opinion? Run through their sorting grids and reinforce the differences between them.

5 Finding out about ethics and balance in journalistic writing

Whole-class teaching

Explain that journalists have a code that requires them to represent people and events accurately and evenly by writing balanced reports, which respect the people being written about. They must not favour one point of view over another or write their own opinions. If they do, it is called *bias*. Discuss why this is important, making links to current news stories.

Discuss how a sports story, for example, could be told in different ways by different journalists by:

- selecting certain information and leaving other bits out
- emphasising certain information – making it stand out
- *burying* certain information a long way down the story
- choosing to use quotes that favour one version of the events
- using words and phrases that make one side look better than the other.

Read/pair/share

Software u6
Explore: Text 3;
Pupil Book
pp39–40

Ask the children to read the football reports in their Pupil Books to identify bias and balance and discuss the questions in *Activity 2*. Show the annotations on the software.

Review

Discuss the children's responses. Draw up a code of conduct for journalists with the children.

6 Using direct speech and reported speech

Whole-class teaching

Software u6
Explore: Text 4

View the annotations on the news report about a girl who was lost in the jungle, to demonstrate the difference between direct speech (the exact words used framed in speech marks) and reported speech (a representation of what was said – not the exact words so no speech marks).

Grammar work

Pupil Book
pp40–41

Explain how journalists use direct and reported speech to develop a story, and that the children will need to use these in their own journalistic writing.

Ask children, independently, to complete *Activity 3* in the Pupil Book.

 Each group can complete the appropriate set of sentences.

Review

Check the children's understanding of direct and reported speech. Discuss how journalists carefully have to choose which words they will report.

7 Building a newspaper report

Shared reading

Software u6
Explore: Text 5

Read *Who Stole our Goal Posts?*. Discuss the way this newspaper report is constructed using the annotations.

Whole-class teaching

Software u6
Explore: Text 6

Tell the children that they are going to write a report about an incident in which a ship with no crew on board was found drifting off the coast of Scotland. The rescue helicopter pilot has been interviewed by a reporter. Read the interview and identify the main points together, before looking at Annotation set a.

Write/pair/share

Ask pairs to compose a headline and the first paragraph for the report, agreeing an audience, e.g. a school newspaper or a local newspaper.

Demonstration writing

Software u6
Explore:
Workpad 6

Write the first few lines of the report explaining your choice of vocabulary and sentence structure. You may wish to use the model in Workpad 6.

Independent writing

Ask children to write their own newspaper report based on the interview.

Review

PCM 6b

Discuss what the children have learned about writing a newspaper report. Check that they have included the features discussed and ask them to start listing these features on PCM 6b.

8 Exploring radio news reports

Whole-class teaching

Software u6
Explore: Text 7

Listen to the radio report *iGoal* about inflatable goalposts and ask the children to identify the similarities and differences with newspaper reports, e.g. radio reports heard, not read by audience, no pictures, both can include quotes from interviews given by the reporter.

Independent note-making

Software u6
Explore: Text 7

Play the audio clip again, asking children to note the features which will help them to construct a radio news report later on.

In pairs, children share their notes.

Collect important points on the board from the pairs for future reference.

Shared reading

Software u6
Explore: Text 7

Listen to the *iGoal* report again and look at the transcript on page 2. Use the annotations to show how it follows a particular structure.

Group discussion

Software u6
Explore: Text 7

Listen to a second radio news report *Speed Restrictions Near School* on page 3 of the software. Ask children, in groups, to discuss how it follows the pattern for shaping a news report. A transcript with annotations can be displayed on page 4.

Review

PCM 6b

Together summarise the features of radio news reports and the format that they can take. Allow the children to continue making notes on radio news report features on PCM 6b.

9 How a radio report is made

Write/pair/share

Software u6
Explore: Text 8;
Pupil Book
pp42–43

Tell children they are radio journalists. A press release has arrived at the news desk and they must make a broadcast by the end of the lesson. Read the press release and ask them to write questions that they will ask the staff at the Bordon sanctuary, referring them to *Activity 4*.

Shared listening

Software u6
Explore: Text 8

Turn to page 4 and listen to the radio journalist's interview with the staff at the Bordon sanctuary about the albino hedgehog. Children can compare the questions she uses with the questions they made up.

Revise the structure of the radio report: starts with a line that grabs the reader's attention, the story is expanded, an interview is introduced, and a summary of the story is made.

Think/pair/share

Software u6
Explore: Text 8

Listen to the interview again. Ask children to make notes to help them write the news report, then share them with a partner. They should also decide on a section of the interview to use.

Independent writing

Software u6
Explore:
Workpad 8

Ask the children, in pairs, to write their radio news report using the same structure as above. They can use the writing frame in Workpad 8 for support.

Group work

Children read their news report in groups as if they were on the radio (a partner could read the interview section). Ask them to comment on each other's performance.

Review

Software u6
Explore: Text 8

Turn to page 5 and listen to the radio journalist's report on the albino hedgehog story based on the interview listened to earlier. Compare it with the children's reports. What have the children learned about radio reports?

Phase plenary

Check that children have grasped the main features of newspaper and radio reports.

 Children understand balance and bias in journalistic writing and know that newspaper and radio reports have similar and different features.

 Children can identify balance and bias in journalistic writing and can attempt to write newspaper and radio reports based on their features.

 Children can discuss the effects of balance and bias in journalistic forms and confidently write newspaper and radio reports and reflect on them.

Phase 3: *Create*

10 Collecting important information for a newspaper report

Role play/Note-making

> Pupil Book pp43–44; PCM 6c

Explain that when writing a report it is important to interview people involved or witnesses to the event.

Tell the children they are going to role-play the alien landing when the journalist arrives on the scene and interviews people. In groups, they will take it in turns to play different witnesses: a police inspector, a child, a teacher, a resident and a doctor. The *witnesses* should refer to the responses in *Activity 5* in the Pupil Book. All children will need to make notes for writing a report in a later session.

 These children could use PCM 6c for support.

Review

Ask a few children to share their notes. Have they included enough information to write a report? Praise children for including interesting quotes.

11 Writing a balanced newspaper report in the public interest

Think/pair/share

Ask children to read their notes to a partner. Remind them that they will be writing a balanced newspaper report and give them time to rehearse their plan orally.

Independent writing

> Software u6 Plan

Ask children to plan their newspaper report and include quotes and an *angle* to help them approach the story, reminding them of their audience. Some children could use the planning frame on the software.

Demonstration writing

> Software u6 Write

Explain that the children are ready to write their report. Demonstrate writing a part of the report. It need not be the opening paragraphs. You may wish to use the modelled writing on the software.

Independent writing

> Software u6 Write

Give children time to write their newspaper report on the alien landing. They may use the blank writing template on the software.

12 Developing language for a newspaper report

Whole-class teaching

Read out some children's work and model ways of offering constructive comments to help the writer.

Remind them to:

- write a headline that captures interest and sets the tone
- put who, what, where and when in the first few sentences
- choose quotes that support the viewpoint of the story or give balance
- choose vocabulary carefully, e.g. *visitors* or *intruders*
- select the most important information.

Independent writing

Give children time to develop their writing, making changes in response to comments made earlier.

Guided writing

Work with groups to develop their language and sentence choice to enrich their news reports.

Independent writing

Software u6
Practise

Emphasise the importance of high quality presentation and the need to edit and proofread. Offer children an opportunity to make illustrations if appropriate.

Children can work through the exercise in *Practise* where they choose the correct way to punctuate sentences.

Review

Ask children to read their newspaper reports with a partner, then talk about what they enjoyed writing, what went well and how they overcame any challenges.

⑬ Planning a radio news report

Group discussion

In groups, discuss what might happen next when the authorities become involved with the alien. Each group appoints a scribe, chairperson and observer.

Listen to the groups' ideas and encourage them to tell the story of the alien.

Role play

Allow children to hotseat the key people in the story. Other children ask questions and take notes as if they were reporters.

Think/pair/share

Pupil Book
p45

Ask the pairs orally to plan their radio news report, referring them to *Activity 6*. Their partner should give feedback and check that the report has a clear structure and tells a full story.

Ask children to jot down a rough plan for their radio news report.

⑭ Writing a radio news report

Class discussion

Remind children of the key features of writing a radio news report made in Session 8.

Independent writing

Pupil Book
p45;
Software u6
Explore:
Workpad 8

Ask children to write their radio news report on the alien landing, referring to *Activity 6*. Some children could use the radio report writing frame in Workpad 8.

They should read the report aloud so they can hear what it sounds like. Encourage partners to give honest and positive feedback and for writers to respond to it.

Guided writing

Work with small groups, focusing on the structure of their reports and the use of quotes.

Review

While reading out the features of radio news reports, ask children to read quietly their own reports to see if they have included these features. Have they included at least one interesting quote from a *witness*?

⑮ Unit plenary: recording a radio report

Independent writing

Children edit and proofread their work, making changes to their alien landing radio news report with a partner.

Read/pair/share

Ask children if they remember how the radio journalist in the earlier radio reports used her voice. In pairs, they can practise reading out their report bearing in mind these techniques:

- Volume and pitch of voice rises to indicate a new story and falls at the end of the story.
- Tone of voice indicates, at the beginning, what sort of story it is, e.g. light-hearted or serious.

Review

Record the children's radio news stories. Play them back and evaluate how effectively they have been written and presented:

- Was there a clear five-part structure?
- Was the interview quote used well?
- Did each voice rise and fall?
- Did the tone indicate what sort of story it was?

Ask children what they have learned about journalistic writing. What were the challenges of writing newspaper and radio reports?

Use the assessment sheet for **non-chronological report** writing on page 172 to help you assess the children's reports.

What next?

 Create a radio broadcast, with news, features and sports reports to be made available in the library or on the school website. Send it to the local radio station.

 *Activity 6a* asks children to write a review of a children's radio or television programme. They may want to write a review of a music CD.

Homework Book p12

 *Activity 6b* asks children to design and write a review of an electronic game for an electronic game magazine (*Fab Games*), then write a letter to the editor of the magazine, explaining why the review should be printed.

Homework Book p13

 This group can develop skills through writing a sports report about a game in the school.

 Inspire the children to write their own school newspaper. Send a copy home to each of the children's carers at the end of term.

If you liked these texts you could read:

Newspapers for children, e.g. *First News*

Suitable children's news websites, e.g. *CBBC Newsround*

Watch the early evening television news regularly with carers

Learning outcomes

Children can:
- evaluate the effect of language features of different journalistic forms
- experiment with writing different journalistic forms
- use features of oral presentation in a journalistic radio report
- appreciate the skills and responsibilities of journalists.

7

2 weeks

How to Write Like an Author

Genre: Different authorial voices and styles

Objectives for this unit

Speaking and listening: Use a range of oral and aural techniques to investigate the writing styles of different authors, including drama and reading with expression.

Reading: Identify and describe the writing styles of different authors.

Writing: Write an imaginative story experimenting with some of the author techniques identified.

PNS Framework objectives

1. Speaking: Use a range of oral techniques to present … engaging narratives	**8. Engaging with and responding to texts:** Read extensively and discuss personal reading with others, including in reading groups; Sustain engagement with longer texts, using different techniques to make the text come alive
2. Listening and responding: Listen for language variation in informal contexts; Analyse and evaluate how speakers present points effectively through use of language and gesture	**9. Creating and shaping texts:** Use different narrative techniques to engage and entertain the reader; Select words and language drawing on their knowledge of literary features
7. Understanding and interpreting texts: Understand underlying themes, causes and points of view	**10. Text structure and organisation:** Express subtle distinctions of meaning by constructing sentences in varied ways

Unit overview

This unit is designed to last two weeks. During the unit, children will compare the writing of two authors and write a chapter for a story based on the techniques used by one of them.

Phase 1: *Engage (sessions 1–3)*

Children begin to identify a range of author techniques including point of view, narrative voice, language choice and use of dialogue.

Phase 2: *Explore (sessions 4–5)*

Children compare two authors, exploring their distinctive styles and continuing to identify author techniques.

Phase 3: *Create (sessions 6–10)*

Children write a narrative experimenting with some of the identified author techniques.

Prior learning

Check that children can already:

- identify some features of fiction text, e.g. character, theme, setting, dialogue, point of view
- discuss their responses to books, e.g. in guided reading or literature circles
- plan a narrative and develop a character
- speak clearly, appreciating an audience's needs.

Cross-curricular links

Citizenship: Children's rights – human rights

Resources

Texts: *The Suitcase Kid* by Jacqueline Wilson, *The Reptile Room* by Lemony Snicket, *The Bad Beginning* by Lemony Snicket

Software 6, Unit 7

Pupil Book 6, Unit 7, pp46–52

Homework Book 6, pp14–15

PCM 7a–b

Optional: copies of *The Suitcase Kid*, *The Bad Beginning* and other books by Jacqueline Wilson and Lemony Snicket

---

Phase 1: *Engage*

 1 Introducing author techniques

Introducing the text

Software u7 Warm up

The children will be looking at texts written by two authors to explore the techniques they use in their writing.

Show the *Warm up* sequence which refers to books by Jacqueline Wilson and 'Lemony Snicket' (Daniel Handler). Share what the children know about these authors.

Shared reading

Software u7 Explore: Text 1

Discuss what the children know of Jacqueline Wilson, e.g. the audience she usually writes for, her style, themes she uses.

Read *I is for Ill*. Briefly discuss the audience that Jacqueline Wilson is writing for, her style (e.g. the narrative describes the character's feelings and is written in a personal, informal way), and the themes she uses, i.e. the effects of divorce on families. Show the annotations on the software.

Responding to the text

Pupil Book pp46–49

Ask the children to read *I is for Ill* independently and complete *Activity 1* in the Pupil Book.

 Each group can complete the appropriate set of questions.

Review

Software u7 Explore: Workpad 1

Share some of the children's responses.

Using Workpad 1, make notes on the techniques that Jacqueline Wilson uses.

 2 Finding out more about author techniques

Class discussion

Software u7 Explore: Workpad 1

Discuss briefly what they have learned about Jacqueline Wilson's techniques, e.g. types of sentences she uses, vocabulary choice, point of view, use of dialogue. Look again at the grid on Workpad 1. You can use the model workpad.

Shared reading

Software u7 Explore: Text 2, Workpad 1

Read the second passage from *The Suitcase Kid*, *Q for Questions*, and discuss Wilson's range of author techniques. Show the grid again and ask children if the same techniques have been used. Fill in other techniques used in this passage. Discuss how Wilson reveals the character's feelings by using questions that emphasise annoying situations in Andy's life. How does the reader know who is asking each set of questions? Discuss the chapter heading. Show the annotations on the software.

Write/pair/share

PCM 7a

Ask children, in pairs, to fill in their own grids on the writing techniques for Jacqueline Wilson.

 These groups should give an example from the text for each technique identified.

Review

Discuss why the techniques Wilson chooses to use and the themes she writes about are effective for her audience. Check that the children can give examples from the texts to highlight the techniques used.

③ Finding out about other author techniques

Class discussion

Remind children of the Lemony Snicket discussion at the beginning of Session 1. Explain that the author's real name is Daniel Handler, but his pseudonym is Lemony Snicket. Share what the children already know about him, e.g. the audience he writes for, his style, the themes he chooses to use.

Shared reading

Software u7
Explore: Text 3

Read the passage from *The Reptile Room*, Book 2 in the series. Explore the text and the techniques the author uses.

How do the children's names give you a clue that this might not be a realistic story? Find the names of places. What do they mean? How do these names make you feel?

Discuss the words that Snicket uses to describe the road, the field, the trees and the river area.

Do the words Snicket uses to describe the Baudelaires' lives make the reader side with them? Why?

What advice does Snicket give the reader in the last paragraph? Does he really want the reader to do this?

What sort of person is the author? What does he look or sound like? Why do you think this?

Group discussion

PCM 7a;
Software u7
Explore: Text 3

Ask the groups to discuss the writing techniques used in the passage. Elect a spokesperson for each group to feed back. Ask all the children to complete the second column on PCM 7a. Show Annotation sets a and b on the software.

Review

Software u7
Explore:
Workpad 3

Fill in the grid showing Lemony Snicket's techniques, based on the feedback from each group. Are there any similarities between the authors' techniques? The children will compare the authors' techniques more closely later.

Phase plenary

Check that the children can identify the range of techniques of the two authors.

 This group can describe some of the techniques that authors use.

 This group can identify a range of author techniques and make reflective personal responses to them.

 This group can discuss a range of author techniques and make detailed personal responses to them.

Phase 2: *Explore*

④ Comparing how authors use different techniques

Group discussion

Software u7
Explore: Text 4;
Pupil Book
pp49–50

Show children the passages from the openings of *The Suitcase Kid* and *The Bad Beginning*. Elect a chairperson, recorder and spokesperson for each group. Ask the children to discuss the similarities and differences between the two authors' techniques, using the questions in *Activity 2* in the Pupil Book as prompts.

Class discussion

Software u7
Explore: Text 4,
Workpad 4

Ask the children to share and discuss the differences and similarities. Start to develop a list of techniques each writer uses set alongside each other in a grid. (You can use the annotations and the grid in Workpad 4.) Focus on the use of the narrator, the way the characters are handled, the use of settings, how events are depicted, and the style of language and types of sentences used.

Role play

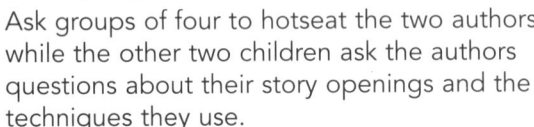

Ask groups of four to hotseat the two authors while the other two children ask the authors questions about their story openings and the techniques they use.

 Children from these groups who are role-playing the authors should attempt to explain in detail why they have used their particular techniques.

Review

Share some of the role plays with the class. Children should now be able to express their knowledge of different author techniques. Discuss whether the techniques used by Lemony Snicket would work for the Jacqueline Wilson story and vice versa. Why?

Homework

Homework
Book
pp14–15

 *Activity 7* asks the children to decide which passage was written by which of the two authors and why they know this. (Sentences 2, 3 and 7 are written by Lemony Snicket; the others by Jacqueline Wilson.)

5 Exploring complex sentences in authors' writing

Class discussion

Remind children that Lemony Snicket uses complex sentences to give the reader information and to develop ideas. Explain that one type of sentence he uses is the relative or embedded clause.

> **Software u7**
> **Explore: Text 3;**
> **Pupil Book**
> **p51**

Use Annotation set c to provide examples in *The Reptile Room*. Point out the example of the complex sentence formed from simple sentences in *Activity 3* in the Pupil Book.

Sentence work

Ask the children to write a complex sentence with an embedded clause for each set of simple sentences in *Activity 3* in the Pupil Book.

> **Pupil book**
> **p51;**
> **Software u7**
> **Practise**

Each group can complete the appropriate set of questions.

They can then complete the exercise in *Practise*, sorting phrases into coherent sentences.

Review

Share some of the children's complex sentences, asking them to explain what they did to add the embedded clause. Discuss how the children can use complex sentences in their own writing to give variety.

Phase plenary

Check that the children can identify the different techniques that authors have used and why they have chosen to use them.

 This group can identify some authors' techniques and make personal responses to them.

 This group can understand and give reasons why writers use different author techniques.

 This group can evaluate, compare and contrast authors' techniques.

Phase 3: *Create*

6 Writing a story opening in the style of an author

Class discussion

Display the openings of *The Suitcase Kid* and *The Bad Beginning* and make available the grid on Workpad 4 giving the writing techniques used by Wilson and Snicket.

> **Software u7**
> **Explore: Text 4,**
> **Workpad 4**

Group reading

Discuss how both texts are forms of informal writing, but have different styles. To allow children to see and hear the differences more closely, ask them, in groups, to take turns reading aloud sections from each passage. They should think about how to use oral expression to highlight the differences, e.g. Wilson's passage uses more dialogue, so more varied expression would be used. Discuss how the language varies in each, giving examples.

Demonstration writing

Briefly discuss how the two authors' techniques affect the way the stories are read aloud and how this might help children writing in their style.

> **Software u7**
> **Explore: Text 5**

Model writing a few lines for an opening to a story in the style of either author. You can use one or both of the story openers in Text 5. The story opens with a scene showing children and adults arriving at a school. The characters take a long look at the school before entering and are met in reception by the head teacher.

Independent writing

Ask the children to write this scene in the style of either author, referring to the relevant list of techniques. They then share each other's writing and check whether their partner has used some of the author's techniques.

> **Software u7**
> **Explore:**
> **Workpad 4**

Review

Read out some of the children's openings and celebrate the most effective writing. Can the class say which techniques each child has used?

7 Choosing and establishing techniques

Class discussion

Software u7
Explore:
Workpad 4

Revisit previous examples of the authors' writing. Briefly review the main techniques that each author uses to show the role of the narrator, how the characters and their thoughts and feelings are portrayed, how setting is dealt with, how and what type of language is used. Keep Workpad 4 displayed so children can view it during their planning.

Explain that the children will be planning and writing a chapter of a story in the style of one of the two authors.

Demonstration writing

Software u7
Explore:
Workpad 5

Remind children that, before writing in the style of an author, they will need to think in the same way as their chosen author. Explain that it is important to establish the techniques they will use before writing.

Model how to list the techniques to be used for writing the chapter. You can use the model for Jacqueline Wilson on Workpad 5.

Independent writing

**PCM 7a;
Software u7**
Explore:
Workpad 5

Ask the children to look at their completed PCM sheets and decide in which author's style they would like to write. Their choice may depend on how confident they feel about being able to treat the narrator, characters and setting, and use of language in the same way as the author.

Ask them to list the points they need to consider when writing their chapter starting with the same sentence: *As I am writing in the style of (author's name), I am going to: …* You can display Workpad 5.

Review

Ask the children to contribute their lists of points. Encourage them to start thinking about the characters and plot they would like to include in preparation for Session 8.

8 Planning to write the story chapter

Class discussion

Hide the chart of techniques and briefly quiz the children on these. This could be played as a class activity, delegating an author's techniques to each half of the class. This reinforces the style they need to produce and allows them to concentrate on planning the scene setting, introducing the characters and establishing a plot.

Demonstration writing

Pupil Book
p52;
Software u7
Plan

Discuss the points in *Activity 4* in the Pupil Book which children will need to consider, depending on which author they have chosen.

Model writing a plan for a story in the style of one of the authors. You can show one or both of the modelled plans on the software.

Independent writing

**PCM 7b;
Software u7**
Plan

The children should plan their chapter. They can use the list of questions on PCM 7b or refer to the plan on the software.

 Work with this group to help them plan their story chapters or, if preferred, continue a chapter based on the opening written in Session 6.

Review

Ask the children to share their plans with a partner. They should check to see that the plans follow the points of technique for each author. Encourage them to suggest improvements to the plans and apply other techniques from the same author if applicable.

9 Writing a chapter in the style of an author

Class discussion

Discuss some of the children's plans and let them talk about the decisions they have made. Praise children who continue to look at the lists of techniques while completing their plans.

Demonstration writing

Software u7
Write

Explain that the children will now use their plans to write a chapter of their story. Remind them that if they are in the style of Jacqueline Wilson, they should use simple sentences and everyday language; if writing in the style of Lemony Snicket, longer complex sentences should be used. Model writing the start of a chapter, based on one of your plans from Session 8. You can use the section of a chapter written in the style of Lemony Snicket in *Write*.

Independent writing

Software u7
Write

Allow children time to write their chapter. Remind them to look back at the various lists and grids, to help them model their writing on the style of the authors. They can use the blank writing frame on the software.

Review

Give children, in pairs, time to read aloud a section of their writing they are pleased with and explain the author techniques they are experimenting with.

 This group can evaluate the effects of these author techniques on an audience.

10 Unit plenary: completing the writing

Independent writing

Allow children time to finish their writing.

Group discussion

They should discuss what was most effective and why, and identify the author techniques with which they experimented. Then, in groups, ask them to read each other's final work, and the reflection. They should discuss what was most effective and why, and identify the author techniques with which they experimented.

Display the stories for the class to read.

Review

Discuss what they have learned about author techniques and how they'll use them in the future.

Use the assessment sheet for **fiction** writing on page 170 to help you assess the children's stories.

What next?

 Children could write a chapter in the style of the other author studied in the unit.

 Ask children to compare the books with film and TV adaptations (*A Series of Unfortunate Events* (2005), BBC TV series of Tracey Beaker by Jacqueline Wilson).

 Children could explore a dilemma or conflict in a book by a focus author using drama, e.g. role play, telephone conversations.

 Children could produce an electronic book for writers in Year 5, with hyperlinks to passages from their own writing that exemplify different techniques.

 Children could design a poster or a webpage to persuade others to choose their author to read.

 Children could do an in-depth study or a quiz about a selected author, e.g. Michael Morpurgo or Roald Dahl.

 Visit www.lemonysnicket.com and http://www.bbc.co.uk/cbbc/tracybeaker/

If you liked these texts you could read:

A House Called Awful End by Philip Ardagh

Dizzy by Cathy Cassidy

Learning outcomes

Children can:
- recognise that authors use different techniques in their writing
- recognise that author techniques can have different effects on a reader and the value of this
- experiment with different author techniques in their own writing

8
3 weeks

The Great Debate

Genre: Non-fiction: Presenting a balanced argument

Objectives for this unit

Speaking and listening: Participate in a whole-class debate using the language of debate.

Reading: Study how effective arguments are constructed in journalistic writing.

Writing: Write a balanced report on a controversial issue.

PNS Framework objectives

1. Speaking: Use a range of oral techniques to present persuasive arguments; Participate in whole-class debate using the conventions and language of debate, including standard English

2. Listening: Analyse and evaluate how speakers present points effectively through use of language and gesture

7. Understanding and interpreting texts: Understand underlying themes, causes and points of view

9. Creating and shaping texts: In non-narrative texts, establish, balance and maintain viewpoints

11. Sentence structure, punctuation: Express subtle distinctions of meaning, including hypothesis, speculation and supposition, by constructing sentences in varied ways

Unit overview

This unit is designed to last three weeks. During the unit, the class will read persuasive texts and balanced arguments, participate in an oral debate and write an argument.

Phase 1: *Engage (sessions 1–4)*

The class reads and responds to a persuasive text and a balanced report.

Phase 2: *Explore (sessions 5–7)*

Children explore arguments on paper and through debate, and analyse discursive reports, identifying formal and persuasive word, sentence and text level features.

Phase 3: *Explore (sessions 8–9)*

Children prepare for and participate in whole-class debate.

Phase 4: *Create (sessions 10–15)*

The class extracts information from opposing texts and organises ideas into a plan for a written balanced argument.

Prior learning

Check that children can already:

- understand and use features of persuasive language
- listen, consider and respond to alternative points of view
- communicate a point of view
- recognise the differences between formal and informal voice
- construct complex sentences.

Cross-curricular links

Citizenship: Choices; In the media

Resources

Texts: *Mobile phones – good or bad?* by Sarah Vittachi, "Expert spells it out" from *The Guardian*, "Posturing on lifestyle" from *Herts and Essex News Online*, "A good sport" from *The Guardian*

Software 6, Unit 8

Pupil Book 6, Unit 8, pp53–59

Homework Book 6, pp16–17

PCM 8a–d

Prepared cards for connective words and phrases for Session 5 Class discussion

Samples of guides and leaflets presenting balanced arguments

Phase 1: *Engage*

 1 Introducing points of view

Introducing the texts

Software u8
Warm up

Show the *Warm up* sequence, introducing the theme of mobile phones.

Explain that the children will be undertaking spoken and written forms of argument, exploring how *new* technology can affect children. Do the children know what written arguments reflecting opposing viewpoints are known as? (Discussion texts). A balanced argument is where two sides of an argument are presented equally. However, in many real discussion texts, the writer often favours one side, e.g. commercial adverts give a one-sided view of a product as they are designed to persuade customers to buy the item.

Think/pair/share

Ask pairs to discuss the advert in *Warm up*, focusing on these questions:

- What are the benefits of owning a mobile phone?
- How does the advert succeed in persuading you?
- Is there anything wrong with using mobile phones? What are the risks?
- Why isn't this mentioned in the advert?

Present the question: Should children be banned from owning mobile phones?

Class discussion

Divide the class in two: one side considers the arguments for children owning mobile phones, the other considers arguments against. Ask children, in pairs, to prepare three statements. Teacher chairs the feedback, taking one argument at a time from either side. (Emphasise the importance of listening to each other's point carefully in order to present a good counterargument.)

Review

Check that children have understood the differences between persuasion and argument. Do they understand what makes an effective argument when debating an issue? How might debate be useful in everyday life?

2 Identifying arguments in a discursive report

Shared reading

Software u8
Explore: Text 1

Remind children about the arguments they presented for and against children's use of mobile phones.

Introduce the article *Mobile phones – good or bad?* which focuses on the safety of mobiles. Explain any unfamiliar vocabulary.

Class discussion

Software u8
Explore: Text 1

Ask children: What are the arguments posed against the safety of mobiles? What are the arguments for?

Divide the class in two to represent *For* and *Against*. Reread the section *Are mobile phones safe?* asking each side to give a signal on hearing a statement supporting their side. Highlight the opposing arguments on screen using two colours or use Annotation set a on the software. Draw out inconclusive statements that could be interpreted as either for or against.

Read/pair/share

PCM 8a

Ask children to continue reading the article in pairs highlighting the opposing arguments using two colours on PCM 8a. Inconclusive statements could be marked with a question mark.

Shared writing

Software u8
Explore: Workpad 1

Model how to draw together the points highlighted on to Workpad 1 showing for and against statements (discussing how some points made could be interpreted to support either side). Add notes showing any useful details, e.g. research findings.

Write/pair/share

PCM 8b

Ask pairs to continue to record points on PCM 8b.

 This group can record the main arguments.

 These groups can record the main arguments and further details relating to these arguments.

Review

Check that children understand the overall conclusion that the discussion text makes. What point of view does the writer take? Is the argument balanced or does it lean more towards a single viewpoint? Take a vote, encouraging children to express their own viewpoints in response to the report. (Children will be using their frames later.)

Homework

Homework Book p16

Activity 8a asks children to highlight the powerful words and phrases that the author uses in *Mobile phones – good or bad?* to persuade the reader.

③ Responding to arguments in a discussion text

Whole-class teaching

Recap on what children know about argument and discussion. Remembering *Mobile phones – good or bad?*, pose questions, e.g. Why are some laboratory tests unreliable in telling us about the effects of mobile phones on the health of human beings? Demonstrate how to skim and scan the text to locate specific details.

Responding to the text

Pupil Book pp53–54

Ask children to work in pairs or as a guided group to complete the appropriate questions in *Activity 1* of the Pupil Book.

 Each group can complete the appropriate set of questions.

Review

Pick up on the questions that children found most challenging. Compare answers from question 5 of each group, making sure that children explain and justify their answers.

④ Exploring argument through role play

Shared reading

Software u8
Explore: Text 2

Explain that they will be experiencing informal argument through role play. Read the article and quotes from *Expert spells it out*, with children reading in role the responses of the professor and the parents.

Role play

Pupil Book p55

Ask pairs to role-play a short scene, where a child is trying to persuade their parent to buy them a mobile phone. Refer them to *Activity 2*.

Ask them first to improvise the scene, then to plan and rehearse the argument between the parent and child. (Children may refer to some of the arguments from Session 3.)

Review

Software u8
Explore: Text 2

Observe a selection of role-played scenes. How did each side try to persuade the other? How effectively were the arguments put forward? Check that children understand how it is important to listen to the argument before presenting a counterargument. Use the annotations on the software to review the work of this phase.

Phase plenary

Check that children understand the nature of arguments in discussion texts and how they differ from persuasive texts that offer a single viewpoint.

 Children can orally identify the arguments for and against in a written argument.

 Children can identify and note down the arguments for and against in a written argument.

 Children can identify the arguments in a written argument and evaluate how effective they are in putting over the author's point of view.

Phase 2: *Explore written arguments*

5 Exploring formal language, conjunctions and connectives in discussion texts

Class discussion

Software u8
Explore: Text 3,
Workpad 3

Display the text for children to read aloud in a formal, persuasive voice, showing the annotations. Then model how to communicate the main ideas from the text using informal language (as if talking to a friend). You can use the example on Workpad 3. A blank version is also provided.

Think/pair/share

Software u8
Explore: Text 2;
PCM 8a;
PCM 8c

Ask pairs to identify the formal text and language features in either *Mobile phones – good or bad?*, or the first section of *Expert spells it out*, using PCM 8c. Ask: Why did the author use formal language? What language features make the text sound logical?

Exploring vocabulary

Software u8
Explore: Text 1,
Practise

Look again at *Mobile phones – good or bad?*. Ask children to identify what it is about the language that makes the discussion text sound logical (the use of connectives and conjunctions). Highlight, using colour, the conjunctions and connectives in the article and stress their importance in showing these logical relationships, or use Annotation sets b and c.

Children can work through the activity in *Practise*, choosing appropriate connectives to form complex sentences with opposing points of view.

Class discussion

Software u8
Explore: Text 1

Prepare cards each with half of a logical sentence, or a conjunction or connective. Give out the cards to individual children. Ask them to form *human sentences* to show how logical relationships can be communicated through the use of complex sentences (using conjunctions). Confirm this by revisiting the annotations.

Think/pair/share

Pupil Book
pp55–56

Ask pairs to use conjunctions and connectives orally to create their own *logical* sentences in *Activity 3*. Check that children use the most appropriate conjunction or

connective to reinforce the logical connection between the two arguments in each case.

Ask children to share their sentences, orally, while their partner suggests improvements, then record the sentences.

■ This group completes the set of sentences in the first box.

● This group completes the sets of sentences in the first two boxes.

▲ This group completes all the sentences in all three boxes.

Review

Ask children to choose their best sentence to read aloud in an appropriate voice. The class evaluates whether or not the sentence communicates a logical relationship and offers alternative ways of communicating the idea.

6 Exploring stock phrases in discussion texts

Class discussion

Explain that there are many *stock* language structures used in discussion texts. Identify examples of these from articles read or from children's prior knowledge (e.g. *Some people say*, *New evidence suggests*, *On the other hand it is thought*), and ask children to read these aloud using the appropriate voice. What are the effects of these words and phrases? Record these stock phrases in a class phrase bank.

Introduce a new issue for discussion and write this on the board: *Should children be banned from having televisions in their bedrooms?*

Remind children how to plan an argument: introduce the issue, note points for and against, add any more useful information against relevant points, and summarise.

Think/pair/share

PCM 8b

Give children time to consider the arguments for and against this issue. They could use the argument frame on PCM 8b.

Model the use of phrases from the class phrase bank to compose sentences centred on the issue of TVs in bedrooms.

Ask pairs orally to compose their own sentences on the same subject, using the bank of stock phrases.

Listen to examples performed in the appropriate voice, discussing the impact of the sentences and suggesting improvements as necessary.

Children can then record the rehearsed sentences.

Review

Ask some children to read out their rehearsed sentences. Ask children to identify a phrase from each one that they would most like to use in their own discussion writing. Recap on the effects of using such phrases on a reader.

 ## ⑦ Using language prompts in arguments

Class discussion

Remind children that formal debates and written arguments use impersonal language to state viewpoints.

Look at the list of language prompts from Session 6 and model the use of two of them to state an argument for the *TVs in bedrooms* issue, e.g. *Some people argue that children have the freedom to choose which programme they would like to watch if they have TVs in their bedrooms*, then a counterargument, e.g. *On the other hand, some people feel that parents and carers are unable to monitor the kinds of programmes that children watch.*

Think/pair/share

 **Pupil Book p57**

Ask pairs to practise debating the original issue of mobile phone safety using *Activity 4* – each child takes turns to use the language prompts for stating arguments and those for counterarguments.

Remind children that in many discussion texts a writer will present all points for one side of an argument then all those from another.

Independent note-making

PCM 8b

Using PCM 8b, ask children to write notes and ideas in preparation for planning and composing a simple written argument about the safety of mobile phones.

Phase plenary

Review the language features and structure of arguments. Check that children understand that formal language is often used in arguments and that stock phrases and certain language prompts are used to present arguments and counterarguments.

 Children can understand that discussion texts include formal language, stock phrases and language prompts and that connectives and conjunctions are used to link ideas and sentences together.

 Children understand that discussion texts usually include formal language, stock phrases and language prompts and are beginning to use connectives and conjunctions to link ideas and sentences together.

 Children can identify and use formal language, stock phrases and language prompts, and can readily use connectives and conjunctions to link ideas and sentences together.

Phase 3: *Explore arguments in debate*

⑧ Preparing for debate

Whole-class teaching

Explain that they will be participating in a debate considering whether or not children should be banned from owning mobile phones.

Divide the class equally into two groups: those in favour of banning children's use of mobile phones and those against.

Group discussion

PCM 8b

Ask children on either side to work in small mixed ability groups to prepare their arguments on PCM 8b.

Children should take a note of evidence to support their argument, e.g. research findings, statistics (refer back to the shared texts). They may also research using the internet and class library for further facts and arguments.

Write/pair/share

Pupil Book p57

Once they have noted their arguments, ask pairs to write and practise using the language of debate (referring to the language prompts in the Pupil Book).

Review

Review the process of debating on the issue. Establish who is to speak for which side and who is undecided, ensuring that all the class know that they will have a chance to contribute.

9 Participating in the debate

Class discussion

Recap on the work done in Session 8 and then lay the ground rules before carrying out the debate.

- Acting as chairperson, allow a group at a time from either side to debate the issue, while the rest of the class observes to evaluate the effectiveness of the arguments presented.
- Then ask groups from each side to join together, so that a whole class debate can occur.

Review

Round off the debate with observers voting to decide the winning side. What was effective about the presentation of arguments? How could these be improved?

Phase plenary

Check that children understand the purpose of debate and the features that are common to both spoken and written forms of argument. What are the differences? Which form is most effective and when?

 Children can attempt to present arguments for an oral debate.

 Children can present arguments for an oral debate, using language prompts and connectives and conjunctions to link ideas together.

 Children can present arguments for an oral debate, using language prompts and connectives and conjunctions, and refer to evidence to support their arguments.

Phase 4: *Create*

10 Comparing arguments and exploring an issue

Whole-class teaching

Explain that they will be writing a guide for parents, showing a balanced argument about the effects of computer games on children.

Think/pair/share

Ask pairs to discuss the pros and cons of children playing computer games.

Tell the children that they will be comparing two texts which hold opposing viewpoints about the effects of computer games on children.

Shared reading

Read the article *Posturing on lifestyle*. What are the main arguments put forward in this article? Is it a balanced argument? What are the counterarguments to the proposal that computer games make children unhealthy? As a class, note the arguments used in the text on Workpad 4. Show the annotations on the software.

> **Software u8**
> Explore: Text 4, Text 5, Workpad 4

Read the article *A good sport*. How does the viewpoint of this report differ from *Posturing on lifestyle*? Is this a balanced report? To what extent does it show two sides of an argument? Show the annotations on the software.

Write/pair/share

> **PCM 8b;**
> **Pupil Book**
> p57–58

Ask pairs to reread *A good sport* and note the main arguments on an argument frame.

Ask them to decide which side of the argument they think is true and to practise stating their viewpoint using the language prompts in the Pupil Book. Model this first, if necessary.

Finally, ask them to write a sentence to state their viewpoint, using one of the language prompts.

Review

Discuss some of the sentences and ask the class to evaluate whether it persuasively states the children's viewpoints. Have they chosen the best language prompt? Does it include evidence from research? Are the ideas linked in a logical way?

Homework

> **Homework**
> **Book**
> p17

 Activity 8b asks children to list the benefits and drawbacks of on-screen entertainment. This will prepare them for the debate work they will do in Session 11.

11 Gathering ideas for a debate

Whole-class teaching

Explain that the class will be having a debate. Divide them into two equal groups: those for and against the argument that: *Computer games are bad for children*.

In groups, ask children to prepare arguments either for or against the issue, noting ideas on the whiteboard, flipchart or poster paper. Record points and elaborate, noting facts/research where possible.

Ask children to select a statement that they will put forward. They should compose the sentence using debate language.

Drama

> **Software u8**
> Explore: Workpad 5

Make a *decision alley* to allow children on either side of the argument to present their statements; one child walks down the middle of the alley and makes a decision based on the strength of arguments given.

In preparation for writing, ask children to select three arguments from each of the opposing sides, drawing on the information gathered. Record these on to Workpad 5. Include points and any elaboration.

Review

Ask children to create sentences showing two sides of an argument, using the connecting phrase *on the other hand* and connective *however*. Check that children have produced arguments supporting their position for the debate.

Planning a balanced argument

Whole-class teaching

Explain that they will be using all the ideas they have explored so far to plan their parent guides on whether computer games are bad for children. Show some examples of guides. Explain that it is important to keep in mind what is appropriate for the intended audience and purpose when planning for writing.

Demonstration writing

> **Software u8**
> Plan

Taking turns and referring to the skeleton notes they made in Session 11, ask children to imagine that they are presenting their arguments to a child's parent. With the children acting as parents, ask them to decide whether or not the arguments are suitable for a parent's guide and how the arguments might need to be reworded for this audience.

Discuss revisions needed with purpose and audience in mind. Remind children that a good discussion text always includes an introduction and a conclusion. Discuss the kinds of points that could be made in these sections. Show how to bullet point ideas on the *Planning a guide for parents* plan and display the modelled version.

Independent writing

> **PCM 8d;**
> **Software u8**
> Plan;
> **Pupil Book**
> p59

Ask children to plan the introduction, main points and conclusion of their guide on PCM 8d or the blank planning frame on the software, drawing upon all their notes and those in *Activity 5*.

Review

Ask children to evaluate each other's plans – speakers explain plans and listeners evaluate: Are the points made appropriate for the audience and purpose? How could the plan be improved?

Writing a balanced argument

Demonstration writing

> **Software u8**
> Write

Model the introduction and the first main paragraphs of the balanced argument on page 1 of *Write* – demonstrate how to rehearse sentences aloud prior to writing to check they make sense and sound strong. Model the use of complex sentences. Make explicit the importance of considering the purpose and audience as you write. Emphasise that the guide must present a balanced report.

Independent writing

> **Pupil Book**
> p59;
> **Software u8**
> Write

Ask children to write their own introduction and a main paragraph using their plans to structure points and using *Activity 5*. They may use the blank writing frame on the software.

Continuing writing

Demonstration writing

> **Software u8**
> Write

Model the opposing arguments and concluding paragraph (page 2 on the modelled text), focusing on the use of complex sentences and the conditional form.

Independent writing

> **Pupil Book**
> p59;
> **Software u8**
> Write

Provide time for children to complete their written arguments, referring to *Activity 5*.

Class discussion

Discuss the importance of presentation. How might their guide be presented? What images would support the purpose of the text? What headings or subheadings are needed and how should these be presented? Might some statistics be shown in separate text boxes?

Independent writing

 Pupil Book p59

Ask children to complete their guides, bearing in mind the points raised about presentation. Encourage them to check and amend their drafts, as necessary, using *Activity 5*.

Once children have edited their first drafts, they can design the layout of their guides for their final versions.

 **15 Unit plenary: responding to writing**

Independent writing

 Pupil Book p59

Give children time to complete their guides. Remind them to proofread and edit for presentation.

Responding to writing

Display the guides on the intranet, or on tables around the room. Ask children to imagine that they are new parents finding out about the school and reading a guide. Ask them to read and report back to the writer what was useful about the guide, whether or not the argument was balanced and what they would like to see in the guide next time.

Review

 Pupil Book p59

Encourage children to use the *Remember!* checklist in the Pupil Book with a response partner to assess their work.

Use the assessment sheet for **discussion** writing on page 168 to help you assess the children's parent guides.

What next?

Encourage children to share their guides with parents or carers to get feedback from a real audience.

Photocopy a section of a leaflet presenting a balanced argument and give this out to this group. Ask children to find at least five connectives used to link sentences.

Photocopy a section of a leaflet presenting a balanced argument and give this out to these groups. Ask children to find at least five connectives used to link sentences and to think of alternative connectives that could be used in their place. Can they add any language prompts?

If you liked these texts you could read:

A local newspaper to find arguments relating to issues relevant to your area

An online newspaper website for wider issues

Discussions by young people on http://www.headliners.org/storylibrary/

Learning outcomes

Children can:
- identify and compare viewpoints presented
- argue points of view in a balanced way, both orally and in writing
- retrieve information, make notes, plan and write a balanced argument.

Finding a Voice
Genre: Poetry

Objectives for this unit

Speaking and listening: Use the techniques of dialogue to explore issues and respond to suggestions made when reading and writing poems.

Reading: Understand how poets use different structures to create impact.

Writing: Use varied structures to shape and organise poems.

PNS Framework objectives

1. Speaking: Use the techniques of dialogic talk to explore ideas, topics or issues	**8. Engaging with and responding to texts:** Read extensively and discuss personal reading with others, including in reading groups
2. Listening and responding: Analyse and evaluate how speakers present points effectively through use of language	**9. Creating and shaping texts:** Select words and language drawing on their knowledge of literary features and formal and informal writing
3. Group discussion and interaction: Understand and use a variety of ways to criticise constructively and respond to criticism	**10. Text structure and organisation:** Use varied structures to shape and organise texts coherently
4. Drama: Improvise using a range of drama strategies and conventions to explore themes such as hopes, fears and desires; Consider the overall impact of a live or recorded performance, identifying dramatic ways of building tension	**12. Presentation:** Use different styles of handwriting for different purposes with a range of media, developing a consistent and personal legible style; Select from a wide range of ICT programs to present text effectively and communicate information and ideas
7. Understanding and interpreting texts: Understand underlying themes, causes and points of view; Understand how writers use different structures to create coherence and impact	

Unit overview

This unit is designed to last one week. During the unit, the class will read poems around issues, compare poets' styles and write a poem based on a structure of a poem.

Phase 1: *Engage (sessions 1–2)*
Children read and respond to linked poems by the same poet on bullying.

Phase 2: *Explore (sessions 3–4)*
Children explore poems by different poets about bullying and the environment.

Phase 3: *Create (session 5)*
Children choose an issue, then write a poem that communicates their feelings about it.

Prior learning

Check that children can already:

- discuss their responses to a range of poetry
- identify and discuss various features of a poem, including structure and organisation of the text and the way language is used to create effects
- identify poetic devices, e.g. alliteration, simile, metaphor and personification.

Cross-curricular links

Citizenship: Choices; Children's rights – human rights

Resources

Texts: *Beyond de Bell* by Benjamin Zephaniah, *What's in a Name?*, *Descriptions* and *Putting the Boot In* by Malorie Blackman, *Billy Doesn't Like School Really* by Paul Cookson, *Bully* by John Coldwell, *Give and Take* by Roger McGough

Software 6, Unit 9

Pupil Book 6, Unit 9, pp60–64

Homework Book 6, pp18–19

PCM 9

In this Unit, *Warm up* introduces Session 4.

Phase 1: *Engage*

1 Responding to poems about bullying

Introducing the unit

> **Software u9**
> **Explore: Text 1**

The class will be responding to poems about issues, including bullying and friendship. They will write a poem about an issue that is important to them.

Listen to *Beyond de Bell* on page 1 and ask the class to respond. Listen to the poem again and talk about other ways in which children can be bullied, e.g. by cruel words.

The full text with annotations is available on page 2 for further exploration of the poem.

Shared reading

> **Software u9**
> **Explore: Text 2;**
> **Pupil Book**
> **pp60–61, 63**

Read *What's in a Name?*. The poem is an extract from a story told in verse. Refer children to the poem and *Activity 1* in the Pupil Book.

Use the annotations to discuss the structure, what is meant by the descriptive phrases, the tension at the end and to find similes.

Discuss the slowly unravelling story. How did Davey become the victim of bullying? What was different about him? (He had a frayed collar and a hole in the elbow of his jumper; he was the *new boy*.)

Sentence work

> **Software u9**
> **Practise**

Children can work through the exercise in *Practise*, identifying similes.

Drama

> **Pupil Book**
> **pp60–61, 63**

In groups, ask children to explore the poem through drama. Refer them to *Activity 2*.

Review

Discuss the poem's impact. Is this story more powerful told through poetry than through a narrative? Ask children to pick out powerful images and descriptions.

2 Responding to different styles of poetry on the same theme

Shared reading

> **Software u9**
> **Explore: Text 3**

Read *Descriptions*. Compare it with *What's in a Name?*. *Descriptions* provides snapshots of three characters in the unfolding story. Use the annotations to discover more about this list poem.

Shared reading

> **Software u9**
> **Explore: Text 4**

Read the shape poem *Putting the Boot In*. Check that children understand the meaning of the title's expression. Use the annotations to talk about the impact of this hard-hitting poem. Discuss the shape of the poem (a boot) and what effect this has.

Responding to the poems

> **Pupil Book**
> **pp62–63**

Ask children to answer the questions about the two poems in *Activity 3*.

 Each group can complete the appropriate set of questions.

Phase plenary

Which poem in this phase has made the biggest impression on the children and why?

 Children understand how poetry can be used to communicate thoughts and feelings about issues.

 Children can empathise with another person's position and explore their thoughts and feelings through drama and discussion.

 Children can explain how a poem communicates the writer's thoughts and feelings.

Phase 2: *Explore*

 **3**

Exploring poems by different poets on the same theme

Shared reading

Software u9
Explore:
Text 5, Text 6

Compare the poems *Billy Doesn't Like School Really* and *Bully* which focus on bullying from the perspectives of an observer and a victim.

Use the annotations to explore the structure of both poems. How are they similar or different?

Demonstration writing

Software u9
Explore:
Workpad 6

Model writing additional verses based on the format of *Bully*. You can use the example on Workpad 6.

Think/pair/share

Software u9
Explore:
Text 5, Text 6

Ask pairs to choose a poem from this session and use its pattern to make up additional verses that explore bullying. Those that choose *Bully* may use the frame in Workpad 6.

Review

Ask children to perform their new verses. Allow listeners to offer constructive criticism and identify powerful descriptions and imagery.

 **4**

Exploring an issue through a poem using repetition

Introducing the issue

Software u9
Warm up

Show the images in the *Warm up* sequence contrasting natural landscapes with environmental damage.

Ask children to note the thoughts and feelings that the images inspire, then share their ideas.

Shared reading

Software u9
Explore: Text 7

Read/listen to the poem *Give and Take*. How has the poet presented environmental issues through repetition?

Use the annotations to explore this poem further.

Class discussion

Software u9
Explore:
Workpad 7

Consider how the poet might have planned his poem. Think about the gifts he has focused on and write two lists to show the contrast between what we take from the Earth and what we give back. You can use the example on Workpad 7.

Think of other ideas to add to the lists. What made the poet decide on the ideas that he used?

Demonstration writing

Software u9
Plan

Using the added ideas, model writing new verses based on *Give and Take*. Alternatively, you could develop the structure further, introducing alternative verbs to *give* and developing descriptions and imagery. You can use the example in *Plan*.

Independent writing

Software u9
Plan;
PCM 9

Ask children independently to write new verses based on the poet's format, then perform them in groups. Encourage other group members to give constructive feedback, identifying powerful imagery and making suggestions for improvements.

 This group could use the writing frame in *Plan* or PCM 9.

Review

Ask children to choose an issue which evokes strong thoughts and feelings, e.g. animal welfare, endangered species, poverty or one from the unit. Ask them to collect photographs, newspaper clippings, information from websites, e.g. Friends of the Earth, which focus on that issue.

Homework

Homework Book
p18

 *Activity 9* asks children to complete the planning activity.

Phase plenary

Discuss which structure might be suitable for their poem, e.g. a list or shape poem, or one using repetition. Check what the children have learned.

Children understand that poems can have different structures and are able to write verses, with support, in the style of a poet's particular structure.

 Children can write verses of a poem with an issue using at least one structure studied.

 Children can write verses of a poem with an issue using any structure studied.

Phase 3: *Create*

 **(5) Unit plenary: Writing a poem on an issue**

Demonstration writing

Software u9
Write

Model writing the poem using the software.

Independent writing

Pupil Book
p64

Drawing on all their ideas, children write their poem, using their planning sheet and *Activity 4* in the Pupil Book.

 Children could continue writing one of the poems in the style of the poet studied in Session 4.

 Children can write their poem using a structure other than the ones learned in the unit.

Children may require extra time to complete their poem and review it with a partner, to judge its effectiveness.

They can use the software or an ICT program to present their poem. Display the poems in a class anthology.

Review

Discuss the different types of poetry explored. Listen to some of their work, inviting constructive feedback. Identify powerful imagery, examples of alliteration, metaphor, simile and personification and discuss their effectiveness.

Poetry writing is very subjective, so there is no assessment sheet for poetry writing. Instead, discuss the children's writing with them, either in small groups or individually.

What next?

 Read the rest of *Cloud Busting* by Malorie Blackman to find out what happens to the bully and his victim and discover the surprising twists and turns.

 Children can visit Malorie Blackman's website: www.malorieblackman.co.uk.

 Children can collect other similar poems. Ask them to organise the poems into anthologies, grouped according to theme or style.

 Children could prepare presentations on their chosen issues, using their poems to introduce their talks.

Activity 9b asks children to write their thoughts and feelings about two different situations.

Homework Book
p18

 This group could list their thoughts and feelings about the situations.

 These groups could write a verse of poetry about each situation.

If you liked these texts you could read

Finding Fizz by J. Alexander (novel on bullying)

How Can You Buy or Sell the Sky: the words of Chief Seattle

Brother Eagle, Sister Sky by Susan Jeffers

What Will You Do? by Clare Bevan

Learning outcomes

Children can:

- identify and explain how a poem communicates the writer's thoughts and feelings to the reader
- play with language to form and shape ideas that express their feelings
- write an interesting and engaging short poem that effectively communicates their thoughts and feelings about an issue.

10
2 weeks

Time Travelling
Genre: Short story with flashback

Objectives for this unit

Speaking and listening: Use dialogue and role play to explore the events and characters' feelings in a story with flashback.

Reading: Understand how writers use flashback in stories to create impact.

Writing: Write a short story on an historical event and include flashback.

PNS Framework objectives

1. Speaking: Use a range of oral techniques to present persuasive arguments and engaging narratives

2. Listening and responding: Make notes when listening for a sustained period and discuss how note-taking varies depending on context and purpose

7. Understanding and interpreting texts: Understand underlying themes, causes and points of view; Understand how writers use different structures to create coherence and impact

9. Creating and shaping texts: Use different narrative techniques to engage and entertain the reader; Integrate words, images and sounds imaginatively for different purposes

10. Text structure and organisation: Use varied structures to shape and organise texts coherently

Unit overview

This unit is designed to last two weeks. During the unit, the class will read a complete short story which includes flashback and write their own story using the same technique.

Phase 1: *Engage (sessions 1–3)*
Children read a mystery story and consider how the author has used the narrative technique of flashback.

Phase 2: *Explore (sessions 4–5)*
Children explore the issues that underpin the story, reflect on the story's historical setting and explore it through discussion, drama and research.

Phase 3: *Create (sessions 6–10)*
Children write their own short story on a similar theme, experimenting with narrative techniques such as flashback or time travel.

Prior learning

Check that children can already:

- form opinions and personal responses to text, using evidence from a written or visual text to support and justify responses
- infer authors' perspectives and understand underlying themes
- use and manipulate paragraphs to structure and shape a narrative.

Cross-curricular links

Citizenship: Children's rights – human rights; How do rules and laws affect me; Local democracy for young citizens

Resources

Texts: *Maggie's Window* by Marjorie Darke, News report from *The Morning Post*, June 1914

Software 6, Unit 10

Pupil Book 6, Unit 10, pp65–70

Homework Book 6, pp20–21

PCM 10a–b

Phase 1: *Engage*

1 Setting the scene

Introducing the text

> **Software u10**
> **Warm up**

Show the *Warm up* sequence. Ask the children when they think the events took place (1914). What were the women demonstrating about?

Explain that they will be reading and writing stories set during this time in history. The stories will also feature flashbacks as a literary device. The unit theme is *freedom and responsibility*, focusing on the Suffragette movement.

Shared reading

> **Software u10**
> **Explore: Text 1**

Read the opening section of Part 1 of *Maggie's Window* (page 1 on the software). Discuss the way Marjorie Darke has opened her story, with a scene from the end of the story. What information has she revealed in the opening scene? What do we learn about Maggie's father? Why did Una look at Maggie with *intense sad disappointment*? How do we know that this scene had a big impact on Maggie? Why might Una have been arrested?

Read the next section of the story up to the end of Part 1.

Why were women breaking windows? What do Maggie's parents think about Suffragettes? What does the newspaper heading tell us about Suffragettes? Show the annotations on the software.

Responding to the text

> **Pupil Book**
> **pp65–68**

Ask the children to read *Maggie's Window* and answer the questions in *Activity 1* in the Pupil Book.

 Each group can answer the appropriate set of questions.

Review

Discuss the children's answers. Why does the author reveal in the opening scene that one of Maggie's companions will be arrested? What questions are left unanswered? (The mystery is not what will happen, but who will betray Maggie's companion since we know that Maggie isn't to blame.)

2 Exploring the development of a short story

Shared reading

> **Software u10**
> **Explore: Text 2**

Recap on the story so far. Discuss how the author has introduced the characters and revealed the mystery. We already suspect that the women's activities will end in betrayal and arrest but how will the story develop and who will betray them?

Read Part 2 of *Maggie's Window*.

Why is Maggie unable to sleep? Why does she decide to join Cora and the other women? (She intends to inform her father about their activities.) Why does Una have doubts about inviting Maggie to the meeting?

Encourage the class to point out interesting phrases, descriptions and expressions. Use Annotation sets a and b on the software to provide examples.

What does Una mean when she refers to *our London sisters*? What does Muriel mean when she says she will *ring for some tea*? (She rings a bell so that a maid brings tea.)

What keeps Maggie awake at the end of this section? (She has a moral dilemma; she will either betray her father or the women who trust her; she believes in the right to vote.)

Exploring vocabulary

Software u10 Practise

Children can complete the exercise in *Practise*, looking at examples of words and phrases where the meaning has changed over time.

Role play

Ask a volunteer to hotseat as Maggie grappling with her conscience. Invite the class to question Maggie about her thoughts and feelings.

Independent writing

PCM 10a; Software u10 Explore: Workpad 2

As Maggie, children write a short diary account of the day she was welcomed into Una's circle and her conflict of loyalties.

 This group can use the writing frame on PCM 10a or Workpad 2 which gives opening sentences for support.

Review

Software u10 Explore: Text 2

Discuss how the author has included historical language and detail. Can the children spot historical details in the story extract so far? Examples are annotated in set c on the software (e.g. *the purring gaslight*).

Ask the children to read out any historical language or details in their diary accounts.

3 Exploring the ending of a short mystery story

Shared reading

Software u10 Explore: Text 3

Discuss the story that is being unravelled. What aspects of the plot are unresolved? How might the story end?

Read Part 3. Why does Maggie think Cora betrayed the women? Why does Maggie feel indignant and ashamed? Who does Una believe betrayed them?

Class discussion

Software u10 Explore: Workpad 3

Look at the words "Edith gave a sudden shout: 'Police!'" This is also the first line in the story; the first and final scenes are set at the

same time, giving the story symmetry, and the rest of the story is told in flashback. Discuss the effect of this. You could use the timeline on Workpad 3 to plot how events are unfolded. A modelled version is provided on the software.

Discuss the title of the story *Maggie's Window*. The story gives the reader Maggie's *view* of the events and at the end, Maggie hurls a stone through a window. By throwing the stone, Maggie shows her allegiance. Show the annotations on the software.

Group discussion

Ask groups to discuss the actions of Cora, Maggie and her father (each group could take a character). What motivates them? Are their actions justified? Why did Cora inform the police? What do the group think about Maggie breaking a window? Was her father right to prevent the protest?

Review

Consider the issues that have arisen from the discussion. Talk about the conflicts of interest between the Suffragettes and people like Maggie's father.

Phase plenary

Check that the class understand the different ways in which Marjorie Darke has used time in her story. For example:

- historical language and details to make its setting convincing
- Maggie's memory of the events
- the main part of the story – the middle section – is told in flashback.

 Children recognise whether a story is set in the past, present or future.

 Children recognise narrative techniques that use time in different ways, such as flashbacks or recounting memories.

 Children can identify a range of techniques used by an author to indicate shifts in time between past and present.

Phase 2: *Explore*

4 Exploring historical events through fictional characters

Drama

Ask groups to re-enact the final scene, including Cora observing in the crowd, Una being handcuffed, Maggie's father with his thumb raised and Maggie poised to throw a stone at the window. Shout *freeze* as the drama reaches its conclusion and ask different characters in turn to explain what they are thinking and doing, and why.

Role play

Recap briefly on what took place at the end of *Maggie's Window*. Ask a volunteer to role-play the part of Maggie and invite questions from the class. For example: Why did she throw the stone? Was she worried about her father? What was she hoping to achieve?

Then invite a child to role-play the part of Maggie's father and invite questions. What did he think about the women's actions? Was he shocked to see his daughter? How did he feel when she threw the stone?

Shared reading

> **Software u10**
> Explore: Text 4;
> **Pupil Book**
> p69

Introduce the news reports in *The Morning Post* newspaper. Read and discuss together referring to *Activity 2* or the software. Ask why women might have been banned from entering the Royal Exchange. Talk about the Suffragists who were arrested at Buckingham Palace; what was their crime? Why would they be taken to Bow Street (Magistrates' Court)? What does the word *militant* tell us about the journalist's opinion? Show the annotations on the software.

Review

Explore how the drama in this session has helped the children understand how fiction can show how real events actually happened, and how the characters' thoughts and feelings mirror those of real people.

Homework

> **Homework Book**
> p20

Activity 10a asks children to write a newspaper report outlining the events at the Town Hall in *Maggie's Window*.

5 Researching for a short story

Class discussion

Discuss the planning processes that would have gone into Marjorie Darke's story, e.g. characterisation, plot and structure, historical research.

Ask the children what they already know about the Suffragette movement. What else would they like to find out? Where could they look for information?

Independent note-making

> **Software u10**
> Explore:
> Workpad 4;
> **Pupil Book**
> p69

Ask children to research and make notes on the Suffragette movement in preparation for writing a story set at that time. Children can work independently or collaboratively. The spider diagram on Workpad 4 shows a way to organise making notes. They should list a few bullet points of information about three topics: Emmeline Pankhurst, Emily Davidson and the Buckingham Palace Demonstration, 1914.

Then ask them to find information to answer the questions in *Activity 3* in the Pupil Book.

Think/pair/share

Ask pairs to share their findings and note down any new information from the discussion to share with the class.

Review

Review the information the children found out about the Suffragette movement and ask which sources they used. Discuss which details could be used in a short story like *Maggie's Window*.

Phase plenary

Check what the children have learned during this phase.

 Children understand that using drama and making notes about a subject are useful techniques to use before planning a story.

 Children are aware of the value of drama as a planning tool. They are able to make notes on a subject and later decide which pieces of information are most useful for their needs.

 Children are readily able to empathise with characters during drama. During research, they can quickly select the most useful pieces of information from which to make notes.

Phase 3: *Create*

6 Planning a short story

Whole-class teaching

> **Software u10**
> Explore: Text 4;
> **Pupil Book**
> p70

Explain that the children are going to write a short story on the same theme as *Maggie's Window* starting with a given paragraph. Tell them that they will base the story on *The Morning Post* article.

Read through together the given paragraph in *Activity 4* in the Pupil Book and invite comments.

Think/pair/share

Ask pairs to discuss how the story might unfold, making notes of the different events that could occur. Then regroup as a class to listen to some of the ideas.

Demonstration writing

Software u10
Plan

Drawing on ideas from the class, plan how the story might progress using the planning frame on the software. A model plan is also provided.

Independent writing

PCM 10b

Children begin planning their own version of the story using the planning frame.

Review

Ask the class to comment on the plan you drew up together. Check that there is a clear distinction between the different stages in time. How do the children's plans compare with the one you worked on as a class?

7 Writing a story using flashback

Demonstration writing

Software u10
Write

Write the next paragraph of the story in flashback, modelling how to draw the reader back in time to the scene outside Buckingham Palace. Decide with the class what the role of the characters in the story will be.

Without completing the story, discuss various ways in which you could develop the storyline and draw it to a close. A model paragraph is provided on the software. The given paragraph is provided on page 1 of the software and the continuation is modelled on page 2.

Independent writing

Pupil Book
p70;
Software u10
Write

Children can begin writing their own version of the story, using the paragraph in *Activity 4* in the Pupil Book as a starting point and the blank frame in *Write*.

Review

Review the writing with the class, paying particular attention to the way the story is structured, and where new paragraphs should begin. Check that details are historically accurate.

8 Continuing to write a story using flashback

Independent writing

Children can use this session to complete their story writing.

Read/pair/share

Pupil Book
p70

Ask pairs to share their stories with each other. Check them against *Remember!* in the Pupil Book.

Review

Invite children to read passages from their work and ask for constructive feedback. How have they used time in their story? Is it effective? Are details historically correct?

9 Checking and editing a story with flashback

Think/pair/share

Ask the children to share their stories with a different partner and review each other's writing. They can discuss success criteria, give feedback and judge the quality of their own work. Ask them to pay particular attention to how time is used in their narrative and check that any historical details are accurate.

Independent writing

Allow children to make any changes or improvements.

Review

Review passages from the children's writing (e.g. nominated by their review partner) and draw attention to interesting features. Are there historical inaccuracies? Why is it important for details to be historically accurate?

10 Unit plenary: publishing a story with flashback

Independent writing

Children complete their stories and use them in a class anthology or wall display.

Review

Choose examples of the children's writing that successfully show shifts in time and read them to the class. Discuss why you have chosen these and take feedback.

Use the assessment sheet for **fiction** writing on page 170 to help you assess the children's stories.

What next?

 *Activity 10b* asks children to examine how language changes over time.

Homework Book p21

- Make a storyboard of all the events in *Maggie's Window*.
- After completing the storyboard, dramatise and make a video film of scenes from *Maggie's Window*.

 Prepare presentations on the Suffragettes based on the information found out in Session 5.

If you liked these texts you could read:

Tom's Midnight Garden by Philippa Pearce

Time Switch by Steve Barlow and Steve Skidmore (play using time travel)

Learning outcomes

Children can:

- identify a range of techniques used by an author to indicate shifts in time between past and present
- understand the effects of using the flashback technique in story writing
- structure their own writing effectively and create pace in a short narrative.

11

3 weeks

Walk to School

Genre: Non-fiction, formal writing

Objectives for this unit

Speaking and listening: Listen and write notes on the key points of a non-fiction text; make oral presentations on an issue and discuss their effectiveness.

Reading: Read and respond to non-fiction texts on an issue.

Writing: Write a brochure or a web page using a combination of different non-fiction texts.

PNS Framework objectives

1. Speaking: Use the techniques of dialogic talk to explore ideas or issues

2. Listening and responding: Identify ways in which spoken language varies according to differences in the context and purpose of its use

3. Group discussion and interaction: Understand and use a variety of ways to criticise constructively and respond to criticism

7. Understanding and interpreting texts: Understand how writers use different structures to create coherence and impact

9. Creating and shaping texts: Select words and language drawing on their knowledge of literary features and formal and informal writing; Integrate words, images and sounds imaginatively for different purposes

10. Text structure and organisation: Use varied structures to shape and organise texts coherently

11. Sentence structure and punctuation: Express subtle distinctions of meaning, including hypothesis, speculation and supposition, by constructing sentences in varied ways

12. Presentation: Select from a wide range of ICT programs to present text effectively and communicate information and ideas

Unit overview

This unit is designed to last three weeks. During the unit, the class will read letters and newspaper and website articles and write non-fiction texts on an issue.

Phase 1: *Engage (sessions 1–5)*

Children read and respond to different types of non-fiction texts, including a letter, a newspaper report and a list of instructions.

Phase 2: *Explore (sessions 6–9)*

Children identify and prepare spoken presentations on how to improve their local environment.

Phase 3: *Create (sessions 10–15)*

Children write non-fiction texts using multi-media and employing a hybrid of text types for a website or brochure.

Prior learning

Check that children can already:

- recall the language and organisational features of the main non-fiction text types (recount, report, instructions, explanation, persuasion, discussion) and employ these in their writing
- understand that non-fiction can sometimes employ a hybrid of text types and forms, depending on its audience and purpose.

Curriculum links

Citizenship: Taking part – developing skills of communication and participation

Geography: How can we make our local area safer?

Resources

Texts: *Letter to the Editor* by Karina Law, *First Walking Bus launched in Sittingbourne* from *Kent Messenger* (2006), *Hop on board the Walking Bus* from www.kentwalkingbus.org, *What do you think of the walking bus?*; *Courthouse School walking bus rules for children*, *Letter to parents* from www.foe.co.uk

Software 6, Unit 11

Pupil Book 6, Unit 11, pp71–74

Homework Book 6, pp22–24

PCM 11a–b

Examples of non-fiction texts in different formats, for example, brochures, posters, websites, newspaper advertisements, ideally sharing a similar focus, e.g. promoting a tourist attraction

Mini-whiteboards

Phase 1: *Engage*

 Identifying an issue

Introducing the text

> **Software u11**
> **Warm up**

Watch the *Warm up* sequence on the software, representing children being dropped off at and collected from school. Discuss the problems that are faced in congested areas, by children, parents, other road-users and local residents.

Shared reading

> **Software u11**
> **Explore: Text 1**

Read the letter of complaint. Discuss the tone and format and use the annotations on the software to identify examples of formal and informal language, and negative words.

What was the letter writer's aim in writing this letter and to whom were they addressing their letter? (Point out that although the letter is addressed to *the Editor*, the wider audience is the readership of the newspaper.)

Group discussion

In groups, ask children to discuss who is responsible for the traffic problems. What could be done to improve the situation? Nominate a spokesperson in each group to note down a summary of the main points.

Word work

> **Software u11**
> **Practise**

Review the group discussions as a class. Draw attention to groups who looked at differing viewpoints.

Point out that differing views can be expressed in the same sentence if an appropriate connective is used, such as in discussion texts. Then, show how, in the same sentence, different connectives can be used to convey a subtly different meaning: *Some people think parents are to blame for congestion outside schools, furthermore, others believe councils should do something to improve matters.* This sentence could be used in persuasive writing; the second part of the sentence adds weight to the first part rather than contradicting it.

Children can use the software to pick out appropriate connectives in *Practise*.

Review

Ask children to self-evaluate how they co-operated with one another during their discussions, placing equal importance on listening as well as speaking skills.

Homework

> **Homework Book p22**

Activity 11a asks children to choose different connectives to complete a text.

② Comparing a formal letter with a news report on an issue

Shared reading

Software u11 Explore: Text 1, Text 2

Reread the letter of complaint. Do any of the issues relate to your own school? How does the school avoid traffic-related problems? (For example, requesting that parents do not block driveways or park on zigzag road markings outside the school; employing the assistance of a road crossing patrol (lollipop person).)

Read the news report about one school's solution to the problem of school-related traffic. What does the class think about the idea of a Walking Bus? What benefits does it offer?

Compare the features of the letter and the news report, using the annotations on the software.

Then focus on the other features of the news report and start a class list.

Responding to the text

Pupil Book pp71–72

Ask children to answer the questions in *Activity 1* in the Pupil Book.

 Each group can complete the appropriate set of questions.

Review

Discuss the children's answers to some of the questions. How effective was the news report in reporting the event?

Homework

Homework Book p23

 *Activity 11b* asks children to answer questions for a newspaper report using formal language.

③ Analysing a non-chronological report

Shared reading

Software u11 Explore: Text 3; **Pupil Book** p73

Read the report *Hop on board the Walking Bus* explaining what a Walking Bus is and how the scheme operates in one county in England.

Discuss what type of non-fiction text the report is. Look at the annotations on the software noting the format and the use of persuasive language.

Independent note-making

Software u11 Explore: Workpad 3

Ask the class to listen and write down key points, while you replay the report. Children who need support can use Workpad 3.

Review

Compare the children's information. Have they enough information to explain the Walking Bus scheme to someone who knows nothing at all about it? Agree the key facts that everyone should have in their notes. If time allows, children could present their information in pairs.

④ Analysing a persuasive letter to parents

Shared reading

Software u11 Explore: Text 4

Read and discuss the content and format of the letter from head teacher Peter Brooks written to parents of a school in Maidenhead in England. Briefly, talk about the formal and persuasive language, asking children to find examples. How well has the head teacher explained the scheme? What benefits does he focus on? Show the annotations on the software.

Group discussion

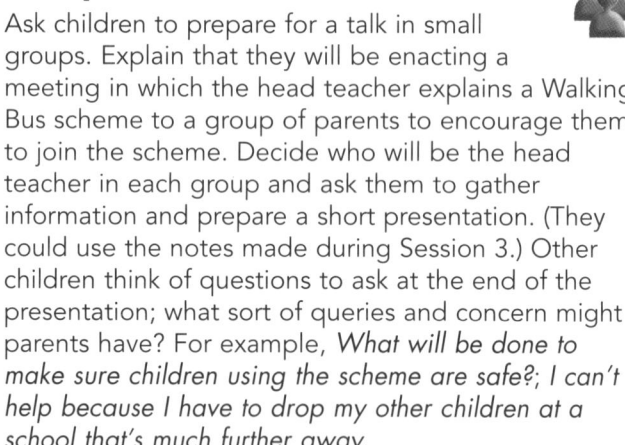

Ask children to prepare for a talk in small groups. Explain that they will be enacting a meeting in which the head teacher explains a Walking Bus scheme to a group of parents to encourage them to join the scheme. Decide who will be the head teacher in each group and ask them to gather information and prepare a short presentation. (They could use the notes made during Session 3.) Other children think of questions to ask at the end of the presentation; what sort of queries and concern might parents have? For example, *What will be done to make sure children using the scheme are safe?*; *I can't help because I have to drop my other children at a school that's much further away.*

Ask the groups to listen without interruptions, while the *head teacher* gives the presentation, before asking the questions and raising the queries they have prepared.

Review

Ask the *head teacher* in each group to comment on how well the *parents* listened. Which questions did they find challenging to answer? Ask the *parents* if the *head teacher* delivered an informative and persuasive presentation. Did they feel encouraged to join the scheme?

5 Analysing safety guidelines

Shared reading

Software u11
Explore: Text 5

Read *Courthouse School Walking Bus rules for children*. Explain that the text is a genuine list of rules written by a school for pupils using a Walking Bus. Which are the most important? Which others could have been included?

Look at the numbered list of instructions on the software and the annotations looking at its features. Do the children think the list was written by teachers, parents or the pupils? (Note the use of the pronoun *we* in instruction 11.)

Group discussion

In groups, ask children to draw up their own list of safety instructions for a *Walking Bus*. Explain that you are looking for evidence that everyone's opinions are heard and respected.

Phase plenary

Review how the groups organised themselves. Did they select leaders or scribes? How did they resolve any disagreements?

Talk about the different types of non-fiction writing in this phase, checking what the children have learned.

 Children understand that non-fiction information can be presented in a number of different formats.

 Children understand how non-fiction can combine media and text types with reference to specific purposes and audiences.

 Children can evaluate the effectiveness of the language, organisation and presentational features of specific non-fiction texts.

Phase 2: *Explore*

6 Comparing informal and formal language

Shared reading

Software u11
Explore: Text 1

Reread the letter of complaint introduced in Session 1. Ask children to point out examples of formal words and phrases (Annotation set a).

Grammar work

Software u11
Explore: Text 6;
PCM 11a

Ask pairs to read the paragraph on PCM 11a and underline examples of informal language. How might they change it so that it has a more formal tone?

Shared writing

Software u11
Explore: Text 6,
Workpad 6

What examples of informal language did the children find? Did they think of ways to change the informal language to a more formal tone?

Discuss the meaning of the colloquial expressions, for example: *What really gets my goat; I'm at the end of my tether*. Point out the use of contractions (e.g. it's, they're, haven't, I'm) and discuss whether they would be appropriate in formal writing. Use the annotations on the software.

Together, change the text on PCM 11a into a formal letter of complaint using Workpad 6 on the software. Decide together who the intended audience will be, for example, a local Member of Parliament or a newspaper editor.

Review

Compare the formal features of your letter with the informal language used on PCM 11a. Are the children beginning to understand the differences between informal and formal language?

Homework

Homework Book p24

Activity 11c asks children to write a formal letter of complaint about a subject of their own choosing.

7 Planning a presentation

Demonstration writing

Software u11
Plan

Discuss the process that the organisers of the Walking Bus scheme must have gone through before the idea became a reality: a) identified a problem; b) considered various ideas to tackle it; c) presented the agreed idea to the local council and local businesses to help fund the scheme; d) enlisted parents' support.

Focusing on the *Walking Bus* idea, model how a plan might be drawn up in preparation for a presentation. A model frame can be found on the software.

Think/pair/share

Software u11
Plan;
PCM 11b

Using the planning frame provided on PCM 11b or the software, ask pairs to think of an idea for an improvement to their community and plan how they will persuade listeners to support their idea.

They should also consider what props they will need, for example: a poster, photographs or video footage illustrating the problem being discussed, a summary of points on a whiteboard.

Review

Discuss how the children found using the planning frame. What aspects did they find useful? What aspects would they change?

 **8** ## Presenting an idea

Think/pair/share

Allow time for pairs to review their plan and rehearse how they will deliver their presentation to a group.

Role play

In groups of about six, pairs can present their ideas. Listeners play members of a school council, school governors' meeting or local Council. They should be invited to ask questions, in role, at the end of each presentation.

Once each pair has presented their idea, the group could vote on the idea that they like best, considering it to be both beneficial and achievable.

Review

Ask groups to report back on the ideas they voted for and explain their reasons.

 **9** ## Exploring different ways of presenting information

Group discussion

Display examples of non-fiction texts in different formats that you have brought in. Ask children to evaluate them in groups, listing the distinguishing features of each. Discuss the children's findings as a class.

Think/pair/share

Ask pairs to focus on one non-fiction format and make a list of its advantages and disadvantages. Children could also try to identify any formal or informal language in each text.

 These children could write formal sentences with connectives to highlight the advantages and disadvantages, for example: *Posters have the advantage of visual impact and accessibility; however, there is a limit to the amount of information that can be included.*

Phase plenary

Check what the children have learned during this phase.

 Children can discern whether formal or informal language is appropriate for particular contexts and audiences.

 Children can identify different features of formal and informal language.

 Children can plan and deliver a presentation using formal language appropriate to the context and audience.

Phase 3: *Create*

 **10** ## Writing an explanatory and persuasive non-fiction text

Shared reading

Software u11
Explore: Text 3

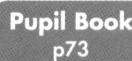

Reread the website article *Hop on board the Walking Bus.* Discuss the purpose of the text: to explain what a *Walking Bus* is and how it operates; to persuade others to join or support the scheme.

Write/pair/share

Pupil Book
p73

Ask the children, in pairs, to compose a similar, non-fiction text of their own explaining what a *Walking Bus* is and how it can benefit the community. Identify the intended audience (parents, teachers, pupils) and purpose (to persuade readers to join or support the scheme). Remind children that the writing will include, in particular, explanation texts and persuasive texts. They can base their writing on *Hop on board the Walking Bus.*

Encourage these children to experiment with different formats for presenting information in addition to the question and answer format used in the model.

Review

Invite pairs to read their writing aloud to the class and invite constructive feedback from listeners. In particular, look at different formats children have used to present information other than the question and answer format used in the model.

Discuss contexts in which the writing could be used, for example, on a website or in a brochure format.

Review

Ask children to share their plans with a partner:

- What idea have they focused on?
- What problems will it help to overcome?
- How does their idea work?
- How will they persuade readers to take part?

 **11**

Planning an information text for a brochure or website

Whole-class teaching

Introduce the final writing task: to create a work of non-fiction employing a hybrid of text types for a website or brochure. The central piece of writing will be explanatory and persuasive but they can also include mock newspaper reports, interviews, surveys, photographs and other features using a variety of media. (Remind children of the non-fiction texts they evaluated in Session 9.)

Independent writing

Pupil Book p74; Software u11 Plan; PCM 11b

Firstly ask them to decide whether they will use the idea of a *Walking Bus* or choose another idea of their own that meets a need in their school or local community. They could look at websites such as the Kent Walking Bus website for other ideas.

Refer them to *Activity 2* in the Pupil Book. They will then need to compile a checklist of the features that will appear in their visual presentation, for example (if focusing on a *Walking Bus*):

- explanatory text
- a list of the benefits
- a survey of how children travel to school
- quotes from people who have benefited from the idea's implementation
- photographs
- (if the presentation will appear on a website page) a video clip showing footage of traffic outside the school at peak times or a Walking Bus in action.

Children can use the planning frame on the software and/or PCM 11b as a starting point. Remind them whether they should use formal or informal writing or both in their presentations.

12

Writing an information text

Demonstration writing

Software u11 Write

Remind children of their writing task and model writing a section of a brochure or website giving information about the Walking Bus or about an issue to help solve a problem in your local area. (You may wish to use the model of a website page provided on the software.) As you write, talk about the features that you are using, e.g. explanatory text to describe the idea, persuasive language to convince the reader, addition of quotes from people who have benefited or will be benefiting from the implementation of the ideas, and so on.

Independent writing

Pupil Book p74

Children use their plans from Session 11 to begin producing the different components of their written presentation. Children who will be writing a website page about the Walking Bus can use the writing frame provided on the software. Remind all children to refer to *Activity 2* in the Pupil Book.

 These children could continue working in pairs, sharing and dividing tasks to produce a single brochure or website page.

Group discussion

In groups, children review their progress and share their ideas making individual checklists of work still to be done.

Review

Discuss the children's progress in the light of their group discussions. Have they remembered which text types require them to write formally or informally?

 **13**

Checking and editing drafts

Independent writing

Pupil Book p74

Children can use this session to edit their work in pairs. Ask them to check that their partner has: a) outlined the problem that their idea will help to overcome, b) explained how their idea works and used persuasive language.

Children can redraft the writing they have completed, implement any agreed changes and discuss the work that remains to be done, considering the best way forward.

Review

Discuss the children's progress and ask them to refer to their checklists made in Session 12 and ensure that the remaining tasks they have given themselves are realistic and achievable.

 ## 14 Publishing an information text

Independent writing

Children should use this session to think about how they will collate their non-fiction texts into a brochure or website page. They should also complete any outstanding writing. Have they checked that they have used informal and formal writing appropriately?

Review

Review the process that children have undertaken in the previous sessions; what challenges have they overcome?

Present examples of children's work and ask the class to identify the different types of non-fiction writing.

 ## 15 Unit plenary: presenting the work

Text presentations

During this session allow the children to present their work in groups, share ideas and receive constructive feedback.

Review

Discuss the different types of formal and impersonal writing the children have explored in this unit. How were these incorporated into their final presentations?

Use the assessment sheets for **explanation** and **persuasion** writing on pages 169 and 173 to help you assess the children's brochures.

What next?

 Children could look on the Internet to find out about Walking Bus schemes operating in other areas.

 Invite a speaker from a public transport industry into school to talk to the children. Ask the children to prepare some questions to ask him or her.

 Invite a local newspaper reporter into school to help children write a news report celebrating a school achievement or event. Children could write reports for a class newspaper or website page using an appropriate IT program. Illustrate the reports by uploading Clip art, digital photographs and scanned images.

If you liked these texts you could read:

The Walking Bus Guide: A Reference Guide for Setting Up and Running a Walking Bus by Tracy Allatt and Sarah Marshall

Learning outcomes

Children can:
- understand how non-fiction information can be presented in different formats combining media and text types with reference to specific purposes and audiences
- evaluate the effectiveness of the language, organisation and presentational features of specific non-fiction texts
- plan a presentation of non-fiction information combining writing with different modes of communication.

12
2 weeks

Plays and Performance
Genre: Playscripts

Objectives for this unit

Speaking and listening: Engage in discussion to explore themes and issues in plays and reflect on and respond to criticism given by others.

Reading: Read and study playscripts to increase understanding of their structure and purpose, contrasting with narrative fiction.

Writing: Write a play scene taking into account features of plays studied.

PNS Framework objectives

1. Speaking: Explore ideas, topics or issues

2. Listening and responding: Analyse and evaluate how speakers present points effectively through the use of language and gesture

3. Group discussion and interaction: Understand and use a variety of ways to criticise constructively and respond to criticism; Adopt a range of roles in discussion and contribute in different ways such as promoting, opposing, exploring and questioning

4. Drama: Improvise using a range of drama strategies and conventions to explore themes such as hopes, fears and desires; Devise a performance considering how to adapt the performance for a particular audience

7. Understanding and interpreting texts: Understand underlying themes, causes and points of view; Understand how writers use different structures to create coherence and impact.

9. Creating and shaping texts: Use different narrative techniques to engage and entertain the reader; Select words and language drawing on their knowledge of literary features and formal and informal writing

10. Text structure and organisation: Use varied structures to shape and organise texts coherently

Unit overview

This unit is designed to last two weeks. During the unit, the class will explore part of a story retelling *Macbeth* and scenes from Shakespeare's *Macbeth* and a play version of *The Railway Children*, and write their own play scene.

Phase 1: *Engage (sessions 1–4)*
Children examine a narrative scene from *Macbeth*, exploring the themes and dilemmas of the main characters.

Phase 2: *Explore (sessions 5–7)*
Children explore through drama how a scene develops by examining *Macbeth* and another playscript (*The Railway Children*).

Phase 3: *Create (sessions 8–10)*
Children invent and write a playscript based on the drama techniques learned.

Prior learning

Check that children can already:

- identify and discuss basic conventions of script writing such as the setting of each new speaker on a new line and the use of stage directions, acts and scenes
- use a range of drama techniques
- use a plan to develop a plot with a simple structure, e.g. beginning, middle and end.

Cross-curricular links

Citizenship: Choices; Living in a diverse world

Resources

Texts: *Macbeth* adapted by Geraldine McCaughrean, *Macbeth*, Act IV by William Shakespeare, *The Railway Children* by E Nesbit adapted by Dave Simpson

Software 6, Unit 12

Pupil Book 6, Unit 12, pp75–82

Homework Book 6, pp25–26

PCM 12a–d

Phase 1: *Engage*

1 Exploring the themes in a Shakespeare play

Class discussion

> **Software u12**
> **Warm up**

Find out what the children know about William Shakespeare (key facts: born April 1564 and died April 1616 in Stratford-upon-Avon; wrote 38 plays; performed for Queen Elizabeth I and King James I; plays first performed at The Globe Theatre in London; plays include *Hamlet*, *Romeo and Juliet*, *Midsummer Night's Dream* and *Macbeth*). Show the *Warm up* sequence. What do children know about his play *Macbeth*?

Shared reading

> **Software u12**
> **Explore: Text 1,**
> **Workpad 1**

Tell the children that, before they study and perform scenes from Shakespeare's *Macbeth*, they will look at a retelling of key scenes. Discuss the themes of the play (murder, war, jealousy, betrayal, broken friendship).

Read *Macbeth Meets Banquo's Ghost*. Note down key points on Workpad 1 (a model is provided). Can the children identify any themes yet? Use Annotation set a to aid the discussion.

Review

> **Software u12**
> **Explore: Text 1**

Point out how the themes within a play scene are often revealed through cause and effect of characters' actions and thoughts as the number of settings that can be shown is limited. Annotation set b points out some examples for you to look at.

2 Examining how the play's themes are revealed through characters

Class discussion

> **Software u12**
> **Explore: Text 1**

Revisit the story of Banquo, focusing on how the personality of the characters is revealed, such as Macbeth's reaction to Banquo's ghost. You can use Annotation set c to highlight the main examples.

Role play

Choose children to hotseat as Lord and Lady Macbeth, Banquo's ghost and the guests at the banquet and answer questions.

Group work

In groups, choose two children to act as Lord and Lady Macbeth and the rest of the group to stand in two lines either side of them to make a conscience alley. As the two characters walk down the alley, ask the children on each side to give advice.

Class discussion

Discuss the dilemmas faced by the characters and the advice given. How does Shakespeare present the themes through the personality of his characters?

Review

Shakespeare has created strong characters to reveal the themes of ambition, greed, evil and deception within his play. Explain that a play often revolves around one main character who interests the audience or who the audience cares about. It also centres on a problem faced by the main character.

3 Identifying dramatic language

Shared reading

> **Software u12**
> Explore: Text 2,
> Workpad 2

Read *Macbeth and the Witches*. Explore what makes it dramatic and again look at the themes, setting and characters, adding these to another Scene development line in Workpad 2.

Exploring vocabulary

> **Software u12**
> Explore: Text 2

Discuss the words and phrases which evoke the use of the senses, e.g. *dark cave* (sight); *stench* (smell), etc. (See annotations on the software.) How do these words increase dramatic impact?

Responding to the text

> **Pupil Book**
> pp75–77

Ask the children to complete the questions about the three witches' scene in *Activity 1*.

Each group can complete the appropriate set of questions.

Review

Share some of the children's answers. Discuss the metaphors used in the witches' scene. What effect do they have?

4 Relating a narrative to a play

Shared reading

> **Software u12**
> Explore: Text 3

Remind children of the text read in Session 3. Read the playscript *The Witches' Spell*. How does it match *Macbeth and the Witches*? Why do they think Shakespeare repeats the verse *Double, double toil and trouble* throughout the spell? How do the children think it should be said each time?

Exploring vocabulary

> **Software u12**
> Explore: Text 3

Look at the word *thrice* in the first line of the First Witch's part. Explain that this is an example of Shakespearean language, and as a class try to work out its meaning and think of the equivalent word or words in modern English, i.e. *three times*.

Word work

> **Software u12**
> Explore: Text 3

Ask the children, in pairs, to look at the highlighted words on the playscript using Annotation set a on the software and write down equivalent modern English words. Later show Annotation set b to check their ideas.

Review

Ask the children to discuss the differences between the narrative and the play scene of the three witches. Why are the characters and their thoughts and actions important in a play? (They convey the storyline and the underlying themes of the play.) What effect do the witches' words have in the play scene? (They build up the theme of evil.)

Phase plenary

Check that the children understand that a play is built up around a theme or themes, and that playwriting involves creating strong characters, powerful images and using dramatic language.

 Children can identify the themes in a Shakespeare play and recognise that plays have strong characters, powerful imagery and dramatic language.

 Children can discuss the themes in a Shakespeare play and explain why plays include strong characters, powerful imagery and dramatic language.

 Children can discuss and compare the themes in a Shakespeare play with those from a narrative version, explaining the effects of powerful imagery, dramatic language and the use of strong characters.

Phase 2: *Explore*

5 Role-playing a scene from Shakespeare's play

Class discussion

Discuss how, in plays, the audience needs to fill in the details of the plot and characters' thoughts, e.g. the mood of the witches' scene is conveyed not by the meaning of their words but how they say them.

Drama

> **Software u12**
> Explore: Text 3;
> PCM 12a

Divide the class into groups of four – one narrator and three witches. Give out PCM 12a and ask groups to prepare for a performance. Tell them that their performance will be for a younger audience and their scene will need to be clear and appropriate. Encourage them to read the stage directions and decide how to use sound effects, basic props, their voices and their actions to portray the setting and mood. Punctuation gives clues to how to say the lines.

Review

Share some of the groups' performances and compare them. Discuss performances that are particularly effective and why.

⑥ Exploring a scene from a modern play

Class discussion

Explain that they are now going to look at a more modern play. Question them about their knowledge of *The Railway Children*.

Shared reading

Software u12
Explore: Text 4

Read the introduction and the scene from *The Surprise Birthday Party*. Discuss the children's responses to the characters and the dilemma.

Responding to the text

Pupil Book
pp78–80

Ask the children to complete the questions about *The Surprise Birthday Party* in *Activity 2*.

Each group can complete the appropriate set of questions.

Review

Discuss the theme of the story and how it's portrayed through the characters' speech and their interaction. Show Annotation set a.

⑦ Performing a dramatised reading of a modern play

Class discussion

Software u12
Explore: Text 4,
Workpad 4

Identify key moments in *The Surprise Birthday Party*. Determine the level of excitement for these key parts and plot them on the "hot" and "cold" graph on Workpad 4.

Group work

Pupil Book
pp78–79;
PCM 12b

Groups should fill in the grid on PCM 12b to describe the characters' feelings and thoughts at each key moment, thinking how the characters' feelings change through the play and how this is shown in the writing.

Drama

Pupil Book
pp78–79

Ask the groups to perform a dramatised reading of *The Surprise Birthday Party*. Give time to practise. Encourage them to read for dramatic effect and convey how each character feels.

Ask the first group to read from the beginning. *Freeze frame* the reading at a key moment and ask how each character is feeling. Ask the next group to continue the reading and rotate around the groups.

Review

Ask the children for constructive comments on the performances. What was particularly effective in revealing the emotions in the play? Did performing it help them understand where/how the author engaged the audience?

Discuss the differences between writing a play scene and a narrative. Use the script to support their opinions.

Phase plenary

Check that children understand how a scene is built up from the beginning to a dramatic moment. How do playwrights create emotional tension? How are characters' personalities shown?

 Children can identify the key points of a modern play through a dramatised reading and pinpoint the emotions of the characters.

 Children can discuss the key points of a modern play through a dramatised reading and relate them to the emotions of the characters.

 Children can relate the key points of a modern play to the emotions of the characters and experiment in conveying these dramatically in different ways.

Phase 3: *Create*

⑧ Exploring stage directions in a play

Class discussion

Software u12
Explore: Text 4

Briefly review the layout of a playscript. Check children's understanding that information to the audience is given through the dialogue and information to the actors is given through stage directions.

Shared reading

Software u12
Explore: Text 4

Show *The Surprise Birthday Party* again, and look at each stage direction. Discuss its purpose. What would happen if they weren't there? What types of words are used in the directions? (Adverbs and verbs). Why are stage directions short?

Grammar work

Software u12
Explore: Text 4

Check children's understanding of verbs and adverbs. Annotation set b shows the verbs and adverbs in the playscript. Discuss their purpose within the stage directions.

Sentence work

Pupil Book
p81

Ask children to practise identifying and using verbs and adverbs in stage directions in *Activity 3*.

 This group can underline the verbs and adverbs.

 This group can write stage directions, adding verbs and adverbs.

 This group can write a script to end the scene, adding stage directions.

Review

Share some of the children's scripts and discuss the stage directions. Which are particularly effective? Why? Write a class list of *top five tips* for writing stage directions.

---

to establish the setting, characters, a problem, a build up in which the problem *comes to a head*, and a resolution.

Before filling in the planning frame, discuss these questions: Where does the scene take place? When? Who is the main character? Who are the other characters and what relationship do they have with the main character? Which props and items of clothing will give the audience a sense of the setting? How will the main character resolve the problem? What happened before the scene? What happens after the scene? You may wish to use the model on the software.

Discuss the tips for scriptwriters at the end of *Activity 4* in the Pupil Book before the children start planning.

Independent writing

Pupil Book
p82;
PCM 12c

Ask the children to decide on their audience and plan their scene using PCM 12c or the blank planning frame on the software and *Activity 4* in the Pupil Book, then swap with a partner. Ask them to suggest a few constructive improvements to each other.

 This group could plan their scene with a partner.

Review

Share some of the children's plans, focusing on those which have a clear opening, conflict or climax and resolution. Capture key points to consider when writing their playscripts.

---

⑨ Planning a play scene

Whole-class teaching

Tell the class they are going to work in groups to write a scene for a play about a special occasion where something unexpected happens and then perform the scene.

Group discussion

Review what they remember about genres and ask each group to choose one to use when writing the playscript. Remind them that information to the audience is given through the dialogue and information to the actors is given through stage directions, and to think about their audience.

Demonstration writing

Software u12
Plan;
Pupil Book
p82

Show them how to plan a scene using the frame on the software. Remind children that, like a narrative, a play needs: an opening

---

⑩ Unit plenary: writing a play scene

Class discussion

Remind children of the key points discussed in Session 9.

Briefly revisit the conventions of writing a playscript: putting the speakers' names in bold or underlining them; starting each new speaker's dialogue on a new line; not using speech marks or speech verbs such as *said*; putting stage directions in brackets and/or italics.

Demonstration writing

Software u12
Write

Demonstrate writing a play scene, referring to the planning notes from Session 9. You may wish to use the modelled writing on the software. Discuss these *tips for screenwriters* while you demonstrate the writing of the scene:

- Use stage directions in brackets to show how characters say things and to tell them how to move (this does not need to be done for every line).

- Read the lines out loud to hear if they sound right.
- Give each character some special feature, e.g. an accent, a phrase to use, a body mannerism.
- Add the title of the play scene.

Independent writing

**Pupil Book
p82;
PCM 12d**

Give the children time to write their play scene, using *Activity 4*, their plan and PCM 12d or the blank writing frame on the software.

Remind them to reread their lines aloud to hear what they sound like, and recheck the tips for scriptwriters.

Ask the children to read their script to a partner, who gives feedback on the use of dialogue, stage directions, and how the action develops. The writer can use the feedback to make changes.

Review

Ask the children to choose effective lines from their partner's script and say why they chose them. Discuss the children's understanding of how to write a play scene, e.g. developing the storyline through the characters' speech and actions, one main character with a problem that's resolved at the end, use of playscript conventions.

Use the assessment sheet for **fiction** writing on page 170 to help you assess the children's play scenes.

What next?

Children can work through the activity in *Practise* where they identify conditional sentences.

Software u12
Practise

Perform some of the children's scripts and make audio versions of their play scenes.

Create a response to the playscript of the witches' scene in *Macbeth* through drawing.

Perform a play scene for other children and parents in the school.

Activities 12a and *12b* ask the children to complete the exercises related to Shakespeare's use of words and language.

**Homework
Book
pp25–26**

If you liked these texts you could read:

Five Children and It by E Nesbit

The Story of the Treasure Seekers by E Nesbit

King of Shadows by Susan Cooper

Mr William Shakespeare's Plays by Marcia Williams

The Lion, the Witch and the Wardrobe by CS Lewis, dramatised by Adrian Mitchell

Learning outcomes

Children can:
- describe the differences between a narrative and a play
- understand characters' dilemmas and themes in a play and how dramatic tension is developed
- shape a script for a play scene using scriptwriting conventions including stage directions and reflect on the effect of their writing on an audience.

13

1 week

Revision: Fiction

Genre: Planning and writing fiction

Objectives for this unit

Speaking and listening: Use discussion to evaluate and respond to each other's writing.

Reading: Read texts to explore features, such as paragraphs and sentence types, to use as models for own writing.

Writing: Attempt short and longer writing tasks in a test situation.

PNS Framework objectives

3. Group discussion and interaction: Understand and use a variety of ways to criticise constructively and respond to criticism

6. Word structure and spelling: Use a range of appropriate strategies to edit, proofread and correct spelling in their own work, on paper and on screen

7. Understanding and interpreting text: Appraise a text quickly, deciding on its value, quality or usefulness

9. Creating and shaping texts: Set their own challenges to extend achievement and experience in writing; Use different narrative techniques to engage and entertain the reader; Select words and language drawing on their knowledge of literary features and formal and informal writing

10. Text structure and organisation: Use varied structures to shape and organise text coherently; Use paragraphs to achieve pace and emphasis

11. Sentence structure and punctuation: Express subtle distinctions of meaning, including hypothesis, speculation and supposition, by constructing sentences in varied ways; Use punctuation to clarify meaning in complex sentences

Unit overview

This unit is designed to last one week. During this unit, the class will practise writing short and longer fiction pieces in preparation for the National Tests.

Phase 1: *Explore and Create (sessions 1–2)*

The class explores the use of paragraphs and variety of sentences to remind them to use these in their own writing.

Phase 2: *Explore and Create (session 3)*

Children plan a longer story taking into account the features of the genre chosen.

Phase 3: *Explore and Create (sessions 4–5)*

Children write and assess a piece of longer fiction writing.

Prior learning

Check that children can already:

- use a range of sentence types
- use paragraphs
- use a plan to guide their writing
- edit and proofread
- write in a range of genres.

Resources

Texts: *The Demon Headmaster* by Gillian Cross, *Dear Diary* by Anna (Year 6 student)

Software 6, Unit 13

Pupil Book 6, Unit 13, pp83–86

Homework Book 6, p27

PCM 13

Mini-whiteboards

Phase 1: *Explore and Create*

1 Using perky paragraphs in a story

Introduction

> **Software u13**
> Warm up

Play the *Warm up* sequence which gives examples of good fiction writing for five different genres.

Ask children to think about what they can already do well in story writing and what they would like to do better. Share with a partner.

Whole-class teaching

> **Software u13**
> Explore: Text 1,
> Workpad 1

Ask children what they know about paragraphs. Remind them that paragraphs start on a new line and are used when someone new speaks or when something new happens, e.g. change of time and place.

Show them the passage from *The Demon Headmaster* and identify uses of paragraphs using Annotation set a. Then show them a passage without paragraph breaks and ask them to identify where they should go using Workpad. A model version is supplied with an explanation for each paragraph break.

Independent writing

> **Pupil Book**
> p83

Children can attempt a short writing task, to be carried out under test conditions, following the prompts in *Activity 1* in the Pupil Book.

Review

Remind children that good writers read their work back to themselves out loud to make changes. Ask them to read their writing to a partner and suggest changes to each other with a special focus on paragraphs.

2 Using smart sentences in a story

Sentence work

> **Software u13**
> Explore: Text 1,
> Practise

Discuss the different types of sentences children can use in their story writing. Explain that complex sentences are smart sentences that help writers to sharpen their writing. Using the passage from *The Demon Headmaster*, ask children to pick out the complex sentences. Reveal them using Annotation set b. Children can now write their own examples in pairs on whiteboards.

Children then complete the activity in Practise in which they organise complex sentences into appropriate paragraphs.

Read/pair/share

Ask the children to review the short story about the supply teacher they wrote in Session 1 and identify with a partner some of the different types of sentences they used. How effective were their sentences? Are there types of sentences that will make their writing smarter?

> **Pupil Book**
> p84

Independent writing

Refer children to *Activity 2* and give them 20 minutes to write another short story, ensuring they include a variety of sentences.

Review

Ask them to read their writing to a partner and suggest changes to each other with a special focus on smart sentences.

Phase plenary

Share and celebrate some interesting sentences.

 Children can attempt to divide their writing sensibly into paragraphs.

 Children can use paragraphs confidently and include a variety of sentences.

 Children can write paragraphs logically and vary the use of sentence types to match the genre and audience of their writing.

Phase 2: *Explore and Create*

③ Guiding genres

Write/pair/share

Allocate different groups or pairs to different genres, e.g. *Science fiction*, *Fantasy*, *Spy thrillers*, *Stories with familiar settings* and ask them to describe the features of their genre.

Software u13
Explore:
Workpad 2,
Text 2

Take feedback on what constitutes each genre and fill in the table in Workpad 2. You can use the model in *Explore* Text 2 to check you have all the features. Remind the children that the features are guides for planning the shape of a story.

Shared writing

With the class, plan a story for the title *The Stranger* using one of the genres above. You may wish to use the model in *Explore* Text 3 which is annotated to show how it uses features from the fantasy genre, or the blank frame in Workpad 3.

Software u13
Explore: Text 3;
Workpad 3

Write/pair/share

Ask pairs to write a story plan for the title *The Stranger* using the planning frame and referring to *Activity 3* in the Pupil Book. In particular, they should:

Software u13
Plan;
Pupil Book
p85

- use some of the features of their chosen genre, e.g. settings, names
- open in a way that grabs the reader's interest
- think of a strong ending which resolves the problem.

You can display the modelled version.

Phase plenary

Give children time to share their story plans with each other. Discuss what they did effectively.

 Children understand that fiction genres use different features and attempt to use some in the planning of their story.

 Children use some of the features in their chosen genre to plan their story, taking into account the audience.

 Children use all the features in their chosen genre to plan their story, taking into account the audience and experimenting with different plots and endings.

Phase 3: *Explore and Create*

④ Writing a longer piece of fiction

Think/pair/share

Tell children they are going to compose a fiction piece of writing. In pairs, ask them to identify three important things to remember when writing a longer piece of fiction writing.

Class discussion

Take feedback and make a list about composing a longer piece of fiction. It might include:

- the effect of the writing on the audience
- using a plan
- choosing a narrative voice – first person often works well
- using paragraphs and a variety of sentences
- using powerful vocabulary
- using dialogue to drive the story forward or to reveal characters and the way they interact
- choosing a detail to identify a character, e.g. *His teeth clicked when he spoke*
- using correct punctuation.

Independent writing

Software u13
Write;
Pupil Book
p86

Ask children to write a story for 45 minutes including about 10 minutes' planning time using the newspaper article about an escaped wolf given in *Activity 4*. They can use the writing frame on the software.

Review

Discuss how the children managed the timed task, e.g. using time well, planning and using the plans to write the story.

5 Unit plenary: assessing a writing task

Class discussion

Software u13 Explore: Text 4

Display an example of a child's longer piece of writing. Ask the children to identify two aspects of the writing that are good and one thing that the author could do to improve it. Summarise what makes this an effective longer piece of fiction, using the annotations.

Independent assessment

Children read their own stories and highlight what they think they have done well and make annotations explaining their choices.

Think/pair/share

PCM 13

Ask children to evaluate their longer piece of fiction writing with other children's writing using the checklist on PCM 13.

Ask children to use their highlighted writing and their conversations with their partner to record what they think they need to do to develop their writing.

Review

Software u13 Explore: Text 5; **Pupil Book** p86

Review the list of points to remember when doing a longer piece of assessed fiction writing as shown in *Remember!* in the Pupil Book and on the software.

Ask children to share what they found they were good at, what skills they need to develop and how they can help themselves to improve their writing in preparation for a test.

Use the assessment sheet for **fiction** writing on page 170 to help you assess the children's stories.

What next?

 Children can write longer pieces of story writing in a different genre.

 Children can make a guide book or poster with advice for Surviving assessment of story writing (SATs).

 Children can make a wall chart with examples of children's smart sentences.

 *Activity 13* asks children to rewrite a story using a range of sentence types, dialogue and powerful vocabulary.

Homework Book p27

If you liked these texts you could read:

Boy Overboard by Morris Gleitzman

Joey Pigza Swallowed the Key by Jack Gantos

Aquila by Andrew Norris

Learning outcomes

Children can:
- plan a piece of fiction, taking into account the genre and audience
- write a piece of short and longer fiction, using simple, compound and complex sentences and include powerful vocabulary and imagery
- identify their successes in fiction writing, see how they can use what they have learned and set personal targets in writing.

Revision: Non-fiction

Genre: Planning and writing non-fiction

Objectives for this unit

Speaking and listening: Use discussion and role play to explore non-fiction texts.

Reading: Read and revise the features of different non-fiction text types.

Writing: Write a discussion text and practise techniques for answering test questions.

PNS Framework objectives

1. Speaking: Use the techniques of dialogic talk to explore ideas, topics or issues

2. Listening and responding: Make notes when listening for a sustained period and discuss how note-taking varies depending on context and purpose

3. Group discussion and interaction: Understand and use a variety of ways to criticise constructively and respond to criticism

7. Understanding and interpreting texts: Understand how writers use different structures to create coherence and impact; Recognise rhetorical devices used to argue, persuade, mislead and sway the reader

9. Creating and shaping texts: In non-narrative, establish, balance and maintain viewpoints; Select words and language drawing on their knowledge of literary features and formal and informal writing

10. Text structure and organisation: Use varied structures to shape and organise texts coherently; Use paragraphs to achieve pace and emphasis

11. Sentence structure and punctuation: Express subtle distinctions of meaning, including hypothesis, speculation and supposition, by constructing sentences in varied ways; Use punctuation to clarify meaning in complex sentences

Unit overview

This unit is designed to last three weeks. During this unit, the class will explore non-fiction texts on a similar theme linked to the Geography topic: the mountain environment. They will practise formulating and answering questions in preparation for the National Tests and will revise the writing skills required to write different types of non-fiction.

Phase 1: *Engage (sessions 1–5)*

Children read and respond to a variety of non-fiction texts and revise the different features of each text type.

Phase 2: *Explore (sessions 6–11)*

Children read and respond to different types of non-fiction texts and gather information to develop a plan for writing a discussion text.

Phase 3: *Create (sessions 12–15)*

Children write a discussion text based on information drawn from non-fiction texts they have read.

Prior learning

Check that children can already:

- recall the language and organisational features of the main non-fiction text types (recount, report, instructions, explanation, persuasion, discussion) and employ these in their writing, when appropriate.
- where appropriate, organise their writing into meaningful and cohesive paragraphs.

Cross-curricular links

Geography: The mountain environment

Resources

Texts: *Eiger Challenge* from www.mariecurie.org.uk, *Sir Ranulph Fiennes' Account* from www.myspace.com, *Helvellyn* from *Pathfinder Guide: Lake District Walks* compiled by Brian Conduit, *What are volcanoes?* and *Living with volcanoes* from *Nature's Fury: Volcano!* by Anita Ganeri, *The Shadow of Vesuvius* by Maureen Haselhurst

Software 6, Unit 14

Pupil Book 6, Unit 14, pp87–92

Homework Book 6, pp28–29

PCM 14a–b

Copies of National Test papers from previous years

Mini-whiteboards

Phase 1: *Engage*

 ① Reading a non-fiction report

Introducing the text

Explain that the class will be studying non-fiction texts on the theme of the Geography topic: the mountain environment and will practise formulating and answering questions in preparation for the National Tests.

The texts compare contrasting mountain locations in the UK and Europe. They focus on the inhospitable nature of particular mountain environments, including volcanic mountains.

Shared reading

> **Software u14**
> Warm up,
> Explore: Text 1

Play the *Warm up* sequence and then read the Internet report *Eiger Challenge*. Talk about the reasons why mountaineers might be motivated to take on such a dangerous and difficult challenge.

Talk about the meaning of the word *Eiger* which means *ogre* in German.

Class discussion

> **Software u14**
> Explore: Text 1

Think about what sort of questions might be asked in a test situation. Ask children to write down their ideas. Discuss their suggestions as a class and consider how marks might be awarded.

Review

Review techniques for answering questions in a test situation. Discuss tips such as answering all the questions, taking account of the number of marks that can be achieved for each question, underlining key words in the question.

 ② Comparing different text types on the same topic

Shared reading

> **Software u14**
> Explore: Text 2,
> Text 1

Introduce the second extract about Sir Ranulph Fiennes' Eiger challenge: a first person account by the climber himself.

Discuss the differences between this text and the former report, before using the annotations for both texts on the software.

Role play

> **Pupil Book**
> pp87–88

In pairs, role-play an interview with Sir Ranulph Fiennes or another mountaineer for a radio or television show. Prompts are provided in *Activity 1* in the Pupil Book.

 **Answering questions relating to non-fiction texts**

Responding to the text
Pupil Book pp87–89

All children can answer the questions in *Activity 2* relating to the texts about Sir Ranulph Fiennes' Eiger challenge. The questions are not differentiated and children should try to answer them all, as they would in a test situation.

Review

Discuss and compare children's responses to the questions. Answers can be found on page xxx.

 **Practice writing task**

Independent writing
Pupil Book p89

Following on from the tasks in previous sessions, children can now attempt a short writing task, to be carried out under test conditions. Ask them to imagine they are a mountaineer and write a recount about a recent challenge, or write about a challenge they faced in real life, referring them to *Activity 3*. Give them 20 minutes to plan and write their recount. Suggest that they spend about five minutes on their planning and that they leave a few minutes at the end of the task to check their writing.

Review

As a class, review and assess one child's piece of writing (anonymously). Alternatively you could produce a sample text yourself that highlights and addresses weaknesses particular to children in your class.

Decide as a class to what extent the writing fulfils the brief. Draw attention to presentation, spelling, grammar and organisation.

 **Revising the features of an instruction text**

Shared reading
Software u14 Explore: Text 3

Introduce the instruction text from a *Pathfinder Guide* which gives instructions for a fell walk in the Lake District. Ask the children to identify the main feature of this text type: instructions, and reveal Annotation set a. Also, explain that the first two paragraphs serve as introductory text, briefly summarising and describing the route that will be taken.

Point out the fact file at the start of the text; what information is presented and why?

Look at Annotation set b to identify and explain the geographical terms.

Look at the points of interest that the writer has included in the instruction text; what is their purpose? For example, a reference to Glenridding's history as a lead-mining village; a tip about boat trips operating from the pier; the name of a stile; information about Charles Gough's memorial stone; information about the site of the alleged first landing of a British aeroplane on a British mountain. While these points are not essential in directing walkers along the route, they are of interest to the reading audience who are primarily tourists.

Unusually for an instruction text, the writer has included a lot of descriptive phrases. Why is this? Ask children to point out some of these, before revealing Annotation set c.

Grammar work
Software u14 Explore: Text 3; Practise

Ask children to identify examples of formal and informal language in the text and write them down. Discuss the language features of the examples they find. For example, *Helvellyn offers a challenging and exciting fell walk* (formal); *Striding Edge looks positively hair-raising* (informal).

Children can work through the exercise in *Practise* where they identify formal and informal sentences.

Write/pair/share
Software u14 Explore: Text 3

Ask pairs to make up questions about the Lake District article, *Helvellyn*. Ask them to include both literal questions (e.g. Where can walkers stop for refreshments?) and inferential questions (e.g. What do you think is the author's favourite part of the walk?). Ask them to consider how many marks might be awarded for each question if they were set within a test situation.

Review

Invite pairs to read aloud their questions for the class to answer.

Phase plenary

Check what the children have learned during this phase.

 Children can formulate and answer questions relating to a variety of different non-fiction text types.

 Children can recognise and identify the language features specific to different non-fiction text types.

 Children understand the language and organisational features of all the main non-fiction text types.

Phase 2: *Explore*

 **Researching the origins of place names**

Shared reading

Software u14
Explore: Text 3

Look again at *Helvellyn* from *Pathfinder Guide* and highlight the place names. What images are conjured up in the children's minds when they read names such as *Striding Edge*, *Dollywagon Pike* and *Coniston Old Man*?

Discuss the meanings of some of the names by identifying clues such as *dale* – meaning valley – in *Langdale Pikes*, *Patterdale* and *Grisedale*; *barrow* – meaning grove or wood – in *Gowbarrow Fell*; *how* meaning hill in *High Spying How*.

Word work

PCM 14a

Ask children to investigate the place names on PCM 14a. Encourage them to look up key words in a dictionary to help their investigation, for example: crag (steep rugged rock or peak); fell (mountain, hill or moor); tarn (small lake). Further information can be found on the Internet or in a dictionary of place names such as the *Penguin Dictionary of British Place Names* by Adrian Room.

 These children may also note the regional significance of particular words, for example: pike *Northern English dialect*, a pointed or conical hill which indicates that a hill with "pike" in its name may well be situated in the North of England, e.g. *Dollywagon Pike*; *Langdale Pikes*.

Review

Check that the children have correctly defined the following terms: dale (valley); barrow (grove, wood); how (hill); tarn (small lake); crag (steep rugged rock or peak); fell (mountain, hill or moor). Discuss the meanings they have uncovered in their investigation of place names. Comments relating to the second exercise can be found on page 116.

 **Writing an instruction text**

Independent note-making

Ask children to think about a walk that they are familiar with, ideally one that they follow regularly, such as the journey to school, or a walk to the home of a friend living nearby. Tell the children that they are going to write a short instruction text giving directions for the walk. They will begin by making a plan, jotting down the directions they follow and any interesting landmarks they remember. Alternatively, they could invent a fictitious walk and make up landmarks that will add points of interest to their writing. Allow them five minutes to complete their plan.

Children may find it helpful to print out a local map using the Internet before they begin their plan, to assist them in recalling the route they will be giving directions for.

Independent writing

Once they have completed their plan, children can begin writing their instruction text giving directions for a local walk using their home or school as a starting point. Allow approximately 15 minutes for the completion of this task.

Checking and editing

If the children used a local map when planning and writing their instruction text, they could mark on it the landmarks or significant points that they referred to. They can review their writing in pairs, checking firstly that they have fulfilled the brief before focusing on spelling, grammar, organisation and presentation. Ask response partners to note any features of instruction texts that have been used in the writing, for example, an opening statement explaining what the instructions are for; imperative verbs, e.g. *walk*, *turn*, *continue*, *take*; language signifying sequenced steps, e.g. *first*, *then*, *next*.

Review

Reflect on how much the children managed to achieve in a short space of time. For those who felt that the writing task went well, why do they think they were able to complete it successfully? Did all the children find it helpful to have a plan to work from? For those children who did not complete the task successfully, what were the problems they faced and how might they have overcome these?

8 Exploring an explanation text

Shared reading

Software u14
Explore: Text 4

Read *What are Volcanoes?* and ask the class what kind of non-fiction text it is. What is the purpose of the text? (To explain the natural phenomena of volcanoes, thereby answering the title question.) Look at the annotations on the software to note other explanatory text features.

Talk about the significance of the origins of the word *volcano*.

Write/pair/share

PCM 14b

Ask pairs to make up questions about the text on PCM 14b and write them on a sheet of paper. Ask them to consider how many marks might be awarded for each question if they were set within a test situation. Each pair can then present their questions to another pair who writes their answers under the questions.

Review

Review the different features of explanation texts.

9 Answering questions relating to an explanation text

Responding to the text

Pupil Book
pp90–91

All children can answer the questions in *Activity 4* in the Pupil Book on *Living with Volcanoes* relating to a discussion text about communities who live under the constant threat of a volcanic eruption. On this occasion, the text should be previously unseen and the children should work under test conditions. The questions are not differentiated and children should be reminded to attempt to answer them all, as they would do in a test situation.

Review

Software u14
Explore: Text 5

Discuss and compare children's responses to the questions, using the annotations to look at the features of a non-fiction text. Answers can be found on page 116.

Homework

Homework
Book
p28

Activity 14a asks children to read an extract about Vesuvius and organise it into paragraphs. They are then asked to write definitions for specialist words in the text.

10 Exploring a persuasive text

Class discussion

Software u14
Explore: Text 6

Review the children's homework task. Reread the text together and discuss what type of non-fiction text it is. Point out that children's organisation of the homework text may differ; there is no one right answer. However, there are places where a paragraph break would not be effective. For example:

Recently, there have been several small earthquakes. They are warning signs.

These sentences should not be separated by a paragraph break because the second sentence qualifies or explains the first. Can the class think of an appropriate connecting word or phrase that could be used to join the two sentences?

Annotation set a reveals where the author, Maureen Haselhurst, used paragraph breaks.

Think/pair/share

Ask pairs or small groups to compare how they have organised the text and explain their reasons for beginning new paragraphs where they have.

Class discussion

Software u14
Explore: Text 6

Revise the features of a persuasive text and ask children to identify examples within the extract, before revealing Annotation sets b and c.

Review

Briefly list the key features of each of the text types you have revised so far in this unit, including recount, instructions, explanation and persuasive texts.

Homework

Homework
Book
p29

Activity 14b revises the use of connectives in different types of non-fiction text.

11 Using a planning frame

Demonstration writing

Software u14
Plan

Remind the class of the opening statement from *Living with Volcanoes*: *About five hundred million people, or one in ten of the world's population, live in places that are at risk from volcanoes.* Explain that they are going to explore the reasons why so many of the world's population live near volcanoes and write a discussion text about it. Using the planning frame provided on the software, plan what information they could include in their writing. Do not necessarily include all the relevant information; just enough to prepare the children for completing the planning frame independently. You may wish to use the model on the software.

Independent note-making

Software u14
Plan

The children can now try completing the planning frame for themselves, beginning with the information you have discussed as a class and adding other relevant information from the passages they have explored.

Review

Children can review their planning frames in pairs, checking that they have identified the key points necessary for writing a discussion text that looks at both the risks and benefits of living near to a volcano.

Phase plenary

Check what the children have learned during this phase.

 Children recognise the general features of non-fiction texts and can demonstrate their comprehension through answering literal questions.

 Children can recall and understand how to approach the reading of non-fiction texts, are aware of a range of questions and how to answer them and can improve their own answers.

 Children can recall and understand the language and organisational features of all the main non-fiction text types.

Phase 3: *Create*

12 Writing a discussion text

Demonstration writing

Software u14
Write

Using the writing frame, model how to structure a discussion text exploring the reasons why people live on or near to volcanoes. Begin by making a statement of the issue you will be discussing. Using the planning frame you completed in Session 11, explore both the benefits and the risks of living near a volcano. Consider what needs to be done to help reduce the risks. Demonstrate how to write a conclusion that summarises your main points and refers back to your opening statement.

Focus on the different connectives you have used or ask the class to help you choose appropriate examples, e.g. *therefore, however.*

Review the structure of your writing with the class. (If you have used the writing frame, your writing will already be organised into paragraphs with a separate focus for each paragraph.) You may wish to use the model text provided on the software.

Role play

In small groups, children could explore the issues that have been unfolding in their reading and in your modelled writing through role play. Ask some of the children to play journalists reporting for a television documentary about communities that live in dangerous, volcanic areas. The remaining children can play farmers and other local people who live and work on or near the slopes of active volcanoes. The journalists can interview the locals about the reasons why they live where they do and how their environment affects their day-to-day lives.

Review

Review the role-play activity as a class. What questions were asked and what answers were given?

13 Practice writing task

Independent writing

Pupil Book
p92;
Software u14
Write

Following on from Session 12, children can now carry out an independent writing task, with the same focus, under test conditions given in *Activity 5.* Allow 45 minutes for children to plan and write their discussion text. Suggest that they spend about 10–15 minutes on their planning and that they leave a few minutes at the end of the task to check their writing.

 These children could use the writing frame to help them structure their writing.

Review

Once the children have submitted their writing for assessment, discuss how they found the experience. What aspects of their writing did they check in their final five minutes, for example, did they check that their writing was legible? That it was organised into paragraphs with an introduction and a conclusion? Did they check their spelling and punctuation for any obvious errors?

Use the assessment sheet for **discussion** writing on page 168 to help you assess the children's writing.

Reviewing and assessing writing

Shared reading

As a class, review and assess one child's piece of writing. Either discuss the completed writing task of one of the children (anonymously) or produce a sample text yourself that highlights and addresses weaknesses particular to children in your class.

Decide as a class to what extent the writing fulfils the brief. Draw attention to presentation, spelling, grammar and organisation.

Think/pair/share

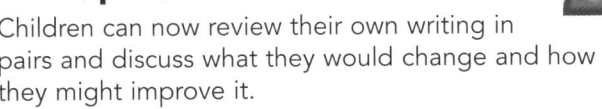

Children can now review their own writing in pairs and discuss what they would change and how they might improve it.

If the children's writing has already been assessed, you could give them an opportunity to redraft their writing, taking into account the points you have discussed as a class and in pairs.

Review

Briefly review the children's achievements in this revision unit and ask them to comment on which aspects of non-fiction writing they now feel more confident about. Are there any areas that need further practice?

Unit plenary: practising the reading section of a QCA National Test for Year 6

Independent writing

At this point it would be appropriate for children to attempt, under test conditions, an example of a non-fiction reading and writing test drawn from previous QCA test materials. For example, the 2004 KS2 Reading Test includes questions about the information text *Sport for All*.

Review

Analyse the children's answers and discuss where they could be improved.

Reflect on all of the main points that children have revised during this unit.

What next?

Investigate the origins of place names in your local area.

Take the children on a local walk to a place of interest using the school as a starting point. Ask them to take notes during the walk, identifying landmarks and jotting down directions for the route you have chosen. They could then write an instruction text giving directions for readers to follow. They could use the Internet to print out a local map and mark on it the landmarks that they refer to.

If you liked these texts you could read:

Violent Volcanoes by Louise and Richard Spilsbury

Volcanoes by Christopher Durbin

Learning outcomes

Children can:
- recall and understand the language and organisational features of all the main non-fiction text types
- recall and understand how to go about reading a non-fiction text, are aware of a range of questions and how to answer them and can improve their own answers
- combine different text types to suit appropriate purposes and audiences
- write non-fiction effectively for a particular purpose and audience, drawing on and combining different language and organisational features as appropriate.

Answers to Pupil Book activities

2 Responding to the texts

Award marks as follows:

1 1 mark for: *exploration* or *he is an explorer.*

2 1 mark for: *nobody* or *it was a solo journey/ expedition.*

3 1 mark for answers relating to *a personal challenge* or *challenge of a lifetime*; 1 mark for: *to raise money for a charity.* Do not award marks for any of the following: *because it was there*; *to overcome his fear of heights.*

4 1 mark for answers that explain how the Eiger is like a giant (metaphorically) in terms of size or danger/threat. (Do not award a mark for answers that simply state that the word means *ogre* in German.)

5 1 mark for: 1938.

6 1 mark for each of the following (up to a maximum of 3 marks): the North Face of the mountain is 6,000 feet high; it consists of vertical rock and ice; it is notorious for rockfalls and avalanches; unstable weather.

7 1 mark for each of the following: Sir Ranulph Fiennes suffers from vertigo; he has a heart condition/has had a double by-pass; he had the fingers of one hand amputated at the half knuckle as a result of severe frostbite. Do not award marks for answers relating to a fear of heights.

4 Responding to the text

Award marks as follows:

1 1 mark for Naples; 1 mark for Seattle.

2 1 mark for each of the following answers (up to a maximum of 3 marks): *the risks were not known at the time that communities were founded*; *volcanoes produce rich, fertile soil which is good for farming/ growing crops*; *because there is nowhere else for them to live*; *volcanic rocks make good building materials*; *heat from hot rocks in volcanic areas is useful for heating water and generating electricity.*

3 1 mark for: *to protect them from rocks hurled out by eruptions.*

4 1 mark for (b) volcanic rock.

5 1 mark for (a) active.

6 1 mark for answers explaining that there is not much farming land in the area; 1 mark for answers explaining that the slopes provide fertile land for growing produce.

Answers to PCM 14a

1 Answers can be found in Session 6 Review.

2 There are probably no definitive answers but the children's research should lead to valuable class discussions.

15

2 weeks

Revision: Poetry

Genre: Reading comprehension (poetry)

Objectives for this unit

Speaking and listening: Discuss responses to a range of poems.

Reading: Identify the different features of poems, including structure, organisation of ideas and the way language is used to create various effects.

Writing: Record key features and personal responses to poems using a planning frame.

PNS Framework objectives

1. Speaking: Use the techniques of dialogic talk to explore ideas, topics or issues

3. Group discussion and interaction: Understand and use a variety of ways to criticise constructively

7. Understanding and interpreting texts: Understand underlying themes, causes and points of view; Understand how writers use different structures to create coherence and impact

Unit overview

This unit is designed to last two weeks. During this unit, the class will explore and compare poems on a similar theme and practise formulating and answering questions in preparation for the National Tests.

Phase 1: *Engage and explore (sessions 1–3)*

Children read and respond to linked poems.

Phase 2: *Explore (sessions 4–5)*

Children explore poems by different poets about creatures great and small.

Phase 3: *Explore and create (sessions 6–10)*

Children analyse poems on a similar theme using a planning frame and practise responding to poems in a test situation.

Prior learning

Check that children can already:

- discuss their responses to a range of poetry they have read
- identify and discuss the various features of a poem, including the structure and organisation of the text and the way language is used to create effects on the reader.

Cross-curricular links

Science: Interdependence and adaptation Section 6: Food chains

Resources

Texts: *The Fly* by Walter de la Mare, *A Fly and a Flea in a Flue* by P. L. Mannock, *Five Eyes* by Walter de la Mare, *Leopard* (Yoruba poem), *The Mole* by Stanley Cook, *Animal Riddle* by Pie Corbett, *Spin Me a Web, Spider* by Charles Causley, *Spider's Song* by Judith Nicholls

Software 6, Unit 15

Pupil Book 6, Unit 15, pp93–96

Homework Book 6, pp30–32

PCM 15a–b

Copies of National Test papers from previous years that include poetry reading, for example: 1999 KS2 Test, which includes the poem, *Spinner*; 2000 Welsh KS2 Test, which includes the poem *City Jungle*

Mini-whiteboards

Phase 1: *Engage and explore*

1 Reading and analysing a poem

Introducing the text

> Software u15
> Warm up

Play the audio-visual version of *The Fly* by Walter de la Mare.

Shared reading

> Software u15
> Explore: Text 1

Read the poem *The Fly*. Ask children to jot down their first impressions of the poem on their whiteboards and show what they have written.

Model how to analyse the poem. The children will have noted that the poem is about a fly but what other themes have they uncovered? For example, contrasts in scale (how tiny things appear large to a fly) and texture (a soft rosebud and a prickly thorn). Ask the children to find words and phrases in the poem to support their written ideas.

Demonstrate how the poem is in three parts. What do they notice about the structure? What do they notice about the number of syllables in each line? (They alternately consist of eight and six syllables, except the final line which has seven.) What effect does this pattern have? (The poem has a regular, gentle rhythm.) Which lines rhyme? Use Annotation set a to draw out examples of rhyming pairs.

Use Annotation set b to show the similes in the poem. Why are they effective? In what way is a mustard seed *as fierce as coals of fire*?

Use Annotation set c to show the metaphors in the third verse. In what ways is a leopard like a wasp? (They have similar colourings; both have intimidating weapons for attack, i.e. a sting, claws and teeth.) In what ways would a dewdrop appear like a looking-glass to a fly?

Discuss the effect of the alliteration: *fierce/fire*; *loaf/lofty*; *specks/salt/see*.

Think/pair/share

The children can explore the similes in the poem they have read. Ask them to think of new similes to complete these lines:

> A rosebud like a …
>
> Its prickle like …
>
> A dewdrop like a …
>
> A hair like …

Class discussion

Returning to the poem, ask children to write down what sort of questions might be asked in a test situation. For example: *What is the poem about?* could at first be considered a little obvious given the title, whereas the poem is, in fact, about the way small things appear to a tiny fly.

Discuss how marks might be awarded. For example, if asked to find similes, for a possible three marks, a child who writes down only two examples may score only two out of the three possible marks. Discuss the routine for reading questions and use examples to model how to identify and underline the key words. Note any references to specific verses or sections of the poem.

Review

Review techniques for answering questions in a test situation. Discuss tips such as answering all the questions, taking account of the number of marks that can be achieved for each question, underlining key words in the question.

2 Comparing contrasting poems on a similar theme

Annotating a poem

> **Software u15**
> **Explore: Text 1**

Ask the children to annotate *The Fly* on screen, highlighting effective words and phrases, identifying examples of rhyme, alliteration, simile, metaphor and any other features they notice.

Allow children, in pairs, to compare the features they have identified and highlight any they have missed.

Shared reading

> **Software u15**
> **Explore: Text 2;**
> **Pupil Book p93**

Introduce *A Fly and a Flea in a Flue* by P. L. Mannock. Ask children to read the poem independently and jot down their initial thoughts about it. Then read and discuss the poem. Compare differences and similarities between this poem and *The Fly*. For example, both have a definite structure; both include rhyme; both include examples of alliteration (although it is more subtle in Walter de la Mare's poem). Ask the class to comment on features such as humour, descriptive phrases and dialogue, then reveal the annotations to confirm their answers. Use Annotation set a to reveal the alliteration, Annotation set b for dialogue, and then Annotation set c to give examples of homophones (words which are pronounced the same way but differ in meaning and/or spelling).

Responding to the poems

> **Pupil Book pp93–94**

All children can answer the questions in *Activity 1* of the Pupil Book. The questions are not differentiated and children should be reminded to attempt to answer them all, as they would do in a test situation.

Review

Ask children to feed back, discuss and compare their responses to the questions. Marking guidance is provided on page 122.

3 Formulating questions about a poem

Think/pair/share

> **Software u15**
> **Explore: Text 3**

Ask pairs to read and annotate *Five Eyes* on screen, noting the structure, highlighting words and phrases of particular interest, and underlining any poetic devices that the poet has used. They can then make up questions about the poem to ask another pair and decide how many marks each question is worth.

In groups made up of two pairs, children can ask the questions they have prepared.

Shared reading

> **Software u15**
> **Explore: Text 3**

Reread the poem *Five Eyes*. While the children talk about the features they found, refer to the annotations on the software. Use Annotation set a to prompt discussion about the setting, Annotation set b to show onomatopoeic words and then Annotation set c to give examples of alliterative words that the poet has used, discussing their effect.

Review

> **Software u15**
> **Explore: Text 1, Text 3**

Compare the poems *Five Eyes* and *The Fly*. Ask the children to comment on similarities and differences they notice between the two poems by the same poet.

Phase plenary

Check what children have learned during this phase.

 Children can discuss responses to a range of poems.

 Children can read and analyse different types of poetry taking into account the main literary features.

 Children can identify the different features of poems, including structure, organisation of ideas and the way language is used to create various effects.

Phase 2: *Explore*

④ Responding to two poems on the same theme

Shared reading

Software u15
Explore: Text 4, Text 3

Read the Yoruba poem, *Leopard*. Point out the regular structure. Using Annotation set a, talk about the impact of the first line in each part of the poem; two words – an adjective and a noun: *Gentle hunter, Beautiful death, Playful killer.* What effect do these phrases have on the reader? Can they find a metaphor in the poem? You can use Annotation sets b and c on the software to aid further discussion.

Discuss the similarities and differences between this poem and *Five Eyes*, a poem on a similar theme.

Responding to the poems

Pupil Book
pp95–96

All children can answer the questions on the poems in *Activity 2* of the Pupil Book. Remind them to attempt all the questions and check their answers carefully when they have finished.

Review

Discuss the children's responses to the questions relating to *Five Eyes* and *Leopard*, referring to the marking guidance provided on pages 122 to 123.

Homework

Homework Book
p30

 *Activity 15a* asks children to read and annotate *The Mole* in preparation for the following session, and then to make up questions relating to the text.

⑤ Analysing a poem

Think/pair/share

Homework Book
p30

Ask pairs to reread the poem *The Mole* in their Homework Books. They can then ask each other the questions they prepared for homework and discuss their answers.

Shared reading

Software u15
Explore: Text 5

Analyse *The Mole*, this time relying on the class to point out more of the main features of the poem. Look at how the sections of the poem focus

on three different themes: use Annotation set a to show key words and phrases in verse 1; the poet uses an underground train line as a metaphor for the mole's tunnels. Annotation set b describes the mole's 24-hour environment, while Annotation set c examines how the mole is seen as prey for other animals.

Review

Discuss how the tone of this poem differs from the tone of *Leopard*. How have the two poets created different effects when both poems focus on hunters and their prey?

Phase plenary

Check what children have learned during this phase.

 Children understand how to go about reading different poems and can answer literal questions based on the text.

 Children can respond to a range of literal and inferential questions relating to poetry texts and have revised strategies to answer them fully.

 Children understand the techniques for answering literal and inferential questions based on poetry texts, and can identify specific lines within the text to support their answers.

Phase 3: *Explore and create*

⑥ Using a planning frame

Demonstration writing

Software u15
Explore: Workpad 5

Present the planning frame *Be a poetry sleuth!* Discuss how it could be helpful as a starting point for analysing a poem. Model how to use the frame to note down the key features of a poem that all the children are familiar with, such as *The Mole*. You may wish to use the model provided on the software.

Independent writing

The children can try using the planning frame for themselves, focusing on a poem of their choice that they have covered already in this unit.

 These children may like to design a planning frame of their own using *Plan* on the software.

Software u15
Plan

Homework

> Homework Book pp31–32

Activity 15b asks children to read the poem *Animal Riddle* and answer the questions relating to it.

 **7** Exploring a riddle poem

Shared reading

> Software u15 Explore: Text 6

Read *Animal Riddle* and ask the class to offer their impressions of the poem. Would they have known the poem was about a badger if the answer had not been spelt out in capital letters? Ask children who think they would have guessed to pick out the words and phrases that gave clues to the answer. Use the annotations on the software to point out some of the clues.

Class discussion

> Homework Book pp31–32

Discuss and compare children's responses to the questions in *Activity 15b* of the Homework Book. Marking guidance is provided on page 123.

 **8** Responding to a poem in a test situation

Independent reading

> PCM 15a; PCM 15b

Ask children to read their poem a couple of times and annotate it, noting the structure, highlighting words and phrases of particular interest, and underlining any poetic devices that the poet has used.

The children can then answer the questions relating to their poem, underlining the key words and paying attention to the number of marks available to them.

 These children can read *Spin Me a Web, Spider* by Charles Causley on PCM 15a.

 These children can read *Spider's Song* by Judith Nicholls on PCM 15b.

Group discussion

> Software u15 Explore: Text 7

Once they have answered the questions, and the PCMs have been collected for assessment, the children could reread their poem in ability groups and discuss the various answers they gave.

Review

Read both poems with the whole class. Ask children to point out ways in which the poems are similar and ways in which they differ. Explain that you will discuss them in more detail, and look at the answers to each question, in the next session.

 **9** Reviewing a marking scheme for comprehension questions

Shared reading

> Software u15 Explore: Text 7

Reread *Spider's Song* and *Spin Me a Web, Spider*. Look at the two poets' descriptions of a spider's web through the key words and phrases using the annotations. Both poets have used words that suggest the web is something precious to be treasured.

Look in greater detail at the second part of *Spider's Song*. What is the *pearled hammock*? Notice the gentle language that the poet has used to describe how the spider traps its victim. Point out the final phrase, *dying sun*; the poet's use of the word *dying* emphasises that the spider's victim is dying, not sleeping.

Class discussion

> PCM 15a; PCM 15b

Refer back to the questions relating to the two poems and discuss how marks would be allocated in a test situation. One way to do this would be to evaluate and mark various real (anonymous) or simulated answers to the questions, as a class, and discuss how they could be improved. Marking guidance is provided on page 123.

 **10** Unit plenary: practising the reading section of a QCA National Test for Year 6

Independent writing

At this point it would be appropriate for children to attempt, under test conditions, an example drawn from previous QCA test materials. For example, the 1999 KS2 Test, which includes the poem *Spinner*.

Review

Analyse the children's answers and discuss where they could be improved.

Reflect on the themes of this unit. All the poems have been about creatures, large and small. What other themes link them? For example: survival, hunters and their prey.

Discuss how the children feel about working under test conditions. Talk about any concerns they may have and discuss ways to help to remain calm and focused.

Please note that there is no assessment sheet for this unit as it's a revision unit; as indicated, marking guidance is provided on pages 122 and 123.

What next?

Children can use the writing frame on the software for the first two activities.

 **Software u15** Write

 Children could try writing an alliterative limerick like *A Flea and a Fly in a Flue*. For example:

A hare and a hen in a hut …

A couple of sheep in a shed …

A dog and a duck in a ditch …

 Children can explore themes from this unit through writing poems of their own. For example, explore the idea of scale by writing a poem about how certain things appear tiny to an elephant.

 Children can revise prefixes and suffixes by working through the exercise in *Practise*.

Software u15 Practise

 Children can collect other poems relating to those from the unit and organise them into anthologies, grouping them according to theme or style.

If you liked these texts you could read:

Who's There? from *Midnight Forest* by Judith Nicholls

Owl by Pie Corbett from *Odd Kettle of Fish* by John Rice, Brian Moses, Pie Corbett, and Lucy Maddison

Learning outcomes

Children can:
- recall and understand how to go about reading a poetry text
- understand that there is a range of literal and inferential questions and how to answer them fully
- read and analyse different types of poetry taking into account the main literary features
- understand the techniques that will help them to answer questions successfully under test conditions.

Answers to Pupil Book activities

1 Responding to the poems

Award marks as follows:

The Fly

1 1 mark for: *a fly*; 2 marks for a more complete answer: *the way (small) things must appear to a fly*.

2 1 mark for: *prickle like a spear*.

3 1 mark for: *a rosebud like a feather bed*.

4 The following words refer to size and scale: *large, tiny, little, smallest, lofty, specks*. Award 1 mark for two correct words, 2 marks for three or four correct words, and 3 marks for five or six correct words.

A Fly and a Flea in a Flue

5 1 mark for: *Limerick*.

6 1 mark for: *flew/flue* or *fly/fly* (noun/verb).

7 1 mark for: *a tube or pipe*.

8 The following words are alliterative: *fly, flea, flue, flee, flew, flaw*. Award 1 mark for three, four or five correct words; 2 marks for six correct words.

2 Responding to the poems

Five Eyes

1 1 mark for answers that include the word *mill* and 1 additional mark for two or more of the following words, *night, cold, old, creaking*. Do not award any marks for answers that do not include the word *mill*.

2 1 mark for any answer along the following lines, *food; titbits/scraps from the bin; meal, mealworm, grain, flour*. Do not award any marks for *cats* or *Hans*.

3 1 mark for answers that include one or two correct words and phrases; 2 marks for three or more correct words and phrases. Answers may include: *Squeaks from the flour sacks, Squeaking and scampering, down they pounce, sniffing snout, lean old Hans he snores away*.

4 1 mark for: *Jill* or *one-eyed Jill*.

5 1 mark for any example of alliteration, such as: *Squeaking and scampering; sniffing snout; Jekkel, and Jessup, and one-eyed Jill*.

Leopard

6 1 mark for: *antelope*.

7 The poet is describing a leopard's contrasting types of behaviour. The leopard is a hunter and a killer, which is revealed when he *crushes the skull* and kills an antelope. However, like other feline animals, he can also be gentle and playful: *His tail plays on the ground*. Award 1 mark for answers that refer to the contrasting types of behaviour; 2 marks for answers that also include appropriate references to the text.

8 1 mark for answers that explain that the spotted robe refers to/is a metaphor for the spotted markings on the leopard's coat/fur.

9 1 mark for: *loving embrace*.

Answers to Homework Book activity 15b

Animal Riddle

1 1 mark for: *a badger*.

2 1 mark for answers that explain the uppercase letters provide the answer to the riddle.

3 1 mark (up to a maximum of 3) for each of the following words: *dark, sleep, torchlight, midnight, moon-lit*.

4 1 mark for: *bundles*.

5 1 mark for: *blinks back at torchlight*.

6 1 mark for answers along these lines: They were disturbed by the noise the badger made when she knocked over the dustbin to get at the food inside.

7 1 mark for: *like a small bear* and 1 mark for: *like an expert barrel-rider*.

8 1 mark for answers along these lines: The body of a badger resembles a small bear but her black and white markings are more like those of a zebra.

Answers to PCM 15a

Spin Me a Web, Spider

1 1 mark for a response indicating *morning*; 1 mark for reference to the line *and hang it with the morning dew*.

2 1 mark for: *spin, spider*.

3 1 mark for answers that refer to the web's appearance which is similar to silver netting; 1 mark for answers that refer to a net as a means for catching something.

4 1 mark for *dew drops that glitter in the sun*; accept *dew drops*.

5 1 mark for answers along these lines: The tone of the poem changes in the last two lines. The fly has an entirely different view of the spider's web which, from the fly's perspective, is a trap rather than a thing of beauty; the fly would therefore happily destroy it if it could.

Answers to PCM 15b

Spider's Song

1 1 mark for answers that refer to *sewing* or *embroidery*; a further 1 mark for any of these words and phrases up to a maximum of 2 marks: *stitched the ivy*; *beaded threads of light*; *a rich embroidery*.

2 Up to 2 marks for answers along these lines: The words of the spider are deceptive; *let me fold you tenderly* sounds like an act of kindness but disguises a sinister meaning as the spider wishes to ensnare its victim in order to bite it/inject it with poison/kill it/eat it. Describing the act of trapping and killing prey as an act of tenderness makes it appear all the more sinister. Award a further 1 mark for answers that explain that the *pearled hammock* is a trap spun from the spider's silk/a cocoon/a *final resting place* for the victim.

3 1 mark for answers that refer to the spider poisoning its prey.

4 1 mark for answers along the following lines: The sounds are soft/quiet/gentle/relaxing; they lull you into a false sense of security; the "s" words make a hissing sound which has a sinister effect.

Name _____ Date _____

Fairytale features

Group fairytales under headings.

Think about the fairytales you know. What features do they have? Do they contain ugly characters who are bad, or tell a story of rags to riches? Write the names of the fairytales in the right feature bubbles. Some fairytales might go in more than one bubble.

Ugly characters who are bad

Animals who can talk

Rule of three (such as three sisters, three guesses)

Small characters who outwit powerful characters

Princesses or princes who have good qualities

Rags to riches/ misery to happiness

Add another feature here.

Genre cards

Stories with familiar settings

Moving home	A new classroom	A stolen object
An irritable old lady	A best friend with a secret	A pet

Fantasy

A dragon	An object to find	A forest that is hiding something
A lake	A small ancient clay bottle that holds a liquid	A secret

Fairytale

A princess	A dungeon in a castle	A key
A greedy, cruel king	A bag of gold coins	A magic mirror

Name _____ Date _____

Genre story plan

Use the boxes to plan your story.

Main character	Character/situation causing problems
Subsidiary character	
Setting	

Chapter 1

Opening (sets scene, introduces characters and establishes problem)	**Build up** (develops problem and shows how main character must act)

Chapter 2

Climax

Chapter 3

Ending (resolves problem and shows how main character has changed)

Name _____ Date _____

Is he a spy?

Find vivid details of characters.

Fill in the spidergram with words and phrases that describe the four main characters in the spy thriller genre. Add more lines if you need to.

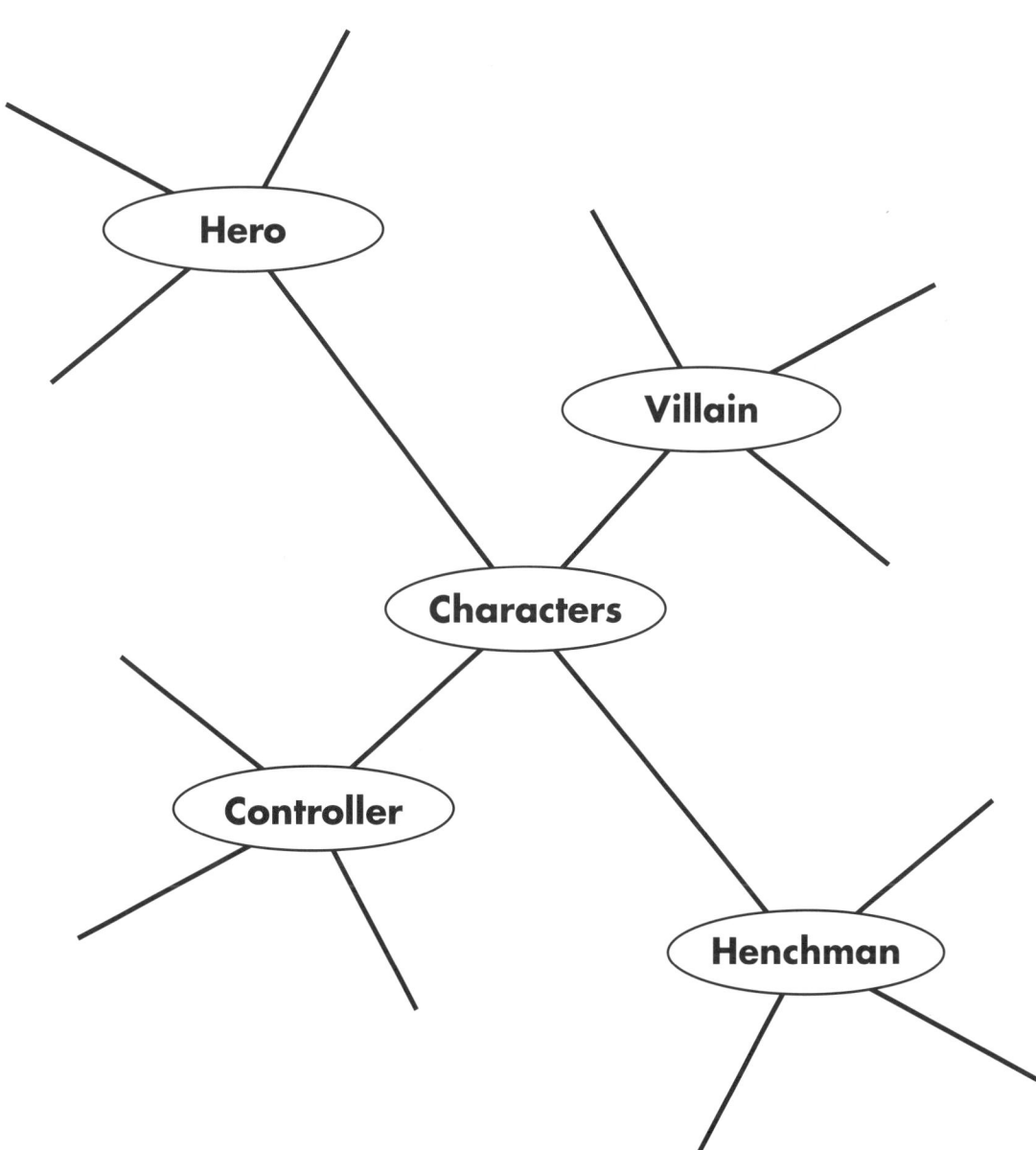

Name _____ Date _____

Design a villain

Imagine an evil villain for a new spy story.

Work in pairs to invent a really evil villain. Draw a picture of them and then fill in the form with your villain's details.

MI5 Data Base of Most Evil Villains – Top Secret

Name: _____

Appearance: _____

_____

_____

Way of speaking: _____

_____

Any other distinguishing features: _____

_____

Type and location of lair: _____

_____

How the villain plans to take over the world: _____

_____

Weak spot: _____

Spy story planning frame

Plan your spy thriller story.

Characters	Setting
Hero	
Controller	
Villain	
Henchman	

Impossible situation

Mission and gadgets

Capture

Evil scheme

Last-second saviour

Name _____ Date _____

Spy plot formula

Plan an exciting spy thriller plot.

Use the flow chart to help you plan the plot for your spy story.

Impossible situation
The spy escapes from an impossible situation with the help of a gadget to grab the reader's attention.

Mission and gadgets
The spy is given a mission to break into an evil villain's lair.

Capture
The spy enters the villain's lair and is captured.

Evil scheme
The villain tells the spy the evil scheme and imprisons the spy (often intending to kill him later). Usually the villain lets the spy watch while the evil scheme is put into action.

Last-second saviour
The spy escapes and stops the plan succeeding at the last second.

© Collins
Primary
Literacy

Personifying objects

Personify an everyday object.

With a partner, choose two objects in the table. How do you think each one would sound, look, move and behave if it were alive? Write some active verbs and verb phrases to show this.

Subject	How does it sound?	How does it look?	How does it move?	How does it behave?
alarm clock	screams screeches yells orders cries	glares stares	shakes nudges jumps up and down pokes	pesters bullies annoys seeks attention
mirror				
toothbrush				
lunch box				

Name _____   Date _____

Creating similes

Write some similes.

With a partner, think of some similes to describe the different types of rain.

Type of rain	Simile
"Spitting" – light rain	*like the soft stroke of gentle fingertips* *delicate as cool silk against my warm skin*
Drizzle	
Unpredictable or intermittent rain	
Shower	
Torrent	
Rainstorm	

Collins Primary Literacy

Name _____ Date _____

Skeleton frame for personification

Record ideas to personify rain.

With a partner, choose a type of rain and write down some active verbs to describe it. How would people respond to this type of rain? In what situations might you see or feel it?

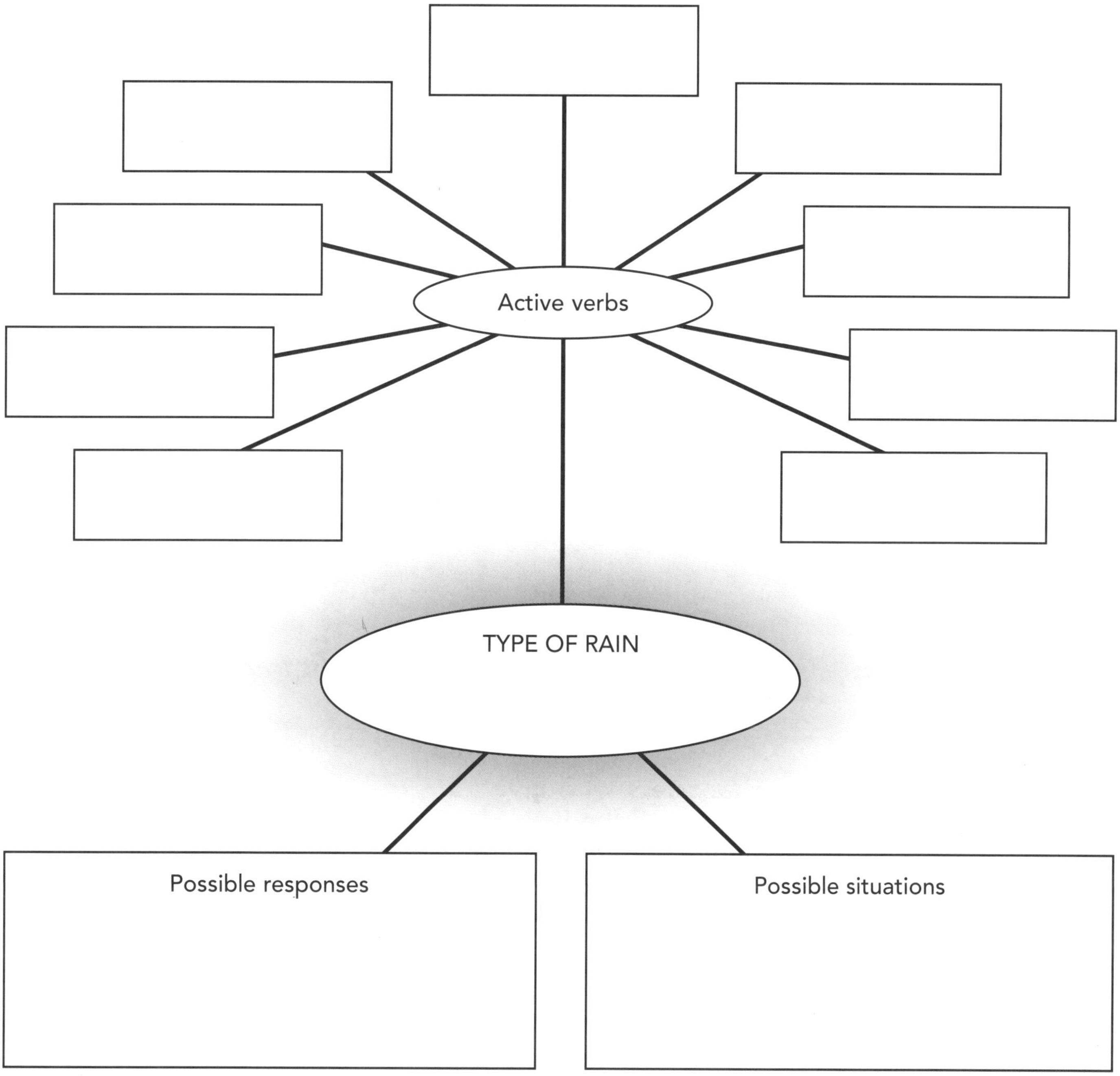

Active verbs

TYPE OF RAIN

Possible responses

Possible situations

Collins Primary Literacy

Name _____ Date _____

Quest adventure cards

Identify the features of a quest adventure.

Cut out these cards and match up the story element to its purpose. Then match these up with the examples from *Bellerophon and the Flying Horse*.

Story element	Purpose in the story	Example in *Bellerophon and the Flying Horse*
Quest	a character who sends the hero on the quest	Chimaera
Hero	where and when the hero must complete the quest	to kill the Chimaera
Quest setter	character who tries to prevent the hero from succeeding in the quest	the end of the quest
Helper	an expedition in search of something	the flight on Pegasus
Menace	the journey to the end of the quest	old farmer and Athena
Journey	characters who give assistance to the hero, for example giving directions, information or gifts like Pegasus	Bellerophon
Trial	a character who completes the quest	King of Lycia

C Collins Primary Literacy

Name _____ Date _____

A quest adventure planned as a branching text

Plan your quest adventure.

Write notes on the two trial choices that Perseus might take to try to reach Andromeda.

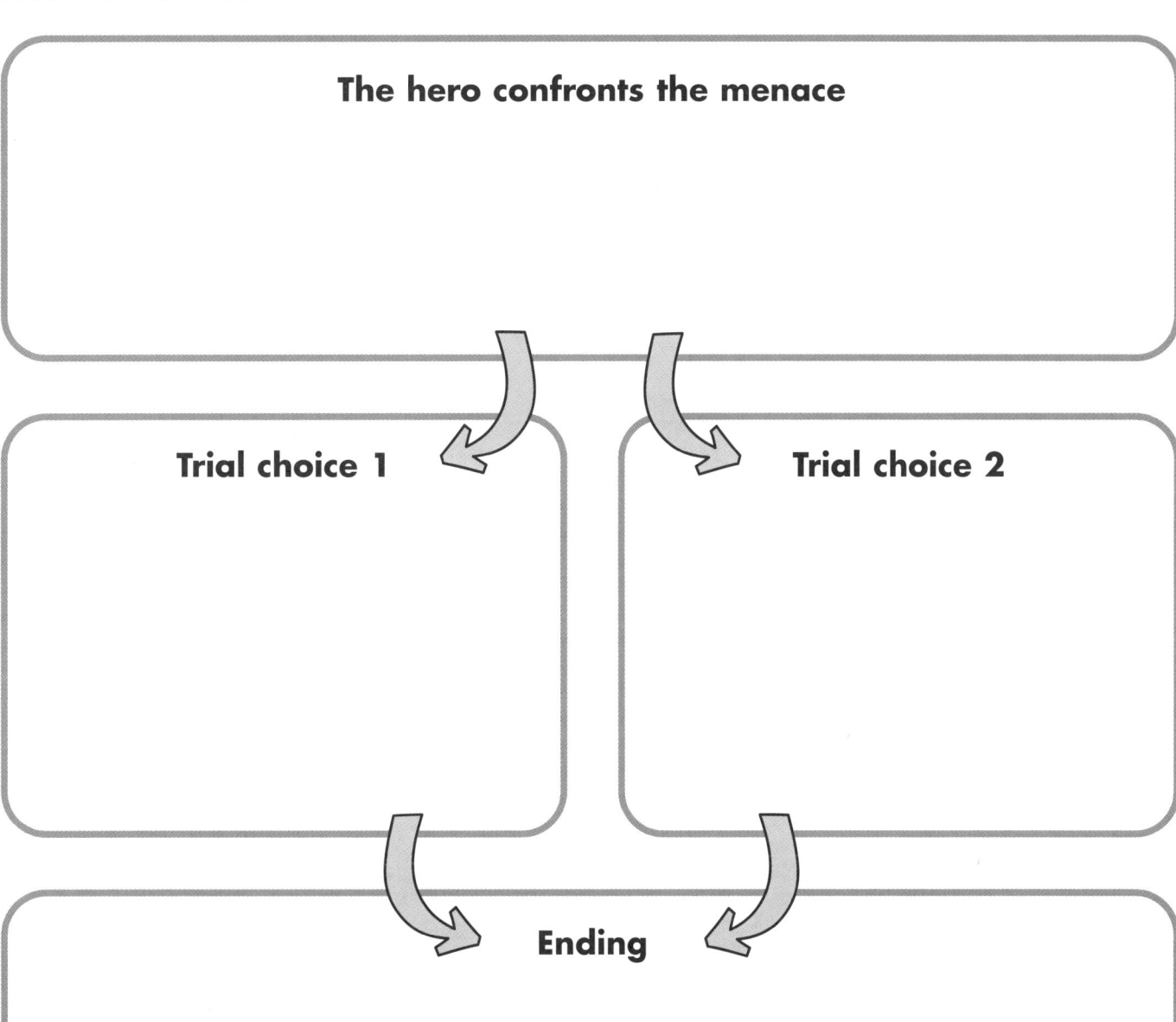

The hero confronts the menace

Trial choice 1

Trial choice 2

Ending

Types of journalistic writing

Name _____

Date _____

Compare different types of reports.

Fill in the grid to compare and contrast different types of report.

Report	Printed text	Sound	Still pictures	Moving pictures	Graphics	Audience/ language	When printed/ broadcast	Comments
TV								
Radio								
Web based								

Name _____ Date _____

Report features

Note the features of newspaper and radio reports.

Write notes on the features of newspaper and radio reports to help you
in your own writing.

Newspaper report features	Radio report features

Collins
Primary
Literacy

Name _____ Date _____

Alien landing report

Make notes for your report.

What happened:

Where:

When:

Who was present:

Name   Age

Occupation

Main points

Suitable quote

Name   Age

Occupation

Main points

Suitable quote

Name   Age

Occupation

Main points

Suitable quote

Name   Age

Occupation

Main points

Suitable quote

Name   Age

Occupation

Main points

Suitable quote

Name _____   Date _____

Author techniques

Write notes on the techniques used by the authors.

 In each box, write down an example from the story that illustrates that technique.

	Jacqueline Wilson	Lemony Snicket
Characters		
Narrative voice		
Language		
Style		
Themes		
Setting		
Illustrations		

Collins Primary Literacy

Name _____ Date _____

Planning frame for a story chapter

Plan your story using these questions.

Answer the questions in the column for the author you've chosen.

In the style of Jacqueline Wilson	In the style of Lemony Snicket
Who is the narrator (main character)?	Who is the main character in the story chapter?
What is the main character's dilemma?	
Who are the other characters involved in the dilemma?	Who are the other characters?
What will be the build-up in the chapter?	What will be the build-up in the chapter?

Name _____ Date _____

Mobile phones – good or bad?

Find arguments for and against.

Read the report and highlight the arguments for and against using mobile phones in two different colours. Put a question mark next to statements that don't fit into either argument.

According to the latest figures, there are over 100 million mobile phone users worldwide. The number of mobile connections is now equivalent to nearly one third of the world population, and there is an entire generation who cannot imagine life without their mobile. But are mobile phones only a good thing?

Mobile phone technology does bring benefits. In countries where land lines are difficult to lay, they enable friends and family to keep in touch. Mobile phones mean that business deals can be done on the move. We use them to call home to say we're safe, that we're going to be late or that we need a lift; moreover, we use them to summon the emergency services potentially saving precious minutes which could be spent finding a land line. Some people owe their lives to mobile phones, which it is argued, has to make them a good thing.

Are mobile phones safe?

Yet debate still rages over mobile phone safety. Can mobile phones damage human health? Some people believe that the electromagnetic radiation emitted by the handsets causes a variety of diseases, ranging from Alzheimer's to cancer. There are also concerns that using a mobile phone can cause changes in brain activity, sleep patterns and reaction times, while research shows that using one when driving significantly increases the likelihood of traffic accidents.

A 2002 study by Finnish scientists indicated that electromagnetic radiation had an adverse effect on human brain cells in the laboratory; however the researchers downplayed the research findings, saying that further study was needed to see if the same would happen with living people. In 2004 the Karolinska Institute in Sweden carried out a study that showed that people who used a mobile phone over a period of ten years or more were four times more likely to develop ear tumours than those who had never used one. Other research has demonstrated that electromagnetic radiation affects the health of mice, but no one knows yet if this also applies to humans.

The UK government-commissioned Stewart Report, published in 2000, reported that there was no evidence to show that mobile phones had adverse health effects, but concluded that it was best to take a precautionary approach to them until more research was carried out. There is still no conclusive research, and therefore no definitive answer.

Children at risk

The report found that children are particularly vulnerable to any adverse effects that may exist. Their nervous systems are still developing, so their growing brains are more likely to absorb any radiation. It recommended that children should only use mobiles in emergencies.

In 2002 a research programme was launched, at a cost of £7.4m, jointly funded by the government and the mobile phone industry, to examine the effects of mobile phone use on health, although manufacturers continue to extol the virtues of mobiles and insist there is no evidence of risk to human health caused by their use.

It seems that, while mobile phones are here to stay, it is still sensible to minimise any potential risks by adopting some helpful strategies. Keep conversations short, make as few calls as possible, and use phones with external aerials. Hands-free kits may help since they reduce the amount of radiation to the brain.

Mobile phones – good or bad? You decide.

by Sarah Vittachi

Collins Primary Literacy

Name _____ Date _____

An argument frame

Prepare an argument.

Record the main arguments for and against the issue on this frame. Remember to include a statement that introduces the issue and a conclusion.

Statement:

FOR	AGAINST

Conclusion:

Discussion checklist

Grade a discussion text.

Use this checklist to help you decide whether an article is a good discussion text.

✓ ✗

Structure

☐ Does the introductory paragraph state the issue clearly?

☐ Are the arguments for and against the issue clear?

☐ Are the arguments supported by examples or factual evidence (for example research findings)?

☐ Are the arguments set out clearly in paragraphs?

☐ Does the final paragraph give a conclusion based on the arguments in the article?

Final structure

☐ Is it mainly written in the present tense?

☐ Are general statements made?
(for example, *Some people believe that …*, *Supporters claim that …*)

☐ Does the argument contain connectives to show cause and effect?
(for example, *as*, *so that*, *because*)

Have connectives been used to:
☐ make links clear
(for example, *therefore*, *consequently*)
☐ introduce more points
(for example, *furthermore*, *in addition*)
☐ introduce opposing viewpoints?
(for example, *On the other hand …*, *However …*)

☐ Is the conditional tense used to suggest possibility?
(for example, *It might/may/could be …*)

Collins Primary Literacy

Name _____ Date _____

Planning a guide for parents

Plan a balanced argument.

Use this skeleton planning frame to plan your parent guide on computer games. Your guide needs to include:

An introductory paragraph (include the purpose of the guide and a statement of the issue that is being debated):

Main paragraphs

FOR	AGAINST

A concluding paragraph (include a recommendation):

Name _____ Date _____

Writing verses for a poem

Write a poem in the style of a poet.

Read the poem *Give and Take*. Make up new verses of your own in the same way.

I give you clean air
You give me poisonous gas.
I give you mountains
You give me quarries.

I give you _____

You give me _____.

I give you _____

You give me _____.

I give you _____

You give me _____.

I give you _____

You give me _____.

I give you _____

You give me _____.

I give you _____

You give me _____.

Name _____ Date _____

Diary writing frame

Write a day in Maggie's diary.

Write a diary entry describing Maggie's thoughts and worries on the day she was welcomed into Una's circle. Continue on a separate sheet.

Friday

What a day I've had today. I can't sleep for worrying about tomorrow!

I was on my way home from school when I bumped into Una. She told me that Cora had sprained her ankle. _____

_____

_____

_____

_____

_____

_____

Collins
Primary
Literacy

Name _____ Date _____

Planning frame

Plan a story using flashback.

Characters
- ⚙
- ⚙
- ⚙

Setting

Opening scene
Time:
Place:
Event:

Flashback
Time:
Place:
Event:

Main story events
- ⚙
- ⚙
- ⚙
- ⚙

Story ending
Time:
Place:
Event:

Formal language

Identify informal language.

1 Underline words and phrases that are examples of informal language.

> You want to know what really gets my goat? It's those kids who hang around the play area outside my house. Actually, half of them aren't even kids – they're teenagers who ought to know better. They mooch about the place, making a racket and dropping litter everywhere. The language they use is shocking. Haven't they got homes to go to? Haven't they got homework to do? It's no wonder that kids today can't read and write properly if all they can find to do is stand around gossiping on their phones or listening to awful music through their headphones. Worse still are the young hooligans who think it's clever to spoil the place with their graffiti. I'm at the end of my tether with it all. I'd move house if I could afford to.

2 Rewrite the informal language you've spotted in more formal language, as in the list started below.

> *gets my goat* – makes me angry
>
> *kids* – children/teenagers

Collins
Primary
Literacy

Presentation planning frame

Plan a presentation.

Imagine you're giving a presentation to persuade people to use your idea for helping your local community. Use the frame to help you plan your presentation.

Identify a need or problem in your community.
What idea will you introduce to make a positive change?
What are the benefits? ✳ ✳ ✳ ✳
How will you persuade others to support your idea? ✳ ✳ ✳ ✳
What will you need to do to make your idea happen? ✳ ✳ ✳ ✳

Name _____ Date _____

The Witches' Spell

Prepare a performance.

Prepare a performance of the witches' spell scene from *Macbeth*. The performance is for younger children.

Scene 1 *[A cavern. In the middle, a boiling cauldron. Thunder. Enter the three WITCHES.]*

First Witch: Thrice the brinded cat hath mew'd.

Second Witch: Thrice, and once the hedge-pig whin'd.

Third Witch: Harper cries: 'Tis time, 'tis time.

First Witch: Round about the cauldron go;
In the poison'd entrails throw.
Toad, that under cold stone
Days and nights has thirty-one
Swelter'd venom, sleeping got,
Boil thou first i' the charmed pot.

After sweating out poison for thirty-one days, under a cold stone, the toad is ready to put in the pot.

All: Double, double toil and trouble;
Fire burn and cauldron, bubble.

Second Witch: Fillet of a fenny snake,
In the cauldron boil and bake;
Eye of newt, and toe of frog,
Wool of bat, and tongue of dog,
Adder's fork, and blind-worm's sting,
Lizard's leg, and howlet's wing,
For a charm of powerful trouble,
Like a hell-broth, boil and bubble.

All: Double, double toil and trouble;
Fire burn and cauldron, bubble.

brinded = brown, with stripes
hedge-pig = hedgehog
Harper = (possibly) a Greek mythical creature
fillet = slice
fenny = from the fens (swampy area)
howlet = baby owl

Name _____ Date _____

How did they feel?

Plot characters' feelings.

As a group, fill in the grid to show how the characters felt during the key moments of the scene in *The Surprise Birthday Party*.

Key moments	What Mr Perks feels and thinks	What Roberta feels and thinks
Perks enters his parlour and finds the pram full of presents and thinks they are from Roberta, Phyllis and Peter.		
Perks finds out that the children have collected presents from people in the village.		
Roberta explains how the children collected the presents and she reads out the messages.		
Roberta, Phyllis and Peter start to leave but Perks calls them back.		

Collins Primary Literacy

Name _____ Date _____

An unexpected scene

Plan a play scene.

Use this grid to help you to plan a scene for a play about a special occasion when something unexpected happens.

Where does the scene take place?	What props will give a sense of the setting?
When is the scene taking place?	**Who are the characters?** *(Keep the number to 2 or 3)*
Who is the main character? *(Any defining characteristics?)*	**Who are the other characters?** *(Any defining characteristics?)*

Opening *(Establish setting, characters and problem)*

Middle *(How problem comes to a head)*

Resolution *(How characters will solve the problem)*

What has happened before the scene?	What will happen after the scene?

Name _____ Date _____

Writing a play scene

Prepare to produce a playscript.

Write down all the details for your play scene.

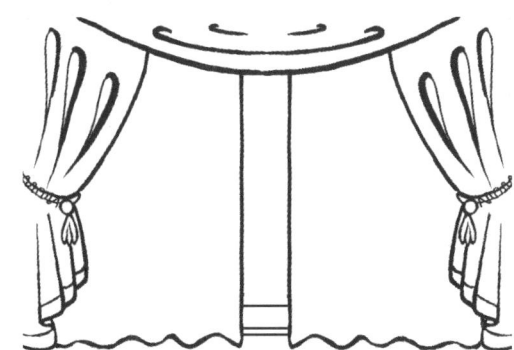

Title of play scene:

Characters in order of appearance:

1.

2.

3.

Opening stage directions (notes for actors and director, such as where characters are, what they are doing, lighting, sound effects)

The curtain rises …

Opening lines (establish setting, introduce characters and the problem)
   Name: (stage direction if needed); what the character says

Collins Primary Literacy

Name _____ Date _____

Assessment checklist

Evaluate longer fiction writing.

GOOD WORK!

Use this checklist to evaluate your own or your partner's work.

✓ ✗

Text structure and organisation

☐ Is the opening clear?

☐ Is there a complication and resolution?

☐ Are the events logically sequenced?

☐ Are there sections and paragraphs that indicate shifts in time, place or focus?

☐ Are adverbs of time used effectively?

☐ Is figurative language used effectively (for example similes and metaphors)?

☐ Are pronouns used effectively?

Sentence structure and punctuation

☐ Is there a variety of connectives to make interesting sentences?

☐ Is there a variety of simple, compound and complex sentences?

☐ Is a range of punctuation used accurately?

Composition and effect

☐ Is the reader told enough about the main events?

☐ Are viewpoints defined and consistent?

☐ Is descriptive vocabulary used?

☐ Is precise language used, such as *hobbled* instead of *walked*, *wept* instead of *cried*?

☐ Is the character developed through action, dialogue and description?

☐ Is part of the story told through dialogue?

Collins Primary Literacy

Name _____ Date _____

Toponymy (the study of place names)

Find out the meaning of place names.

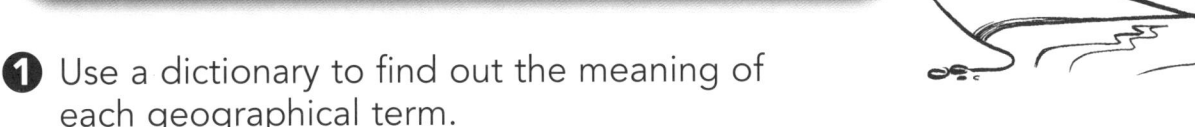

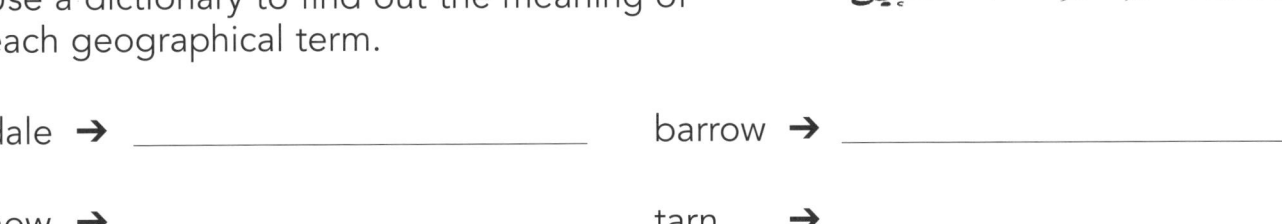

① Use a dictionary to find out the meaning of each geographical term.

dale → _____   barrow → _____

how → _____   tarn → _____

crag → _____   fell → _____

② Now investigate these place names.

Langdale Pikes
Grizedale Forest
Coniston Old Man
Dollywaggon Pike
St Sunday Crag
Patterdale
Gowbarrow Fell
High Spying How

Collins
Primary
Literacy

Name _____ Date _____

What are volcanoes?

Write questions for a test situation.

① Read this passage on volcanoes.

② Write some questions for a partner to answer on a sheet of paper. Remember to think about how many marks will be awarded for each question.

③ Then swap and answer each other's questions.

A volcano is a hill or mountain where molten rock spurts to the surface from deep under the ground. Above ground, the magma is known as lava. A volcano is made up of lava that has cooled and solidified, together with cinders and ash. Volcanic eruptions are among the most violent and spectacular natural events on Earth. Accompanied by red-hot rivers of lava, towering clouds of ash and thick flows of mud, they can devastate the landscape and people's lives.

Volcanoes have been erupting since the Earth was formed 4,500 million years ago. Today, about twenty-five volcanoes around the world erupt every year on land. Some of these active volcanoes erupt almost all the time. Others may only erupt every few hundred years. Some volcanoes erupt with giant explosions. Others erupt more gently, producing fizzing lava fountains.

Volcanoes and the landscape

Much of Earth's surface is made up of rocks that have come from volcanoes. Volcanoes create and build mountains and islands, but they can also be destructive. They cover the landscape with lava, ash and mud, burning and burying plants and destroying animal habitats. Houses, villages and towns may also be buried or burned. In the past, eruptions have killed thousands of people.

Vulcan's island

The word volcano comes from Vulcano, an island off the coast of Italy. The ancient Romans believed that the god Vulcan lived in a volcano on the island, where he made weapons for other gods, such as arrows, armour and lightning bolts. Fiery eruptions from the island's volcanoes were believed to be sparks from Vulcan's forge.

from Nature's Fury: Volcano! *by Anita Ganeri*

Collins Primary Literacy

Name _____ Date _____

Spiders and webs

Analyse a poem.

Spin Me a Web, Spider

Spin me a web, spider,
Across the window-pane
For I shall never break it
And make you start again.

Cast your net of silver
As soon as it is spun,
And hang it with the morning dew
That glitters in the sun.

It's strung with pearls and diamonds,
The finest ever seen,
Fit for any royal King
Or any royal Queen.

Would you, could you, bring it down
In the dust to lie?
Any day of the week, my dear,
Said the nimble fly.

Charles Causley

Read the poem carefully. Then answer the following questions.

1 At what time of day is the poem set and how do you know this? (2 marks)

_____

2 Find and write down two words in the first verse that are an example of alliteration. (1 mark)

_____

3 *Cast your net of silver*

Why do you think the poet has described the spider's web in this way? (2 marks)

_____

4 *It's strung with pearls and diamonds*

What are the *pearls and diamonds* metaphors for? (1 mark)

_____

5 What effect do the final two lines of the poem have on the reader? (1 mark)

_____

Name _____ Date _____

Spiders and webs

Analyse a poem.

Spider's Song

See, I have stitched the ivy
with beaded threads of light,
a rich embroidery, newly hung.
Step on my tightrope,
lie with me;

let me fold you tenderly
in my pearled hammock,
lull you to silken sleep,
sweet dreamer,
under the dying sun.

Judith Nicholls

Read the poem carefully. Then answer the following questions.

1 What human activity does the poet refer to metaphorically when she describes the act of spinning a web? Use words and phrases from the poem to support your answer. (3 marks)

_____

_____

2 *let me fold you tenderly*
in my pearled hammock

Explain the meaning of these two lines and their effect on the reader. (3 marks)

_____

_____

3 How do you think the spider will *lull* its victim to *silken sleep*? (1 mark)

_____

4 *lull you to silken sleep,*
sweet dreamer

What effect does the alliteration in this poem have? (1 mark)

_____

Supporting drama

Drama has long been regarded as an indispensable teaching tool, and it has been given due status in the renewed framework. It promotes better thinking, reading and writing through its ability to engage and motivate children.

The benefits of using drama

You'll see the benefits of using drama in this programme through children becoming:

- engaged, interested and showing lots of enjoyment.
- better thinkers.
- sharper users of the spoken word as they hone up and shape exactly what they want to say in role as a character.

Better writers

Children produce writing which is more powerful because they have been "inside" the situation they are writing about. Their creative impulses are harnessed by this engagement in a "real" situation – and boys are galvanised to write.

Better readers

Children's reading skills improve because they have to use inference and deduction to find the clues to the behaviour of characters in books, and translate these into a "freeze-frame", piece of improvisation or "decision–alley" experience

Drama tools for teaching

What follows is a selection of easy-to-use drama tools for teaching. These are used throughout *Collins Primary Literacy*, and can be used elsewhere in the curriculum so that children become completely at ease with them. The benefits are enormous!

Role play

This is familiar to many teachers and involves a child talking as if they are a character from a story or a representative from a group, for example the builders who want to build a supermarket.

Preparing for role play

It's a good idea to ask the rest of the class or groups to prepare some questions to ask the character as it can "fall flat" if they are asked to think of questions without any prior thinking.

Less experienced children

Less experienced children might rehearse with a teaching assistant listening and offering feedback – this builds up their confidence when they perform in front of the class.

Group role play

Ask a group of children to plan a role-play as one character, rather than just one child. The benefit of this is that the planning beforehand allows children to share their views of the character together.

Whole class in role

This could be used in a Review session. For example, if the children have been studying viewpoint in a novel, ask the whole class to go into role as one character and question them. The class can divide into two, each group taking on a different role – and question each other.

Teacher in role

You get into role as a character, and the class prepare questions. This is particularly good as you can challenge children's views by using empathy to describe the way characters are feeling.

Freeze-frame

Children select a key moment from a story and create a still picture to illustrate what is happening. When you call freeze, children remain still, holding the action for a moment in time. They may have written a caption to go with the frame, which can be displayed near to their acting space.

(See *Improvisation* and *Thought tracking* for ways of further developing freeze-frames.)

Improvisation

Children in a freeze-frame can come to life when you signal to them. Children can improvise a conversation with no prior planning, in role as characters from the story.

Thought tracking

This is when the private thoughts or reactions of a character are spoken publicly. You or a child can tap characters in a freeze-frame on the shoulder – this signals that the child in role must speak their thoughts aloud. This technique is very useful for developing inference and deduction as readers, as the children have to find the clues in the story by re-reading the text and deducting or inferring the views/attitudes of main characters

Decision alley

A central character facing a dilemma in the drama moves slowly between two lines formed by the rest of the group. As they pass each person, those on one side comment aloud in support of a course of action, while those on the other side give reasons against it. At the end of the alley, the character has to make a decision based on what they've heard.

This technique can be used across the curriculum, for example:

- **History** – should the Romans have invaded Britain?
- **Science and Geography** – how can we justify the hunting of seals, or the building of more houses on the flood plains of rivers?
- **PSHE** – what are the consequences of bullying in the playground? How does it feel to be bullied?

Diaries, letters, messages

Written in role by characters that are part of the story, these pieces of writing reveal the power of drama to engage children in writing.

Dynamic duos

These are improvisations of conversations in pairs, with one child acting as a main character who tells a "friend" about what has happened in the story and how they feel about the course of events and the behaviour of others. Allow a few of the conversations to be "overheard" by the class so that children can experience and reflect on the views of others.

Mantle of the expert

In the role of specialists, for example scientists or farmers, the children present what they've learned about a topic.

Meetings

Here you can involve the whole group in the same place at the same time within a dramatic context linked to the text, for example a meeting at the town hall to discuss views for and against the building of a new supermarket.

Hot seating

One or more children can be in role. The rest of the class is forewarned and prepares questions to ask the child/children in role.

Children reflecting on the usefulness of drama as a teaching tool

Review sessions in *Collins Primary Literacy* suggest that children reflect upon the usefulness of different teaching tools. This reflects the concept of children being at the heart of the learning experience, critically evaluating teaching techniques.

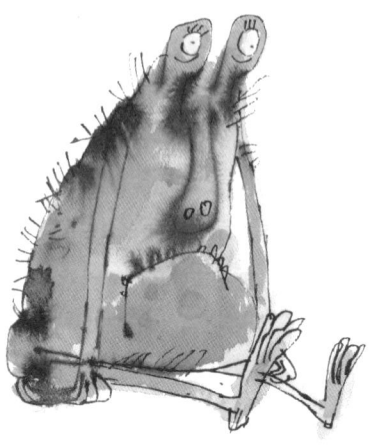

Supporting speaking and listening

Planning for group discussion at Upper Primary

It's a good idea to prepare for this with a class discussion! Discuss class rules for group discussion and together draft a plan for the class to test out.

You might start with a few prompts such as those in the table, and then have a trial run in the context of the discussions suggested in a *Collins Primary Literacy* unit. Then draw up what the children consider to be a workable draft. Come back to it with the class from time to time to remind them of or revise the rules.

Possible plan	Prompt
Be clear about what is to be discussed	Should the group objective be written down?
Decide whether to elect a group leader	Is this a good idea?
Discuss the role of a group leader	Is it to: ● Keep the group on task? ● Make sure children take turns? ● Encourage quieter children?
Decide whether to elect a group scribe	Should it be the same person every time?
Discuss whether a time limit should be placed on the discussion	How much time is reasonable?
Discuss poor behaviour in the group	● What is a "no go" situation? ● Should the group ask for help from the teacher? ● Should they resolve it themselves independently?
Consider what level of noise is acceptable within the class	What is reasonable?
Discuss what would be helpful for you to do as you join a group	What would be helpful?
Discuss how to give feedback	Elect a leader to offer the group's views?
Give feedback by using "jigsawing" (where new groups are formed by each group splitting up by sending an envoy to a new group. The envoy shares the views of their original group.).	Is this effective?

Support for talk in the Lower Primary classroom

The chart below may be more suitable for younger children – although establishing rules for talk is just as important with older children! It's based on advice in the Primary National Strategy for Key Stage 1 and 2.

Talking Together Tips

- Look at the person you're speaking to.

- Everybody should have a turn to speak.

- It's a good idea if one person speaks at a time.

- You don't always have to agree with what someone says.
  Wait until they've finished and say:
  "I agree with what you are saying because…".
  Or
  "I disagree with what you are saying because…".

- Try to speak clearly

- Speak loud enough for the group to hear what you're saying

- Try to be clear about what you mean

- Be pleasant and smile at others in the group

- SHOUTING IS NOT ALLOWED – however strongly you feel!!!

Assessment and progression

Assessing progress in learning

There are different ways of assessing progress in children's learning.

Formative assessment

Formative assessment or assessment for learning (AfL) is most effective when it's embedded in the teaching and learning process.

As part of this process it's essential to share learning goals with children as a standard feature of your classroom routine. Children benefit greatly from knowing the purpose behind what they are learning.

Research shows that formative assessment is most effective when you:

- involve children in their own learning
- provide effective feedback to children
- adjust teaching as a result of assessment
- share with children how they can assess their own progress
- help children understand how to improve.

It is hugely motivating for children to know where they are in their learning and how to move on. It also enhances their self-esteem. This is a key factor in raising children's standards of achievement.

Summative assessment

Summative assessment is carried out periodically, for example at the end of a unit of learning, or year, or key stage. It is a judgement about children's **performance** in relation to national standards.

Learning journey

Collins Primary Literacy and formative assessment

High-quality formative assessment is embedded in *Collins Primary Literacy*, threaded through each unit to create a seamless fabric.

Prior learning

The journey starts with the *Prior Learning* slot at the beginning of every unit which highlights what children should already know and do if the most is to be gained from the unit. Use this opportuntiy to **revise previous objectives** if needed and **revisit strategies for learning**, e.g. effective paired and group work.

Shared objectives

The learning journey continues with your **sharing the objectives with the children** for the whole unit and at each stage of each phase, focusing the children's attention on what it is that they're going to learn.

Assessment is threaded through *Collins Primary Literacy* in the following ways:

- **Modelled writing**, where you walk and talk children through the writing process, showing them first hand what merits a quality piece of writing.
- **Regular reviews** of what children have learned when they are encouraged to reflect on what they've done well and what they need to develop.
- **Joining discussion groups** to listen to views and take part in the discussion, so that you can see and hear what learning has taken place – and take the opportunity to offer oral feedback.
- **Using questioning techniques** such as asking a range of ready- prepared questions to judge comprehension skills.
- **Using peer learning strategies** such as *Think/Pair/Share, Read/Pair/Share* and *Write/Pair/Share* to enable children to learn from each other, and share views and opinions with the class and you.

- **Adopting a "no hands up" approach** to direct questions to certain children after they have had time to talk through the question with another child – this gives you a picture of what children know and can do.
- **Evaluating the use of drama strategies** – asking the children how effective these are for learning, and why.
- **Using talk for learning** by experiencing different types of talk, both formal and informal, and enabling children to assess each other's presentations on their effectiveness.
- **Establishing rules for feedback** by showing children how to comment constructively on each other's writing. This helps children see for themselves what they need to do to improve in their own writing.
- **Promoting reflection**, for example where children are expected to work independently on activities in the Pupil Book and reflect on how well they've managed the task.
- **Scaffolding writing** by using materials on the software so that children can produce better quality pieces.

Collins Primary Literacy and summative assessment

- **Easy-to-use assessment progress charts** are offered for different writing genres so that you can judge children's progress against National Curriculum Levels
- **Assessment criteria are built into each unit** at the end of each phase, and provided in the Teacher's Guide for your guidance. You could show children how to use these assessment criteria to assess their own learning.

Assessing speaking and listening

Your role

Collins Primary Literacy offers many practical suggestions for assessing learning through oral feedback – not only by you but also by the children, who are treated as equal partners in the learning journey.

Collins Primary Literacy's approach to learning supports the concept of the classroom as a workshop – this encourages children's talk and offers you many opportunities to assess learning, thinking and oral skills. Some examples from the Teacher's Guides are given here.

Collins Primary Literacy 3	
Turn their storyboard notes into a story.	**End of Phase Review** Children share their reflections on their work in the unit and report their responses back to the class.

Collins Primary Literacy 4	
Invite one or two groups to role-play interviews to the rest of the class.	**Review** How effective was the questioning? Did the reporter listen to the answers given?

Collins Primary Literacy 5	
Each group presents a "living storyboard" in turn.	**Paired discussion and feedback** Did the events flow in the right order? What are the benefits of visualisation?

Collins Primary Literacy 6	
Ask the children individually to answer the questions in the Pupil Book.	**Review** Ensure the children have understood the text by discussing their answers.

Speaking, listening and drama and the Primary National Strategy

Collins Primary Literacy fully covers the speaking, listening, group interaction and drama objectives in the Primary National Strategy.

The table on page 166 can be used to assess progress to match the key aspects of talk and drama covered in depth throughout *Collins Primary Literacy* Levels 3 to 6.

Assessing reading and comprehension

Your role

Collins Primary Literacy offers a range of strategies to assess comprehension. As well as using drama as a key tool for inference and deduction and exploring motive and themes, you can draw on the many suggestions in the Teacher's Guide and the ready-prepared, differentiated sets of questions linked to most texts in the Pupil Book.

Here are some examples of differentiated comprehension questions.

Collins Primary Literacy 3

 Why do you think Mr Kane needed a *bit of hush*?

 What words describe the roofs and chimneys of Winklesea?

 Would you like to stay in Winklesea? Why/Why not?

Collins Primary Literacy 4

 What is the knight searching for?

 Do you think he'll find what he's searching for?

 Why do you think the knight keeps travelling?

Collins Primary Literacy 5

After reading a selection of advertisements, all groups have to answer these questions:

Who is persuading you?

What do they want you to do?

How do they try to persuade you?

Collins Primary Literacy 6

 Where is the poem *Silver* set? Describe the setting.

 In the poem *Xmas*, why does Wes Magee use the word duvet?

 What do you think Wes Magee thinks of Christmas? What evidence can you find to support your opinion?

Assessing progression in comprehension skills

Collins Primary Literacy covers all the reading objectives in the Primary National Strategy.

The table on page 167 can be used to assess progress to match the key aspects of comprehension.

Assessing progression in writing

Your role

This will very often be through oral feedback in guided and paired writing sessions, through responses to shared writing, modelled writing and activities on the software, and through assessing finished pieces of writing using the assessment sheets provided at the end of the unit in the Teacher's Guide.

The *Remember!* box used in Pupil Book units offers key points to think about and check for both during and after writing.

The *What I have learned* box at the end of every unit summarises the key objectives for writing in a child-friendly way.

Assessing speaking and listening

Year 3/P4	Year 4/P5	Year 5/P6	Year 6/P7
Explains process or present information clearly, with relevant detail	Listens to a speaker & makes notes for different purposes	Identifies formal and informal talk in a presentation	Explores ideas, topics and issues
Justifies views during conversation or whole class discussion	Offers reasons and evidence for their views, considering alternative opinions	Presents a spoken argument, persuasively	Presents persuasive arguments and engaging stories
Uses expanding vocabulary	Tells stories effectively	Tells stories using repetition, recap and humour	Participates in effective whole class debate, using more formal English
Takes different roles in group discussion	Identifies the main points in an argument	Analyses the use of persuasive language	Uses effective listening to make relevant notes
Uses drama strategies to explore stories or issues, and evaluate success	Uses improvisation to develop scripts	Develops skills of effective group work, including decision making	Listens and identifies formal and informal language
	Uses role-play to explore viewpoint, and evaluate success	Uses role-play to explore complex issues and evaluate success	Learns to criticise constructively and respond to criticism
		Performs a scripted scene, making use of theatrical effects	Uses a range of drama strategies to explore theme and evaluate success
			Identify the impact of a live or recorded performance

C Collins
Primary
Literacy

Assessing progress in comprehension

Year 3/P4	Year 4/P5	Year 5/P6	Year 6/P7
Makes notes of the main points in a text	Identifies and summarises evidence from a text	Makes notes and uses evidence to explain events and ideas	Appraises a text quickly to assess its quality and usefulness
Infers characters' feelings through empathy	Deduces reasons why characters behave as they do from their behaviour	Infers writers' viewpoints from what is written and what is implied	Understands underlying themes, causes of events, and point of view
Uses syntax, meaning and word structure to expand vocabulary as they read for meaning	Uses word structure and origins to develop their understanding	Explores how writers use language for comic and dramatic effect	Explores how word meanings change when used in different contexts
Explores how texts appeal to readers	Explores how writers create images and atmosphere	Uses and evaluates visualisation, prediction and empathy to explore the meaning of a text	Recognises rhetorical devices used to argue, persuade, mislead and sway the reader
Identifies how writers make readers respond to their books	Reads and re-reads texts to clarify understanding and response	Compares how a common theme is presented in poetry, prose and other media	

www.collinseducation.com © HarperCollins*Publishers* Limited 2007

	Composition and effect	Text structure and organisation	Sentence structure and punctuation
NC Level 2	**Purpose and features** → Shows insecure grasp of features except through talk; unlikely to show balance → Uses some characteristics of discursive writing, though may not give a balanced view; includes topic words and description → Uses some features of discussion in writing; adds detail to interest the reader and develops arguments on both sides	**Structure of discussion** → Adopts a basic structure → Links some points with "and" → May include an opening and points on both sides, but these may be mixed up	**Sentence structure** → Adopts speech-like sentence structure, mostly joined by "and"; uses tense inconsistently → Extends some sentences with "but" and "so" → Includes longer sentences, using connectives such as "because" or "when"; includes adverbial phrases in different positions; usually writes in present tense **In addition**, confident writers vary sentence openings (e.g. when – "Tomorrow", how – "Quietly"), and include detail with prepositional phrases ("in", "under", etc.) **Punctuation** → Becoming more accurate with use of full stops and capitals → Uses other punctuation marks (exclamation and question marks)
NC Level 3	**Purpose and features** → Writes a recognisable discussion text, though some features absent or undeveloped; covers content unevenly → Includes features to support purpose of persuading, but gives too much or too little detail; uses some impersonal language → Includes most features of discursive writing; writing is relevant for audience; covers content in a balanced way most of the time **Use of vocabulary** → Makes word choices to tell the reader about two points of view – some words reflect spoken language → Includes description to add information, and uses technical language → Uses some well-chosen vocabulary in order to make argument convincing **In addition**, confident writers attempt a more formal style	**Structure of persuasion** → Includes basic introduction followed by series of points on both sides; may not make links between arguments clear → Begins with a clear introductory statement followed by detail about both sides; links arguments with connectives → May change paragraph to link with a new side of the argument, or introduce a new point **Organisation and layout** → May use a layout that is not conventional according to task → Divides arguments into sections; → May include statistics, graphs, images and layout features to support or reinforce arguments	**Sentence structure** → Develops ideas with simple connectives → Uses a wide variety of connectives in sentences; subjects and verbs usually agree → Varies sentence openings by using adverbials or subordinators to structure arguments **Punctuation** → Uses commas in lists → Uses full stops and capital letters with increasing accuracy. → Uses other punctuation where appropriate and also for effect; attempts to use commas to separate sections of a sentence
NC Level 4	**Purpose and features** → Leaves some features undeveloped; balances and paces arguments to ensure reader is informed; occasionally attempts a formal style → May include additional detail to add interest or information; sometimes attempts to adopt appropriate tone and control relevant style → Uses characteristics of text type assertively; presents information clearly, with writer's purpose evident at each stage; shows greater control of formality, though not fully sustained **Use of vocabulary** → Makes arguments using topic words and "accurate" description → Chooses words and phrases for interest and precision → Chooses words and phrases carefully, to add shades of meaning to argument	**Structure of argument** Structures writing with increasing clarity: follows introduction with a series of arguments covering two points of view and a conclusion. May deal with arguments on two sides in two sections, or point by point. **Use of paragraphs** → May include several different arguments in a paragraph → Organises separate points in paragraphs which include a topic sentence; uses connecting words and phrases to organise the discussion for the reader → Shows evidence of "staging" to manage pace and progression, with several paragraphs developing one part of the report; able to draw a reasoned conclusion	**Sentence structure** → Writes longer compound and some complex sentences, with a range of connectives to explain arguments → Includes a variety of complex sentences, with different subordinators, to extend arguments; includes connectives to give order and emphasis within sentences; generally uses pronouns and tenses consistently; varies subjects of sentences; may use future tense to express consequences → Employs range of sentence types to create the desired effect on the reader; makes use of strategies to avoid repetition; produces concise and precise writing; **Punctuation** → Uses punctuation with increasing accuracy; sometimes uses commas to separate clauses → Uses commas to separate clauses → Starting to use a wider range of punctuation where appropriate (for example, dashes and brackets, semi colons and colons)
NC Level 5	**Purpose and features** → Shows evidence of adapting material to support reader's understanding; writes in a style appropriate for task; → Balances and paces argument well; shows awareness of audience through adaptation of writing and presents two viewpoints as well as his/her own; chooses and sustains an appropriate level of formality → Writes well in respect of structure and linguistic features of text type; style is appropriate and shows control **Use of vocabulary** Chooses words to support the purpose with increasing precision, economy and effectiveness	**Structure and paragraphs** → Separates main ideas into sections or paragraphs, which are shaped into stages within the writing; links paragraphs with adverbials or connectives → Produces writing that is well structured and convincing, developing two points of view through whole text; includes paragraphs of different lengths, emphasising the importance of certain parts of the argument → Uses a fully-developed and appropriate structure and layout	**Sentence structure** → Employs a range of sentences – simple, compound and complex–for effect; uses passive constructions to support formal style; uses conditional verbs for arguments → Finds effective ways within sentences to avoid unnecessary repetition: uses rhetorical questions in a formal style → Fluently constructs a range of sentence types; may alter word order to develop themes and sustain reader interest **Punctuation** → Correctly demarcates most sentences, using a range of relevant punctuation → May use punctuation to enhance point of view or add humour → May use punctuation to avoid ambiguity; effectively employs semi colons or colons to structure longer sentences

Name _____ Date _____

www.collinseducation.com © HarperCollinsPublishers Limited 2007

Collins
Primary
Literacy

Assessing writing

Explanation

	Composition and effect	Text structure and organisation	Sentence structure and punctuation
NC Level 2	**Purpose and features** → Shows insecure grasp of features; → Conveys information through labels for drawings, extended captions and lists; uses topic words → Uses some features of explanation writing; adds detail to interest the reader	**Structure of explanation** → Includes some subjective comments or observations → Includes several points of observation and comment → Organises writing to reflect purpose, e.g. a flowchart with pictures and notes; may include an opening statement; uses time connectives to reflect order	**Sentence structure** → Adopts speech-like sentence structure, mostly joined by "and"; uses tense inconsistently → Extends some sentences with "so"; usually writes in present tense → Includes longer sentences, using connectives such as "because" or "when"; includes adverbial phrases in different positions **In addition**, confident writers use adverbials and prepositional phrases ("in", "under" etc) to explain **Punctuation** Becoming more accurate with use of full stops and capitals
NC Level 3	**Purpose and features** → Produces a recognisable explanation text, though some features absent or undeveloped; covers content unevenly; some detail may relate to topic but not to explanation → Includes features to support purpose of giving information to explain, but gives too much or too little detail; uses some impersonal language → Includes most features of explanation; writing is relevant for audience; mostly balanced coverage **Use of vocabulary** → Chooses words to help explain – some words reflect spoken language → Includes description to add information, and technical language → Uses some well-chosen vocabulary to make explanation clearer **In addition**, confident writers attempt a more formal style with generalised vocabulary	**Structure of explanation** → Includes introduction, followed by a series of explanatory points → May write title as a question followed by the process in order; links ideas in several sentences with time and causal connectives; may not end with a concluding statement; → Progresses through main points; writes separate conclusion **Organisation and layout** → May not use a conventional layout → May include separate sections and labelled diagram, if relevant → May change paragraph for each stage of the process; uses sub-headings	**Sentence structure** → Develops ideas with simple connectives → Uses a variety of connectives, including cause and effect; subjects and verbs usually agree → Varies sentence openings with adverbials or subordinators; introduces wider range of causal connectives **Punctuation** → Uses commas in lists → Uses full stops and capital letters with increasing accuracy → Uses other punctuation where appropriate; attempts to use commas to separate sections of a sentence
NC Level 4	**Purpose and features** → Leaves some features undeveloped; balances and paces explanation to ensure reader is informed; occasionally attempts a formal style → May include additional detail to explain; sometimes attempts to adopt appropriate tone and control relevant style → Uses characteristics of text type assertively; successfully combines information and explanation, with writer's purpose clear at each stage; shows greater control of formality, though not fully sustained; maintains a consistent viewpoint **Use of vocabulary** → Includes interesting information, using topic words and "accurate" description → Chooses words and phrases for interest or precision; attempts to use "weasel" words for generalisations (e.g. "usually", "often") → Chooses words and phrases carefully to explain and provide extra information	**Structure of explanation** Structures writing with increasing clarity: follows introduction with a series of elaborated points which explain a process and draw a conclusion **Organisation and layout** → Uses layout features to aid explanation e.g. diagrams → Changes paragraph for each subject in explanation; includes a topic sentence; uses paragraphs to improve overall cohesion → Shows evidence of "staging" to manage pace and progression, with several paragraphs developing one part of the explanation; Uses relevant layout: sub-headings, bullet points, paragraphs	**Sentence structure** → Writes longer compound and some complex sentences with a range of connectives → Includes a variety of complex sentences, with different subordinators, to extend meaning; includes connectives to give order and emphasis within sentences; generally uses pronouns and tenses consistently → Employs range of sentence types to create the desired effect on the reader; makes use of strategies to avoid repetition; produces concise and precise writing; varies type of subject in sentences (pronoun, place, person), and varies subjects of sentences across a paragraph **Punctuation** → Uses punctuation with increasing accuracy; sometimes uses commas to separate clauses → Uses commas to separate clauses → Starting to use a wider range of punctuation where appropriate (for example, dashes and brackets, semi colons and colons)
NC Level 5	**Purpose and features** → Shows evidence of adapting material to inform the reader; writes in a style appropriate for task; → Balances and paces explanation well; shows awareness of audience through use of language or adaptation of task; chooses and sustains an appropriate level of formality → Writes well in respect of structure and linguistic features of text type; style is appropriate and shows control **Use of vocabulary** Chooses words to support the purpose with increasing precision, economy and effectiveness	**Structure and paragraphs** → Main ideas separated into sections or paragraphs, which are shaped into stages of writing; uses layout conventions that are consistent with the task; links paragraphs together with adverbials or connectives → Produces well-structured and convincing writing, including a well-focused introduction and conclusion; maintins cohesion between sections → Uses fully-developed and appropriate structure	**Sentence structure** → Employs a range of sentences – simple, compound and complex – for effect; uses passive constructions to support formal style; uses future tense for hypothetical phenomena → Finds effective ways within sentences to avoid repetition: → Fluently constructs a range of sentence types; may alter word order to develop themes and sustain reader interest **Punctuation** → Correctly demarcates most sentences, using a range of relevant punctuation → May use punctuation to enhance description or clarify meaning → May use punctuation to avoid ambiguity; effectively employs semi colons or colons to structure longer sentences

Assessing writing

Fiction

Composition and effect

NC Level 2

Story in appropriate genre
→ Writes story as if it were spoken
→ Uses greater variety of storytelling language and detail about characters
→ Writes lively story to interest the reader, including description of character and/or setting

Use of vocabulary
→ Uses adjectives
→ Varies verbs, e.g. "said" and "went"
→ Chooses words which show awareness of audience

NC Level 3

Story in appropriate genre
→ Adopts simple style in range of genres – not always successfully managed
→ Writes more clearly, though still some uneven sections
→ Sustains genre and is aware of audience

Use of vocabulary
→ Makes word choices to interest the reader – some words reflect spoken language
→ Includes description to add interest – e.g. detail about setting, powerful verbs
→ Begins to use adventurous vocabulary, including figurative language
→ **In addition**, confident writers develop character beyond description of appearance, show interaction between characters and use details which might explore motive.

NC Level 4

Story genre and audience
→ Sustains genre and may include surprise ending, if appropriate
→ Creates well-developed climax; establishes viewpoint
→ Uses language to hook reader; narrator "speaks" directly to reader

Characterisation and setting
→ Includes description, action and direct speech to make stories more realistic
→ Includes well-chosen words and expanded phrases
→ Develops well-rounded characters throughout story and creates atmospheric settings; implies detail through careful choice of vocabulary
→ **In addition**, confident writers increasingly interlink detail of characters, setting and plot, imply detail about characters and use reported speech effectively

NC Level 5

Story genre
→ Creates changes in pace; interweaves dialogue, action and description effectively
→ Makes narrator's viewpoint clear; adapts and reorganises material for effect
→ Stories well-written in respect of structure and linguistic features of genre; uses direct and reported speech in a well-controlled way; employs effective stylistic devices

Authorial voice and audience
→ Uses varied effects to hook reader: direct address, informal style, repetition for effect
→ Demonstrates increasing control over narrative viewpoint
→ Shows a sustained awareness of reader; the author's view of events and control of story encourages reader to take a view

Text structure and organisation

NC Level 2

Story structure
→ Includes simple beginning, middle and end, with events in correct order using time connectives
→ Includes problem and resolution in plot, though some parts of story may be undeveloped
→ Writes clearer development and ending

NC Level 3

Story structure
→ Includes opening; build up; problems or events; resolution and ending. covers content of story unevenly
→ Links sections of story with time-related words.
→ Writes stronger ending

Use of paragraphs
→ Writes three paragraphs for beginning, middle and end
→ Writes paragraphs for five parts of story
→ May include further paragraphs to show change of time and place; connects paragraphs in different ways

NC Level 4

Structure
→ Uses different types of openings within 5-part story structure
→ Uses specific techniques related to genre; includes shifts in time and place to shape story
→ May include improvisation, for example a parallel plot line

Use of paragraphs
→ Connects sentences within paragraphs, though may not link paragraphs effectively
→ Uses paragraphs to emphasise key aspects and help develop all parts of story equally
→ Writes fluently, with clear links between paragraphs. Shows evidence of pace and progression in "staging", with several paragraphs developing one part of the story.

NC Level 5

Structure and paragraphs
→ Separates main events into paragraphs, which shape stages of writing
→ Makes story convincing; controls paragraphs to shape story
→ Allows a clear theme or message to emerge; varies paragraphs in length and structure

Sentence structure and punctuation

NC Level 2

Sentence structure
→ Writes speech-like sentence structures, mostly joined by "and"
→ Extends some sentences with "but", "so" and "then"; usually past tense
→ Includes longer sentences linked with other connectives, such as "because" or "when"
→ **In addition**, confident writers vary sentence openings (e.g. when – "Tomorrow", how – "Quietly"), and include detail with prepositional phrases ("in", "under", etc).

Punctuation
Becoming more accurate with use of full stops and capitals
Uses other punctuation marks (exclamation and question marks)
Sometimes uses speech marks for dialogue

NC Level 3

Sentence structure
→ Uses connectives to create compound sentences; starts sentences in different ways
→ Uses a wide choice of connectives; subjects and verbs usually agree
→ Writes sentence openings with adverbials or subordinators.
→ **In addition**, confident writers move phrases round in sentences for effect.

Punctuation
→ Uses commas in lists
→ Uses full stops and capital letters with increasing accuracy
→ Uses other punctuation where appropriate, including speech marks; attempts to use commas to separate sections of a sentence

NC Level 4

Sentence structure
→ Writes longer compound and some complex sentences with a range of connectives
→ Includes a variety of complex sentences, with different subordinators, to extend meaning; uses connectives give order and emphasis within sentences; generally uses pronouns and tenses consistently; varies type of subject in sentences (pronoun, place, person), and varies subjects of sentences across a paragraph
→ Uses range of sentence types to create the desired effect on the reader; uses strategies to avoid repetition

Punctuation
→ Uses capital letters, full stops, question, exclamation and speech marks with increasing accuracy
→ Uses commas to separate clauses and phrases
→ Uses wider range of punctuation where appropriate (for example, dashes)

NC Level 5

Sentence structure
→ Employs range of sentences – simple, compound and complex – for effect
→ Finds effective ways to avoid repetition
→ Fluently constructs a range of sentences; may alter word order to develop themes and sustain reader interest

Punctuation
→ Correctly demarcates most sentences, using a range of relevant punctuation
→ May use punctuation to enhance description or clarify meaning
→ May use punctuation to add humour or vary pace

Assessing writing

Instruction writing

	Composition and effect	Text structure and organisation	Sentence structure and punctuation
NC Level 2	**Purpose and features** → Includes features that are becoming clearer but are not sustained; includes informative topic language; uses simple adjectives; → Sometimes makes ambitious word choices; usually uses imperative verb to underline purpose → Writes in a lively style to hold reader's interest; adds detail to make instruction clearer; might refer to the reader	**Structure of instructions** → Includes brief sequence of instructions in order; each instruction is complete and makes sense → Includes an opening or title which inform reader about purpose; uses the structure consistently; → Uses features of layout to support reader's understanding; might include labelled diagrams and lists of ingredients or materials, if relevant	**Sentence structure** → Writes speech-like sentence structures, mostly joined by "and"; may use "you" to introduce each step → Shows some variation in structure; uses time connectives to show order → Uses adverbials or prepositional phrases to give extra information **Punctuation** Becoming more accurate when using full stops and capitals
NC Level 3	**Purpose and features** → Covers content unevenly; may not make links between instructions clear → Includes features to support purpose of giving instructions to interest and inform, but gives too much or too little detail; uses some impersonal language → Uses most features of instructions; writing is relevant for audience; covers content in balanced way most of the time **Use of vocabulary** → Makes word choices to inform and interest the reader – some words reflect spoken language → Uses description to add information, and technical language → Uses some well-chosen vocabulary for clarity and precision **In addition**, confident writers attempt a more formal style	**Structure of instructions** → Follows introduction with points in order; may not make links between points clear; employs different ways to indicate order; uses some layout features → Includes an introduction to interest the reader; adopts appropriate basic structure and layout → May include main and sub-headings and separate conclusion; uses an appropriate layout	**Sentence structure** → Uses simple connectives ("also", "because", "but") to link points within an instruction → Draws on a wider choice of connectives **Punctuation** → Uses commas in lists → Uses full stops and capital letters with increasing accuracy → Uses other punctuation, where appropriate
NC Level 4	**Purpose and features** → Leaves some features undeveloped; balances and paces instructions to ensure reader is informed; occasionally attempts a formal style → Includes additional detail to add information and advice; makes direct appeals to the reader; Sometimes attempts to adopt appropriate tone and control relevant style (e.g. third person and present tense for two player game) → Uses characteristics of text type assertively; presents information clearly, with writer's purpose evident at each stage; shows greater control of formality, though not fully sustained **Use of vocabulary** → Uses topic words and "accurate" description → Chooses words and phrases for explanation or precision → Carefully chooses words and phrases to add shades of meaning	**Structure and paragraphs** Structures writing with increasing clarity: short introduction, a number of points, possibly divided into sections and a short conclusion; uses appropriate layout features → Organises writing appropriately for purpose and audience → Develops some points into short paragraphs to give extra information or explanation → Produces writing that is fluent and progressive with clear links between paragraphs or sections. Shows evidence of "staging", and may include more than one paragraph related to a stage	**Sentence structure** → Writes longer compound and some complex sentences with a range of connectives; may include repetition to ensure clarity → Includes a variety of complex sentences, with different subordinators, to extend meaning; includes connectives to provide order and emphasis within sentences; generally uses pronouns and tenses consistently → Employs a range of sentence types to create the desired effect on the reader; uses strategies to avoid repetition; produces concise and precise writing **Punctuation** → Uses punctuation with increasing accuracy → Uses commas to separate clauses, phrases and items in a list → Starting to use a wider range of punctuation where appropriate (for example, dashes and brackets, semi colons and colons)
NC Level 5	**Purpose and features** → Shows evidence of adapting writing to instruct and explain to the reader; adopts appropriate writing style for task; → Balances and paces instructions well; shows awareness of audience through use of language or adaptation of task; chooses and sustains an appropriate level of formality → Writes well in respect of structure and linguistic features of text type; style is appropriate and shows control **Use of vocabulary** Chooses words to support the purpose with increasing precision, economy and effectiveness	**Structure and paragraphs** → Separates main ideas into sections or paragraphs, which are shaped into stages of writing; uses layout conventions that are consistent with the task → Produces writing that is well-structured and convincing, including a well-focused introduction and conclusion; maintains cohesion between sections → Uses fully developed and appropriate structure; may make other text types clear in different sections, e.g. persuasion in an introduction	**Sentence structure** → Employs a range of sentences; may use whole sentences and bullet points in different parts of text; uses passive constructions to support formal style → Finds effective ways within sentences to avoid repetition → Fluently constructs a range of sentences types; may alter word order to develop themes and sustain reader interest **Punctuation** → Correctly demarcates most sentences, using a range of relevant punctuation → May use punctuation to enhance description or explanation → May use punctuation to avoid ambiguity; effectively employs semi colons or colons to structure longer sentences

Assessing writing

Non-chronological report

	Composition and effect	Text structure and organisation	Sentence structure and punctuation
NC Level 2	**Creates meaning of report through** → Includes features that are becoming clearer but are not sustained; includes topic language related to subject of report and adjectives to inform → Sometimes makes ambitious word choices → Includes detail to interest the reader	**Structure of report** → Adopts a simple structure → May link some events by "and" → Includes opening followed by relevant information; includes pictures or diagrams to give information	**Sentence structure** → Writes speech-like sentence structures, mostly joined by "and"; uses third person inconsistently → Extends some sentences with "but" and "so"; usually writes in present tense (unless writing an historical report) → Includes longer sentences, using connectives such as "because" or "when"; includes adverbial phrases in different positions **In addition**, confident writers vary sentence openings (e.g. when – "Tomorrow", how – "Quietly"), and include detail with prepositional phrases ("in", "under" ,etc). **Punctuation** Becoming more accurate when using full stops and capitals Uses other punctuation (exclamation and question marks)
NC Level 3	**Purpose and features** → Writes a recognisable report, though some features absent or undeveloped; covers content unevenly; some attempts to generalise and classify → Includes features to support purpose of giving information to interest and inform, but gives too much or too little detail; uses some impersonal language → Uses most features of report writing; writing is relevant for audience; balances coverage of content most of the time **Use of vocabulary** → Makes word choices to inform and interest the reader – some words reflect spoken language → Uses description to add information; includes technical language **In addition**, confident writers attempt a more formal style with generalised vocabulary	**Structure of report** → Includes heading(s), an opening and organises information in sections → Writes an introduction that defines subject → Ends with a simple concluding sentence **Organisation and layout** → Groups some information into sections; may not link ideas clearly → Divides information into sections; → May use sub-headings, lists of questions and answers, bullet points or paragraphing	**Sentence structure** → Develops ideas with simple connectives → Uses a variety of connectives in sentences; usually ensures that subjects and verbs agree → Varies sentence openings varied with adverbials or subordinators. **Punctuation** → Uses commas in lists → Uses full stops and capital letters with increasing accuracy → Uses other punctuation, where appropriate; attempts to use commas to separate sections of a sentence
NC Level 4	**Purpose and features** → Leaves some features undeveloped; balances and paces report to ensure reader is informed; sometimes attempts a formal style → Includes additional detail to interest and inform; sometimes attempts to adopt appropriate tone and control relevant style → Uses characteristics of text type assertively; presents information clearly, with writer's purpose evident at each stage; shows greater control of formality, though not fully sustained; maintains a consistent viewpoint **Use of vocabulary** → Includes interesting information using topic words and "accurate" description → Chooses words and phrases for interest or precision; sometimes attempts to use "weasel" words for generalisations (e.g. "usually", "often") → Carefully chooses words and phrases to give interesting information	**Structure of report** Structures writing with increasing clarity: introduction with generalisation and/or classification, followed by information divided into sections and conclusion; uses relevant layout conventions **Use of paragraphs** → Changes paragraph for each subject in report; includes a topic sentence → Uses paragraphs to improve overall cohesion → Shows evidence of pace and progression in "staging", with several paragraphs developing one part of the report	**Sentence structure** → Writes longer compound and some complex sentences with a range of connectives → Includes a variety of complex sentences, with different subordinators, to extend meaning; includes connectives to give order and emphasis within sentences; generally uses pronouns and tenses consistently; varies type of subject in sentences (pronoun, place, person), and varies subjects of sentences across a paragraph → Employs a range of sentence types to create the desired effect on the reader; uses strategies to avoid repetition; produces concise and precise writing **Punctuation** → Uses punctuation with increasing accuracy; sometimes uses commas to separate clauses → Uses commas to separate clauses → Starting to use a wider range of punctuation where appropriate (for example, dashes and brackets, semi colons and colons)
NC Level 5	**Purpose and features** → Shows evidence of adapting writing to interest, involve or inform the reader; adopts appropriate writing style for task; → Balances and paces report well; shows awareness of audience through use of language or adaptation of task; chooses and sustains an appropriate level of formality → Writes well in respect of structure and linguistic features of text type; style is appropriate and shows control **Use of vocabulary** → Chooses words to support the purpose with increasing precision, economy and effectiveness	**Structure and paragraphs** → Separates main ideas into sections or paragraphs, which are shaped into stages of writing; uses layout conventions that are consistent with the task; links paragraphs together with adverbials or connectives → Produces writing that is well-structured and convincing, including a well-focused introduction and conclusion; maintains cohesion between sections → Uses fully-developed and appropriate structure	**Sentence structure** → Employs a range of sentences – simple, compound and complex – for effect; uses passive constructions to support formal style → Finds effective ways within sentences to avoid repetition: → Fluently constructs a range of sentence types; may alter word order to develop themes and sustain reader interest **Punctuation** → Correctly demarcates most sentences, using a range of relevant punctuation → May use punctuation to enhance description or clarify meaning → May use punctuation to avoid ambiguity; effectively uses semi colons or colons to structure longer sentences

www.collinseducation.com © HarperCollins *Publishers* Limited 2007

Collins Primary Literacy

Assessing writing

Persuasion

Composition and effect

NC Level 2

Purpose and features
→ Shows insecure grasp of features except through talk and visual elements
→ Includes some characteristics of persuasion; topic words and description
→ Uses some features of persuasion; detail to interest reader

NC Level 3

Purpose and features
→ Produces a recognisable persuasive text, though some features absent or undeveloped; uneven coverage
→ Includes features to support purpose of persuading but gives too much or too little detail; uses some impersonal language
→ Includes most features of persuasion present and relevant for audience; covers most content in a balanced way

Use of vocabulary
→ Chooses words to persuade the reader – some words reflect spoken language
→ Uses description to add information; includes technical language
→ Uses some well-chosen vocabulary for clarity and precision, e.g. in advertising slogans

In addition, confident writers attempt a more formal style or a colloquial style for effect; they can sustain a point of view that is not their own

NC Level 4

Purpose and features
→ Leaves some features undeveloped; balances and paces arguments to ensure reader is informed; occasionally attempts a formal style
→ May add additional detail to argument by explaining or advising; makes some attempt to adopt appropriate tone and control relevant style
→ Uses characteristics of text type assertively; presents information clearly, with writer's purpose clear at each stage; shows greater control of formality, though not fully sustained; maintains a consistent viewpoint

Use of vocabulary
→ Makes persuasive points made using topic words and "accurate" description
→ Chooses words and phrases to persuade: uses powerful or emotive vocabulary;
→ Carefully chooses words and phrases to add force; attempts to use "weasel" words for persuasive purposes; increases range of persuasive sentence openings

NC Level 5

Purpose and features
→ Shows evidence of adapting material to persuade the reader; writes in a style appropriate for task;
→ Balances and paces argument well; writer shows awareness of audience through use of language or adaptation of task; chooses and sustains an appropriate level of formality
→ Writes well in respect of structure and linguistic features of text type; style is appropriate and shows control

Use of vocabulary
Word choices support the purpose with increasing precision, economy and effectiveness

Text structure and organisation

NC Level 2

Structure of persuasion
→ Adopts basic layout
→ Links some points by "and"
→ May include an opening and several points to persuade the reader; organises material to reflect purpose e.g. leaflet or poster

NC Level 3

Structure of persuasion
→ Includes basic introduction followed by series of persuasive points; may not make links between arguments clear
→ Includes clear introductory statement followed by persuasive detail; links arguments by connectives
→ May change paragraph to link with a new persuasive point

Organisation and layout
→ May not use a conventional layout
→ Divides arguments into sections;
→ May use statistics, graphs, images and layout features to support or reinforce arguments

NC Level 4

Structure of argument
Structures writing with increasing clarity: introduction followed by a series of arguments and a conclusion; uses layout relevant to task e.g. newspaper article, letter, flyer. In certain tasks, may attempt to counter an opposing view

Use of paragraphs
→ Includes several different arguments in a paragraph
→ Organises separate points in paragraphs, which include a topic sentence
→ Shows evidence of pace and progression in "staging", with several paragraphs developing one part of the persuasive text

NC Level 5

Structure and paragraphs
→ Separates main ideas into sections or paragraphs, which are shaped into stages of writing; uses layout conventions that are consistent with the task; links paragraphs together with adverbials or connectives
→ Produces well-structured and convincing writing, including a well-focused introduction and conclusion; maintains cohesion between sections; orders paragraphs to emphasise argument; uses paragraphs of different lengths to emphasise importance of certain parts of the argument
→ Uses fully-developed and appropriate structure and layout

Sentence structure and punctuation

NC Level 2

Sentence structure
→ Writes speech-like sentence structures, mostly joined by "and"; inconsistent use of tense
→ Extends some sentences with "but" and "so"
→ Includes longer sentences, using connectives such as "because" or "when"; includes adverbial phrases in different positions; usually writes in present tense

In addition, confident writers vary sentence openings (e.g. when – "Tomorrow", how – "Quietly") and includes detail with prepositional phrases ("in", "under" etc). Deliberately repeats some words to make a point

Punctuation
→ Becoming more accurate with full stops and capitals
→ Uses other punctuation (exclamation and question marks)

NC Level 3

Sentence structure
→ Develops ideas with simple connectives
→ Uses a variety of connectives in sentences; subject and verbs usually agree; uses imperatives to persuade
→ Varies sentence openings, with adverbials or subordinators, to structure arguments; uses questions to make arguments

Punctuation
→ Uses commas in a list
→ Uses full stops and capital letters with increasing accuracy
→ Uses other punctuation, where appropriate, for effect; attempts to use commas to separate sections of a sentence

NC Level 4

Sentence structure
→ Writes longer compound and some complex sentences with a range of connectives relevant for persuasion.
→ Includes a variety of complex sentences, with different subordinators, to extend meaning; varies types of sentences for impact: uses imperative, and rhetorical questions; uses connectives to give order and emphasis within sentences; generally uses pronouns and tenses consistently; varies type of subject in sentences (pronoun, place, person), and varies subjects of sentences across a paragraph, may use future tense to express consequences
→ Employs a range of sentence types to create the desired effect on the reader; uses strategies to avoid repetition; produces concise and precise writing;

Punctuation
→ Uses punctuation with increasing accuracy: sometimes uses commas to separate clauses
→ Uses commas to separate clauses
→ Starting to use a wider range of punctuation where appropriate (for example, dashes and brackets)

NC Level 5

Sentence structure
→ Employs a range of sentences – simple, compound and complex – for effect; uses passive constructions support formal style where relevant; uses conditionals for effect; includes sentences that are deliberately ambiguous
→ Finds effective ways within sentences to avoid unnecessary repetition:
→ Fluently constructs a range of sentence types; may alter word order to develop themes and sustain reader interest

Punctuation
→ Correctly demarcates most sentences, using a range of relevant punctuation
→ May use punctuation to enhance point of view or add humour
→ May use punctuation to avoid ambiguity; effectively uses semi colons or colons to structure longer sentences

Assessing writing

Recount

Name _____ Date _____

Composition and effect

NC Level 2

Purpose and features
→ Includes features that are becoming clearer but are not sustained; includes topic language and names of people and places
→ Makes some ambitious word choices
→ Writes in a lively style to hold reader's interest; adds detail through description

NC Level 3

Purpose and features
→ Produces a recognisable recount, though some features absent or undeveloped; covers content unevenly
→ Includes features to support purpose of re-telling, but gives too much or too little detail
→ Uses most features of recount; writing is relevant for audience; balances content coverage most of the time

Use of vocabulary
→ Makes word choices to interest and inform the reader – some words reflect spoken language
→ Includes description to add interest and information; uses technical language
→ Uses well-chosen vocabulary for clarity
In addition, confident writers attempt a more formal style

NC Level 4

Purpose and features
→ Leaves some features undeveloped; balances and paces recount to ensure reader is informed; sometimes attempts a formal style
→ Includes additional detail to interest and inform; sometimes attempts to adopt appropriate tone and control relevant style
→ Uses characteristics of text type assertively; presents information clearly, with writer's purpose evident at each stage; shows greater control of formality, though not fully sustained; maintains consistent viewpoint

Use of vocabulary
→ Includes interesting information, using topic words and "accurate" description
→ Chooses words and phrases for interest or precision
→ Carefully chooses words and phrases to add shades of meaning

NC Level 5

Purpose and features
→ Shows evidence of adapting writing to interest, involve or inform the reader; uses appropriate writing style
→ Balances and paces recount well; shows awareness of audience through use of language or adaptation of task; chooses and sustains an appropriate level of formality
→ Writes well in respect of structure and linguistic features of text type; adopts appropriate style; puts forward a point of view implicitly or explicitly

Use of vocabulary
Makes word choices to support the purpose with increasing precision, economy and effectiveness

Text structure and organisation

NC Level 2

Structure of recount
→ Includes brief opening followed by sequence of chronological events, all given equal importance
→ Organises writing more clearly using time connectives; includes opening that tells reader "where" and "when"
→ Uses simple layout conventions to support the facts about an activity or visit

NC Level 3

Structure of recount
→ Starts with basic introduction followed by some main events, which are not clearly linked
→ Starts with clear opening which includes details of who, what, where, when and why; follows with series of events in order
→ Attempts a satisfactory ending; uses side headings for clarity
In addition, confident writers might change paragraphs for a new event or the conclusion;

NC Level 4

Structure of recount
Structures writing with increasing clarity: introduction followed by series of chronological events and a conclusion; uses layout conventions where relevant

Use of paragraphs
→ Changes paragraph for change of time or event; includes a topic sentence
→ Uses paragraphs to contribute to overall cohesion
→ Shows evidence of pace and progression in "staging", with several paragraphs developing one part of the report

NC Level 5

Structure and paragraphs
→ Separates main events into sections or paragraphs, which are shaped into stages of writing; consistently uses layout conventions that are consistent with the task; links paragraphs together with adverbials or connectives
→ Produces well-structured and convincing writing that maintains cohesion between sections
→ Uses fully-developed and appropriate structure and layout

Sentence structure and punctuation

NC Level 2

Sentence structure
→ Writes speech-like sentence structures, mostly joined by "and"
→ Extends some sentences with "but" and "so"; writes in past tense
→ Includes longer sentences, using connectives such as "because" or "when"; includes adverbial phrases in different positions
In addition, confident writers vary sentence openings (e.g. when – "Tomorrow", how – "Quietly"), and include detail with prepositional phrases ("in", "under" ,etc).

Punctuation
Becoming more accurate with full stops and capitals
Uses other punctuation (exclamation and question marks)
Sometimes uses speech marks

NC Level 3

Sentence structure
→ Develops ideas with simple connectives
→ Uses a variety of connectives (including time connectives) in sentences; subjects and verbs usually agree
→ Varies sentence openings with adverbials or subordinators.
In addition, confident writers move phrases round in sentences for effect.

Punctuation
→ Uses commas in lists
→ Uses full stops and capital letters with increasing accuracy
→ Uses other punctuation, where appropriate, including speech marks, if relevant to the recount; attempts to use commas to separate sections of a sentence

NC Level 4

Sentence structure
→ Writes longer compound and some complex sentences with a range of connectives; attempts reported speech, if relevant., e.g: biography
→ Includes a variety of complex sentences, with different subordinators, to extend meaning; includes connectives to give order and emphasis within sentences; generally uses pronouns and tenses consistently; varies type of subject in sentences (pronoun, place, person), and varies subjects of sentences across a paragraph
→ Employs a range of sentence types to create the desired effect on the reader; uses strategies to avoid repetition

Punctuation
→ Uses punctuation with increasing accuracy; sometimes uses commas to separate clauses
→ Uses commas to separate clauses
→ Starting to use a wider range of punctuation where appropriate (for example, dashes and brackets, semi colons and colons)

NC Level 5

Sentence structure
→ Employs a range of sentences – simple, compound and complex –for effect; uses passive constructions to support formal style
→ Finds effective ways within sentences to avoid repetition
→ Fluently constructs a range of sentence types; may alter word order to develop themes and sustain reader interest

Punctuation
→ Correctly demarcates most sentences, using a range of relevant punctuation
→ May use punctuation to enhance description or clarify meaning
→ May use punctuation to add humour or avoid ambiguity; effectively uses semi colons or colons to structure longer sentences

Notes

Notes